*23-13*

# SOCIETY, SCHOOLS AND PROGRESS IN CHINA

# SOCIETY, SCHOOLS & PROGRESS IN CHINA

BY

## CHIU-SAM TSANG, B.A., M.A., Ph.D.

*Dean, Faculty of Arts, Chung Chi College,*
*The Chinese University of Hong Kong*

THE QUEEN'S AWARD
TO INDUSTRY 1966

## PERGAMON PRESS

OXFORD · LONDON · EDINBURGH · NEW YORK
TORONTO · SYDNEY · PARIS · BRAUNSCHWEIG

PERGAMON PRESS LTD.,
Headington Hill Hall, Oxford
4 & 5 Fitzroy Square, London W.1

PERGAMON PRESS (SCOTLAND) LTD.,
2 & 3 Teviot Place, Edinburgh 1

PERGAMON PRESS INC.,
44–01 21st Street, Long Island City, New York 11101

PERGAMON OF CANADA LTD.,
207 Queen's Quay West, Toronto 1

PERGAMON PRESS (AUST.) PTY. LTD.,
19a Boundary Street, Rushcutters Bay, N.S.W. 2011, Australia

PERGAMON PRESS S.A.R.L.,
24 rue des Écoles, Paris 5ᵉ

VIEWEG & SOHN GMBH,
Burgplatz 1, Braunschweig

Copyright © 1968 Pergamon Press Ltd.

First edition 1968

Library of Congress Catalog Card No. 68–21109

*Printed in Great Britain by A. Wheaton & Co., Exeter*

08 012843 2 (flexicover)
08 012844 0 (hard cover)

92044

# Contents

# Comparative Studies

*An Introduction to the Series* "Society, Schools and Progress"

*By* EDMUND KING

THIS volume is one of a mutually supporting series of books on SOCIETY, SCHOOLS AND PROGRESS in a number of important countries or regions. The series is intended to serve students of sociology, government, and politics, as well as education. Investment in education, or satisfaction of the consumer demand for it, is now the biggest single item of non-military public expenditure in many countries and an increasing proportion in all the rest. The systematic use of education to achieve security, prosperity, and social well-being makes it imperative to have up-to-date surveys realistically related to all these objectives; for it is impossible to study one effectively without reference to the others or to assess the objectives without reference to education as the chosen instrument.

Comparative studies of all kinds are in vogue. We find university departments of comparative government, law, religion, anthropology, literature, and the like. Some comparison is taken for granted in a contracting world of closer relationships. But not all comparative studies are forward-looking or constructive. Comparisons based solely or mainly on backward-looking interests can have their own kind of respectability without necessarily drawing lessons for the present. However, some contemporary comparisons show utility as well as interest or respectability, particularly when observers are enabled to analyse social organization, formative customs, value systems, and so forth.

More important still are area studies based upon a comprehensive survey of a whole culture, showing the interpenetration of its technology, government, social relationships, religion, and arts; for here we see our neighbours making man—and making him in an idiom which challenges our own assumptions and practices. This concerted and conscious making of posterity by a multiplicity of interlocking influences is perhaps mankind's most astonishing feature—at least on a par with rationality and speech, and inseparable from them. As the last third of the twentieth century begins, however, we are witnessing the struggle of competing educational prescriptions for the whole future of mankind.

## THE MAKING OF THE FUTURE

The most important studies of all in the world today are those undertaken with a view to modifying deliberately the formative conditions in which our children and their descendants will live —that is to say, their education. In the pre-industrial past there was plenty of time for the slow evolution of civilization and technology. Even in this century people used to think of societies and education as growing empirically and evolving. Today's world cannot wait upon the spontaneity that sufficed yesterday. It is often said that the Industrial Revolution is entering on its second and more important phase—the systematic application to social relationships of mechanized and urban-style abundance, with a corresponding transformation of all learning opportunities.

Certainly that is the dream of the hitherto underprivileged majority of mankind. All countries are involved in this social stocktaking and reckoning for the future, no matter whether they are called socialistic or capitalistic. In any case, the pace of change is so fast everywhere that some co-ordination or phasing of development is accepted as a critical responsibility of statecraft in all countries.

## THE TRANSFORMATION OF EDUCATION

In relation to education, this sequence of events has already been attended by remarkable changes. Education used to be undertaken largely at home, by society at large, by working relationships, or by voluntary organizations. Now it is a publicly regulated, publicly financed activity for the most part. It is provided as a necessary service by an expanding range of public employees. Of course unofficial people and social groups continue to take a keen interest, especially in their own children; but increasingly it is the State which co-ordinates and directs the process for all children. In some countries the State claims a monopoly of education; in most others that claim is hotly resisted, though inevitably the State is conceded a growing share in the partnership.

In any case, the State or its professional subsidiaries will assume a mounting responsibility for the allocation of funds, for increasingly expensive instruments and premises, for ensuring fair distribution of opportunity, for preventing the waste of talent, for safeguarding economic and social well-being, and for setting the national priorities into proper order. Therefore, no matter what education has been in the past, the logic of the Industrial Revolution has turned it into publicly regulated and publicly provided activities, directed towards the deliberate construction of a more satisfactory future.

That commitment is now implicitly indivisible within any one country. It is also accepted that internationally, too, everyone's education is likely to be to the advantage of everyone else in the long run. For this reason alone, international comparisons and assessments are of the utmost importance.

Whole countries are finding that their external context is changing in unprecedented ways. The emancipation of formerly subject peoples is a conspicuous example. Another instance is seen in the large regional developments whereby food production, commerce, and mutual protection are ensured in "developing countries"—usually with some notable reliance on educational improvements. Even quite powerful and well-established countries (like several in Western Europe) co-operate increasingly with their neighbours for commercial and political reasons; and all these changes necessitate some adjustment of school orientation and programmes, if only for the interchange of personnel. Apart from such specific instances, it is increasingly obvious that no education anywhere is worth the name unless it is viable in world terms.

Great though these adjustments are between sovereign nations, the changes that transcend all national boundaries and apply to all school systems alike are even more radically influential. In all countries, the area of education monopolized by the schools and other formally instructive institutions is diminishing in relation to educative forces outside. For example, the first public television programmes in the world began in 1936; yet within 25 years television and radio absorbed almost as much of children's time and interest (taking the year all round) as the formal school hours in a number of countries. The appeal of such external influences may be greater than the schools'. The universal teacher problem accentuates the change.

In any case, all instruction offered in school is largely conditional for its success on subsequent reinforcement. This it does not always get in a world of expanding opportunities and experiences for young people, which challenge schools' previous prerogatives and sometimes their precepts. A whole new range of "service occupations" provides alternative perspectives. Furthermore, technological and social change necessitate much professional retraining and personal reorientation in all advanced countries. There is far less idea of a once-for-all preparation for life. Learning the unknown is taking the place of teaching the certainties.

In all countries we share this uncertainty. Deeply rooted though we all are in our own ways of life, our scrutiny of the future becomes increasingly a comparison of our hypotheses and experiments. No really adequate answers to any educational or social problem can be determined within one country's confines any longer. Comparative Education is above all the discipline which systematizes our observations and conclusions in relation to the shaping of the future.

COMPARATIVE EDUCATION IN GENERAL

Comparative studies of education are necessarily based upon existing practices, institutions, and background influences which have shaped the present variety of educational idioms throughout the world. It is essential to acquaint ourselves with the most important systems, not as alien phenomena but as variations upon the preoccupations of every family and every school in our own country. To be both civilized and scientific we must try to "feel inside" the common human concerns of our neighbours. By this transference of sympathy we achieve some sort of detachment which will enable us to appreciate our own involvement in circumstances—quite as much as theirs.

What adds up to education in our own country is as confused a tangle as any to be found in those other countries where we more easily assume the role of critical advisers. Much of it is habituation, and much is emotionally bound rather than rational. Advice and rational planning that do not take account of these actual influences on education at any one place and time are unscientific as well as failing in humanity. From a practical point of view too they will fail, because they lack a sense of the local and topical dynamic. We must know the living present. It is this that gives momentum to the future and conditions it. Thus, even at this first or informative stage of Comparative Education, we are made analytically aware (not only descriptively) of today's climax of forces. We inevitably envisage some possibilities for the future—if only with reference to our own reactions and purposes.

Therefore, though Comparative Education must go on to study particular problems (such as control or university expansion), it must begin with area studies or dynamic analyses of concurrent influences such as this series provides. Without awareness of what "education" seems now to be to its participants, no student or planner can effectively share in the shaping of the future. He may have falsely identified his "problems". He will probably misjudge their topical significance. On the basis of unrealistic generalizations he will certainly fail to communicate acceptable advice. The climax of local culture which amounts to education in any one place is emotionally more sensitive even than language issues or religion, because it includes within itself these very influences and many others.

## THE PURPOSE OF THIS SERIES

SOCIETY, SCHOOLS AND PROGRESS are here surveyed in the world's most significant countries—significant not simply for reasons of technological or political strength, but because of the widely relevant decisions in education now being taken. Since the end of the Second World War a ferment of reform has been going on. No reform takes place in the sterile conditions of a laboratory. In the social field not even research can be isolated and sterilized. Experiment in education involves all the untidiness and unpredictability of human responses, which are the source of all creative ingenuity. Every planner or theorist, every student of "problems" that seem abstract and general enough, needs an opportunity of studying again and again the forensic application of his theories.

Nevertheless, so that some general study may be made of frequently recurring tendencies and problems, the books in the SOCIETY, SCHOOLS AND PROGRESS series are arranged in a fairly uniform pattern. They all begin with the historical and institutional background. They then go on to describe administration, the school system, family influences, and background social forces in much the same order of progression. Thus it is easy to make cross-references from one volume to another. Cross-cultural analysis of particular problems or interests is facilitated, but always in relation to the living context which so often reveals unexpected pitfalls or opportunities.

After this second or "problem" level of cross-cultural analysis in detail, the serious student can go on to a third stage. He can assess as a dynamic whole the collective preparation for the future of each of the countries featured. This third level of assessing orientation, or of planning, is not always marked by logic alone within any one of the countries concerned; but an international survey of discernible trends can be of great practical importance. The evolving form of the future can at least be surmised and continuing research can guide it.

Public investment in education (and consumer demand still more) has often been a precarious venture from the half-known into the unsuspected. Yet buildings, teachers, and the children's lives may be committed for generations. For this third level of comparative analysis it is therefore necessary to work closely with specialists in other disciplines, such as economists and sociologists. But the specialist in Comparative Education gives insight and information to them, just as he receives from them. Making the future is no project for any one man, any one discipline, any one interpretation.

This brings us to a last general point. It is more important than ever to have soundly based comparative studies of education, because the relevance of even the best of systems has limits imposed by time. Reorientation and retraining successively throughout life will be the experience of most people in advanced countries for generations to come. That trend is already evident at the most educated levels in the United States, Sweden, Britain, and some other countries. All human roles are being transformed too, not just subjects and occupations. Therefore it is useless to rely on what has been done, or is being done, in schools. We must try instead to think of what will be required, and to observe experiments now being undertaken on the very frontiers of education, where new matrices, new media, new elements, and methods of learning are being revealed.

The less settled educational patterns of "developing countries" (where most of mankind live) make it easier for them to be radical. They can by-pass the institutions, methods, and curricula of older-established school systems in their eager pursuit of unprecedented but valid objectives. This is all immediately important to us, because the whole world's educative relationships are being transformed, our own along with all the others. For that reason, one or more of the books in each batch of volumes published in the SOCIETY, SCHOOLS AND PROGRESS series will deal with a developing country, whose experience is particularly relevant in assessing education's contribution to the future.

## THE PARTICULAR CASE OF CHINA

For obvious reasons a comparative study of China is both fascinating and instructive. If there had been relatively little change in recent years the same might have been said, for China represents an ancient and prolific civilization whose message continues to influence profoundly the most numerous people on earth, and has also exerted great power over the development of Japanese culture to this very day. However, the changes which have overtaken the Chinese way of life and its external connections in this century intensify our interest incalculably.

In the first place, slow-paced and intermittent reaction to the Western barbarians during previous centuries suddenly accelerated and became more acute at the beginning of the twentieth with the establishment of a Republic. China's neighbour Japan also revealed the possibility of using the formal education system of the West not only to achieve national resurgence but to challenge Western imperialism and eventually Western technology. The difficult development of the Chinese Republic, its humiliation by the treaty powers and Japanese encroachment, did not prevent the gradual spread of regard for Western education's advantages, as shown in the United States, in Japan, and in some European countries. Internal challenges were thus produced in China between the venerable old and upstart new, between the literary tradition and the scientist returning from abroad, between Confucianism and its competitors, between a minority of innovators and the majority of a 650 million population. All these tensions provide a wealth of material for cross-cultural comparisons even within the one country.

More remarkable than ever is the story since the establishment of the People's Republic in 1949, for that event and all the rapid changes since have made China pivotal in world affairs. The establishment of a communist system of government over the greater part of the Eurasian land mass in itself represents a challenge to any previous thought about human relationships; but the vagaries of political subdivision and reinterpretation have transformed Chinese politics into front-page news and day-by-day television comment. At the same time the immense efforts at public education, with the production of a million university students on top of a huge if uncertain structure of primary and secondary schools, demand urgent appraisal by all educators in other lands. Indeed, public education outside the schools may in the long run have more to teach non-Chinese observers throughout Asia than what the schools themselves do. Western countries have generally used their schools to accelerate their existing progress and intensify or modify existing development; for Asian countries it may seem necessary to copy the Chinese experiment in total transformation. Nuclear status and political hegemony are persuasive neighbours, especially as China represents the hungry majority of mankind.

It is against this dynamic background that Dean Tsang recounts and analyses the events of recent years in his native country. He has had highly responsible experience inside the People's Republic and in Hong Kong. With an American doctorate, and being an expert on Western education too, he communicates as few others could the immense upheavals of Chinese consciousness during the cultural revolution of recent years.

# Preface

THERE are many ways to present the system and problems of education in China, in the framing of topics and in the arrangement of chapter sequence. The scheme which the present author uses is not one of his choice, but was suggested to him by the editor of the Society, Schools and Progress Series as one to be followed for the purpose of facilitating comparison among the countries under study. If it were not because of his desire to comply with the wishes of the publishers he would have taken a different course which might be more appropriate for the Chinese situation. He is happy, however, that he can take part in this joint undertaking, the significance of which, he hopes, may be comparable to the series of Studies on the Making of Citizens in different countries under the editorship of Charles E. Merriam of Chicago University in the late 1920's and early 1930's.

To write in Hong Kong on China today, close as it is in space and time, is not so easy as it may seem. What makes it difficult is not so much the solicitation of facts or supply of data, but the interpretation of their meaning in the light of China's historical and social setting and their significance for today and implications for tomorrow. Looking over the development in China during the past seventeen years, some are allured by her many virtues and others are disgusted by her many defects. Numerous Western writers have published books and articles on contemporary China. In spite of the fact that they are outside observers, who are supposedly more detached, diversity of views has been apparent. It seems that some kind of bias is inevitable in a world which is now so widely divided, with divergent concepts of values in accordance with their respective ideologies. As a Chinese who has been brought up, in the main, in the Chinese culture and in the

Chinese background, the author has no claim to personal objectivity. However, he does not intend to use his writing to defend his country and his people for national pride, nor to "sell" his country and his people to cater to Western interests. He hopes, however, that his view represents a Chinese point of view, though he must admit that a Chinese point of view does not imply a better point of view. It is his hope that his presentation will help to bring about a better understanding of the Chinese situation, both for the future of the Chinese people and for the good of the rest of the world.

The author was in Communist China but has now left it. If he had not shared some of the ideals cherished by the Chinese People's Republic, he would not have been there in the first place. On the other hand, if it were not because of something there which he fundamentally dislikes, he would not have left it to choose a life of exile. So in this book which presents his analysis, whatever shortcomings there may be, he hopes that it is an honest account as it is intended to be and bears no resemblance to propaganda literature which aims either to speak "for" or "against" the Chinese régime.

Hong Kong where this book was written is an interesting place. There are assembled here all kinds of people with different political alignments. In their attitude toward China, on one extreme, there are loyalists to the Nationalist régime, agents of the Taiwan government, and refugees from the Chinese mainland; and on the other, Chinese Communists, Communist agents and Communist fellow-travellers. The labour force, for instance, is divided into "left-wing" and "right-wing" labour unions. Side by side with the free world enterprises are the Communist banks, Communist stores, Communist newspapers, Communist cinemas, Communist schools, etc. Being a colony of the United Kingdom which recognizes Communist China, the Hong Kong Government officially and legally refers to Communist China as "China", and Nationalist China only as "Taiwan". In spite of this, the political commercial, and cultural activities of the United States, China's confirmed No. 1 enemy, are very active in Hong Kong. It is, indeed, a great meeting place of Communists, pro-Communists, non-Communists, and anti-Communists of all shades and of all national origins. In the course of writing, as the author looks out of his window over his desk, every day he sees in front of him the passing trains of the Canton–Kowloon Railway which bring Chinese passengers and foreign visitors in and out of China, and loads of freight cars with livestock and refrigerated meat from China to feed the millions in Hong Kong. This rail link between the free world and the iron curtain of China through a border which is only fifteen miles away from the writer's desk, is symbolic of the peculiar situation at which his observations are made.

The latest event in China is the purge which is known as the Great Proletarian Cultural Revolution led by the army group and came to the open in April 1966. However important this event is and whatever it may lead to, it should not be over-magnified because of its recency. In the opinion of the writer, this episode is only a development of what has been going on in China and it rather serves to substantiate some of the observations made in the various chapters of this book than to contradict them. If this episode of the Great Proletariat Cultural Revolution, or any episode in Communist China for that matter, leads to very serious consequences, there should be no surprise. Anything is liable to happen in a totalitarian state. If it does, it simply reflects on the precarious nature of the dictatorship which makes all seeming stabilities essentially unreliable.

It is usually the place in the Preface to acknowledge the help the author has received. Though he has received considerable help from his Chinese friends in Hong Kong in checking on certain data and in the preparation of the manuscript, he feels it unfair to them to get their names involved in a book of this nature. The names of a few non-Chinese colleagues could be mentioned who showed an interest in his book at the initial stage of writing. But he would rather tender them his appreciation by sending them his complimentary copies when the book is published. He wishes, however, to record his thanks, in a formal way, to the East-West

Center of the University of Hawaii, whose invitation he accepted as Senior Specialist and Visiting Professor in 1965, and where he had the opportunity and facilities to do a part of this research. He expresses appreciation of the generosity of the Union Research Institute of Hong Kong for letting him use its library.

# CHAPTER 1

# The Historical Background

IN ORDER to understand present-day China, her society, her schools, and her progress, one must take a good look into her history—both her history of the long past and her history since the impact of the West a little over a century ago. Failing to take note of the long accumulating national experience of the Chinese people, one can not hope to understand their struggles and aspirations nor see the meaning and significance of the social, political, economic, and cultural movements in China either to the Chinese people or to the rest of the world.

Books on Chinese history are so numerous that they can fill many libraries. Even in the English language alone, there are more books on Chinese history than one can possibly read. A sketch of China's historical background here, which is short, as it is bound to be, cannot claim to have anything to add to the already voluminous stock of knowledge on the subject. Whatever merit there is will lie in the reorientation of its presentation in the interest of the general topic under consideration and in the light of the problems of the contemporary world as observed by one who has been brought up in the Chinese background, sharing the Chinese experience as its national, since the turn of the twentieth century.

Before we start on Chinese history, let us have a brief account of her geography as a background to a background.

## GEOGRAPHY

The homeland of the Chinese, which they call *Chung Kuo*, the Central Kingdom, is in that part of the world which has been known to the Westerners, however, to whom the centre of the world is Europe, as the Far East. Disregarding fractional exactness, its land stretches in latitude from 18°N in the Island of Hainan to 53°N in the Amur River in Manchuria, and in longitude, from 73°E in Sinkiang to 135°E at the mouth of Ussuri River. It covers an area of 95,970,000 square kilometers or 37,054,054 square miles.[1] It is not an empire made up of scattered islands or dominions far separated from one another, but a compact continental area in eastern Asia which, for thousands of years, was cut off from the rest of the continent in the west by vast mountain masses, by deserts in the north, and protected in the east and south by the waters of the sea.

Within the boundaries of China are arrayed numerous physiographic features which include almost every known type of topographic expression, with plateaux, table lands, basins, steppes, deserts, plains, islands, peninsulas, mountains, hills, rivers, lakes, and a long coast. The landscape, as a whole, is a slope which runs from the north-west to the south-east, with three major river systems, flowing from west to east, the Huang Ho (Yellow River) in the north, the Yangtze River in the middle, and the Pearl River or Si Kiang in the south, forming the three main river basins in China proper where most of the Chinese people live. This is the home of the Chinese people wherein they developed through many many centuries past their independent civilization, isolated from the rest of the world, with but casual contacts with Western Asia and Europe, though with considerable influence over their neighbouring races and lesser states. Commenting on China with a land of this dimension, E. T. Williams once said: "Holding dominion over palm and pine, and every variety of soil and climate, her agricultural products were more varied than those of other lands, and, equally rich in animal and mineral resources, she had raw materials for every kind of manufacture and has given the world some of its most important industries."[2] The Chinese have always been

[1] See *People's Handbook, 1965*, published by the Ta Kung Pao, Peking.
[2] E. T. Williams, *China, Yesterday and Today*, Thomas Y. Crowell Co., New York, 1927, p. 7.

happy and contented with their land which is valued as a gifted geographic inheritance.

The Chinese population is now estimated to be approximately 700 million.[3] There are nations in the world with territories as vast as or even vaster than that of China, but none with a population so huge and yet so homogeneous in colour, in race, in history, in culture, in language, and in the general modes of life. There are national minorities in China to be sure, but they form but a very small fraction of the population. The minorities present no such sharp contrast as the Negroes in the United States, the whites in South Africa, the French in Canada, or the Moslems in India. Now when the days of Western colonization of China and the threat of international partition are probably gone, and when the Chinese people have awakened from a long sleep and regained their respectable nationhood, this massive people of a massive land may in time become a formidable force in the arena of the world for good or for evil. What is happening in China cannot be ignored. It will have far-reaching effects not only to the Chinese but also to their neighbours and to the rest of mankind.

## HISTORY

The history of China, for the purpose of our study, may be presented under the following periods : (1) Ancient China, that is, the Pre-Chin Period up to 220 B.C.; (2) China from the Chin Dynasty to the Opium War, that is, a period of 2000 years of perpetual dynastic history from Chin Shih Huang to Emperor Tao Kwang, 220 B.C. to A.D. 1840; (3) The dissolution of the Dynastic Empire, that is, from the Opium War to the Fall of the Ching Dynasty, 1840–1911; (4) The Chinese Republic up to

[3] According to the statistics given by the Chinese People's Republic in the *People's Handbook of 1965*, published by the Ta Kung Pao, Peking, in October 1965, the population in China in 1957 was 656,630,000, with Taiwan and overseas Chinese population excluded. The 1965 Report of the United Nations indicated that Mainland China has a population of 686 million in the middle of 1964.

the birth of the Chinese People's Republic, 1911–49; and (5) China in the last two decades, 1949–66.

## ANCIENT CHINA

By Ancient China is meant the period from the earliest time of Chinese history to the unification of China in 221 B.C. by Chin Shih Huang, sometimes known as Shih Huang-ti, of the Chin Dynasty. It is generally known as the Pre-Chin Period. It includes and ends with the *Chun-Chiu Chan-Kuo* period, the period of "Spring and Autumn" and the "Warring States", where the Hundred Flowers Bloomed and the Hundred Schools Contended in Chinese thought and philosophy. It was in this *Chun-Chiu Chan-Kuo* period that lived China's greatest thinkers: Confucius, Lao-tze, Chuang-tze, Mo-tze, Hsun-tze, Mencius, Han Fei-tze, and a long roll of philosophers who are familiar to the Western world. This period is important to us in our understanding of China, because it laid the foundation of Chinese society and Chinese culture which has characterized the Chinese as distinct from other peoples. The political and ethical ideas of those thinkers concerning human relationships have greatly affected the people's ways of thought and the ways of life in the family, in society, and between the govern and the governed.

To go back a little, China's earliest inhabitants probably came from the central part of Asia. But exactly when and from where they moved over is still not ascertained. The earliest civilization was believed to have developed along the Yellow River basin in North China. They developed farming which has remained to be the chief means of livelihood, and farming has been the main use of the land. There have been famines, floods, and warfare which necessitated migration from one part of the land to another, but, on the whole, the people have stayed close to their soil, making theirs a civilization both stable and static, as all agrarian civilizations are.

Although the physical features of the Chinese are very unique, there can be no claim that the Chinese are a pure race. Intermarriage with the neighbouring tribes and minority races was bound to happen. As the Chinese people propagated into a much huger population than their minor neighbours, it was natural that the Chinese type remained predominant, especially as the features of the bordering peoples were of the same Mongol type, with black and straight hair, brown eyes, yellow skin, broad face, medium stature, and less hairy.

Some people are sceptical of the historical accounts of Huang Ti, the Yellow Emperor, who is dated back to 4554 B.C. But most people would accept as authentic China's dynastic history starting from the first Tang Dynasty under Emperor Yao of 2332 B.C. It is also generally accepted that the dynasties in line of succession up to the Ching Dynasty have been fourteen in number : namely, Tang, Yu, Hsia, Shang, Chou, Chin, Han, Tsin, Sui, Tang,[4] Sung, Yuan, Ming, and Ching. Some historians have doubts regarding the authenticity of the stories about the great emperors Yao, Shun, and Yu of the respective Tang, Yu, and Hsia dynasties, but their images as the most public-minded and exemplary sovereigns have affected the lives of the Chinese people for thousands of years no less than if they were proven historical figures. But beginning from the Shang Dynasty, which is sometimes called the Yin Dynasty, there are ample supporting evidences from recent excavations for the authenticity of the historical records. There is no doubt that, by then, the Chinese had attained a fairly high stage of civilization. The history of the Chou Dynasty is kept in a much fuller written record. The Chou Dynasty was formed in 1122 B.C. and was finally overthrown by Chin Shih Huang in 221 B.C. There was a line of forty emperors who ruled in succession for 900 years, which makes Chou by far the longest dynasty in Chinese history.

The Chou Dynasty is significant in these ways : (1) Being long, it was able to establish firmly a pattern of life which no short dynasty could ever do. (2) It was the period of feudalism in

4 There are two dynasties with the same name, Tang, but they are thousands of years apart. The second Tang Dynasty dates A.D. 618–960.

China. When the Chou Dynasty collapsed, feudalism was abolished. The abolition of feudalism in China was ahead of Europe by almost 2000 years. (3) The dissolution of the Chou Dynasty took a long time. It took centuries. Confucius's main effort was to try to save it by means of historical criticism through the writing of the annal "Chun-Chiu" which covers the period from 770 to 481 B.C. When he failed to save it from dissolution by his ethical approach, the conditions in the country went from bad to worse until the different states within the empire were in constant war. The subsequent period from 403 to 221 B.C. is known in Chinese history as *Chan-Kuo*, the Period of the Warring States, which was ended by the unification of China by Chin Shih Huang. Coincidentally, the period in which Confucius (551–479 B.C.) and Mencius (372–289 B.C.) lived was quite close to the period of Socrates (469–399 B.C.) and Plato (427–347 B.C.), which is known in European history as the Golden Age of Greece.

Confucius may be said to be the champion of familism and feudalism. Filial piety to parents and loyalty to the emperor were the two great canons of the codes of personal and social life. Out of these grew the ideals of the *Chun-Tsze* or the princely man, and the virtues of propriety, righteousness, obedience, faithfulness, modesty, chastity, charity, self-respect, mutual-respect, and public-mindedness. The Confucian ideals and teachings enjoyed supremacy in China for over 2000 years. It is true that there were times when other ideas came in, particularly the ideas of Buddhism, but they supplemented Confucianism rather than contested it. It is because of this social and cultural foundation laid in the Chou Dynasty that the pre-Chin history becomes the more significant in our understanding and interpretation of the Chinese revolution today.

Although feudalism as a political system was abolished over 2000 years ago, it is claimed that feudalism as a social and ethical system has persisted in Chinese society and still dominates the Chinese mind. According to the Chinese Communists, the remnants of feudalism still exist in China in the economic life, social life, and in art and literature. Effort must not be spared to combat its revival. Feudalism is placed with imperialism and capitalism as objects of struggle as stated in the First Article[5] of the Common Programme adopted by the Chinese People's Political Consultative Conference in September 1949. Indeed feudalism, in as much as it is native and deeply rooted, will be the more difficult for the Communists to deal with.

## FROM CHIN TO CHING

Chin Shih Huang terminated a chapter of Chinese history and opened a new one. He abolished feudalism and established a unified government with absolute central authority. For 2000 years since his death, Chinese historians condemned him from the standard of the Confucian concept of a sovereign. But modern Chinese historians of late, since the rise of nazism, fascism, and communism, have been speaking more kindly of him. He was ruthless. He burned all books except those on agriculture, medicine, and divination, and buried alive 300 scholars. All weapons of war and sharp implements were confiscated and only one cutting knife was allowed for ten households and even then it was chained so that it could not be taken away. Whispering was punished by execution in the market place. But he accomplished much. He completed the construction of the famous Great Wall of over 5000 li (about 1300 miles) to guard against invasion from the north. He unified the written language, standardized measurements, and required the axles of carts and chariots to be of the same length for use on the national roads. He divided the whole country into thirty-six provinces, a

[5] "The Chinese People's Republic is a state of the new democracy which is People's Democracy. It exercises the democratic dictatorship of the people which unites people of all classes and all races of the state under the leadership of the working class, founded on the alliance of the workers and peasants. It opposes imperialism, feudalism, and bureaucratic capitalism in its struggle for the independence, democracy, peace, unity, and prosperity of China."

system of division which is largely followed to the present day. He put in order a country which had been for almost 500 years in a hopeless state of confusion, strife, and turmoil, an accomplishment which no one at his time had the ability to attain. The fact that he could achieve all this in his lifetime is marvellous. Whether one likes him or not, it is indisputable that he was the first to have brought about the unification of China.

Chin Shih Huang was for 25 years king of the Kingdom of Chin, one of the seven kingdoms contesting for supremacy, before he became emperor of the Chin Empire. He died in the 37th year of his reign, the last 12 years of which were in the status of emperor. In spite of the shortness of his reign, he left behind him the marks of a strong central government, though his name is always associated with despotism and with contempt. The simple-mindedness and naïvity of the dictator is amply shown in his assumption that an empire founded by force without regard to human nature could last forever and be succeeded to by his son and his son's sons to ten thousand generations. It turned out, however, that his empire survived only 3 years after his death. In the 3rd year of the reign of his son, the Chin Dynasty was overthrown by several rebels, the strongest of whom was Liu Pang who established the Han Dynasty, which lasted for over 400 years from 206 B.C. to A.D. 264.

It is not our business here to outline the historical events of the dynasties from Chin to Ching, however interesting they may be to the student of Chinese history. It may be mentioned here that there were nine dynasties[6] which stretched the span of 2130 years from the founding of the Chin Dynasty in 221 B.C. to the fall of the Ching Dynasty in A.D. 1911. With the exceptions of the Yuan Dynasty which was ruled by the Mongols and the Ching Dynasty which was ruled by the Manchus, all the dynasties were ruled by the Chinese, each under one family in one surname.

[6] Chin (221–207 B.C.); Han (206 B.C. to A.D. 264); Tsin (A.D. 265–580); Sui (A.D. 581–617); Tang (A.D. 618–959); Sung (A.D. 960–1279); Yuan (A.D. 1280–1367); Ming (A.D. 1368–1644); and Ching (A.D. 1644–1911).

As in all dynastic histories, there were certainly times of order and disorder, of expansion and invasion, of civil and foreign wars, of prosperity and depression. These again do not concern us particularly in our present discussion. What interests us in the long period is not the rise and fall of dynasties but the final termination of dynasties as dynasties. At this turning point, which is within the lifetime of many of us, including that of the author, one must appreciate the change that has taken place in the minds of those who had been schooled in dynastic government as the pattern of life for thousands of years. The forces which pressed for change and the inertia which tried to retain the old were equally strong. Indeed, this inertia was seen in the events following the establishment of the Chinese Republic, the most spectacular of which were Yuan Shi-kai's attempt to become emperor in 1915 and the reascension of the disposed emperor, Hsuan Tung, in Peking, in 1917. The installation of the Manchukuo in Manchuria by the Japanese as a puppet state from 1932 to 1945 was not without its historical basis.

Why such a great change took place as the termination of thousands of years of dynastic rule, we shall learn in the next period of history, the period from the Opium War to the birth of the Chinese Republic. We may note in passing that the Chinese people have been accustomed to change of dynasties. They are not particular about one dynasty or another. They say that whoever is emperor, they have to pay tax. They are also accustomed to a certain amount of despotism so long as it is not too unbearable. To rule over the Chinese is not a difficult task. The masses of the Chinese people have been taught by the sages of feudalistic society and nurtured in thousands of years of dynastic government to submit instead of rebel, to forbear instead of complain.

Throughout the dynasties, although the power was vested with the throne, scholars and gentry played an important role in the actual administration of government. Most of them came from the ranks of the common people. The system of selection of the talented by recommendation from the localities was used in earlier times. Beginning during the Sui Dynasty (A.D. 581–617) the system of selection by examination began to be used, it was perfected in the Tang Dynasty (A.D. 618–959) and thereafter continued down to almost the last days of the Ching Dynasty. It was a system of selecting the most talented in the country for the service of the State as well as keeping the talented preoccupied with prescribed classical and literary learning, so that their endeavour to win social and political privileges also lessened the chance of their engagement in subversive activities. Concerning the latter point, Li Shih-min, first emperor of the Tang Dynasty, was so delighted with the examination system that he said : "Now the scholars of the whole world will hereafter fall within my target."

In this examination system, which some Western scholars have called the Chinese Civil Service Examination system, the successful candidates were awarded titles of scholastic distinction : *Hsiu-Tsai* "The blooming talents", *Chu-Jen* "Promoted Man", *Tsin-Sze* "Advanced Scholar", and *Han-Lin* "Forest of Pens", which were comparable with the academic degrees in the West. Except for a short period of time when the government was corrupt and when such titles could be bought by financial subscription, the examinations were very fairly administered and the holders of such titles enjoyed considerable public esteem. The part that scholars and intellectuals played in Chinese government has been considerable, much more so than in the West, particularly as there was no religious priesthood which could bring pressure on politics in China.

The education which the intellectuals received in the past was literary and classical in nature. Schooling was confined to a very small group who aspired towards public status and officialdom. Except for the ambitious, schooling was not of much concern to the working people. Their skills in making a living, whether in farming or as artisans, were learned by actual occupational participation or by apprenticeship. It must be pointed out here that education should not be identified with literacy. While the Chinese were mostly illiterate, that did not mean that they were uneducated in the sense that they were savages or that they were uncultured. They were fully exposed to social and ethical culture through the influence of the literati who lived among them. Indeed, the traditional culture went so deep into the lives of the masses of the people that they took it for granted without question.

For 2000 years, in spite of various setbacks, Chinese society was, in general, progressive. This progress included the arts and crafts, philosophy and literature, science and technology. Since Chinese economic life was essentially agricultural and the Chinese mentality was one of looking back to the golden days of the past, according to the teachings of Confucius who advocated the return to the ways of the ancients, Chinese society was essentially static and conservative in nature. So social progress was more truly an enrichment of the traditional culture than a departure from its ways. One could say that if a man had fallen asleep in the Han Dynasty and woken up in the Ching Dynasty he would not have found family life, village life, and social life in China strange to him. He could have found them reading the same books, eating the same food, putting on the same attire, taking the same attitude to their emperors, using the same utensils, speaking the same language, and sharing the same ideology.

There have always been virtuous emperors and vicious emperors, as there have been good dynasties and bad dynasties. The last of the emperors, Kuang Sui and Hsuan Tung, were definitely not bad emperors. Kuang Sui was anxious for reform, and Hsuan Tung was too young to be good or bad, as he ascended to the throne at the age of 3 and abdicated it at the age of 6. The Ching Dynasty was the last dynasty but not necessarily the least. If history was left to run its free course, the overthrow of the Ching Dynasty could have meant the rise of another dynasty. The abrupt termination of dynastic history can only be explained by the totally new situation that had arisen, that of the impact of the West which we shall take up in the following section.

The beginning of modern Chinese history is usually dated from the Opium War in 1840. Although this period is short, with only 127 years up to the time of the present writing, compared with China's long history of thousands of years, its significance is out of proportion to the time it covers, even when we admit that one is prone to exaggerate the importance of his own day. Since the theme of this book is contemporary China, it is fitting that we dwell a little more on this modern period which, for convenience, we shall subdivide into three periods as captioned in the three following sections. We shall first show how the chain of events, starting with the Opium War, brought about the downfall of the Ching Dynasty. Then we shall outline the major affairs of the Chinese Republic—shall we call it the first Chinese Republic?— which survived the two world wars. Finally, we shall review some of the happenings in the Chinese People's Republic, which some people call Communist China, up to the year 1966. We shall now start with the period commencing with the Opium War.

## FROM THE OPIUM WAR TO THE FALL OF
## THE CHING DYNASTY

The period of 70 years, 1840–1911, from the Opium War to the fall of the Ching Dynasty, may be called the transitional period from the old dynastic era to the republican era. In time it was still within the Ching Dynasty in the reign of the last five emperors; but in significance it may be called the prelude of a different social order.

To start China's modern history with the Opium War does not imply that China had no contacts with the West before that time. The first Christian missionaries from Persia, the Nestorians, arrived at China's capital, Chang On, as early as A.D. 500. Marco Polo reached Peking in A.D. 1275. The Portuguese first arrived in 1516 and settled in Macao in 1557. Ricci, an Italian Jesuit, came to Peking in 1601. The Russians first entered the valley of Amur in 1644, and China's first treaty with a Western power was made with Russia in 1689. As for the British, their first vessel called at Canton in 1637, 200 years before the Opium War, and was followed later by Macartney's embassy to Peking in 1793 and Emherst's embassy in 1816.

Before we come to the Opium War it may be worth while to bear in mind that Chinese society before the Opium War was not so deplorable, nor its government so bad, as it was in later years. The society was integrated, the people were satisfied with their livelihood, the country was in a period of relative prosperity, and the government was enjoying considerable prestige. The early decades of the nineteenth century in China were not long after the celebrated reign of Emperor Chien Lung who was on the throne for 60 years from 1736 to 1795. If we recall that American Independence was declared in 1776 and the French Revolution broke out in 1789, we can see that the Chinese during the Chien Lung period had cause to believe that their country was not incomparable with the Western countries at that time. There was much in China for the Chinese to be proud of, just as there was much in the behaviour of the fortune-seeking sailors who came to Chinese shores in these days for the Chinese to despise. The Chinese did not care about Western ways of life; they wanted to be left alone and did not want to be bothered. When their doors were knocked, they refused to open. They wanted to close their own doors to dream their own dreams.

The Opium War brought to the Chinese a shocking experience. It was the first combat with the West which resulted in national humiliation and hatred. The door was forced open; but, unfortunately, the issue at stake was one of opium traffic. We shall not discuss the details of the conflict nor of its rights and wrongs, but the result was that China lost the war to Great Britain. In the Treaty of Nanking signed in 1842, which the Chinese called the first unequal treaty, Hong Kong was ceded to Great Britain. Five ports—Canton, Amoy, Foochow, Ningpo, and Shanghai—were opened to foreign trade, 21 million taels of silver were paid for indemnity, etc.

That was neither sufficient to teach China the lesson she needed to learn nor to satisfy the Western powers' appetite for expansion, so a series of conflicts ensued. The Second Opium War with Britain broke out in 1856, starting as a British redress for a grievance due to the disrespect shown to the British flag in Canton. France joined the war as Britain's ally because a French priest was killed in Kwangsi Province. The Treaty of Tientsin was signed in 1858; since both sides were unsatisfied, war was resumed. Peking was occupied by the Anglo–French allies, Emperor Hsien Feng fled for refuge. The magnificent palace, the Yuan Ming Yuan, was looted and burned to the ground. The Treaty of Peking was signed in 1860 with a heavier indemnity and more concessions. Then followed the war with France in 1864, the war with Japan in 1895, and the Boxer Uprising in 1900 in which armies of eight foreign powers joined in alliance. They captured Peking and drove the emperor, Kuang Sui, and his royal household away as fugitives.

We need not go into the details of the conflicts. But in the series of conflicts the result was more humiliation, more indemnities, more concessions of territories, and more special rights to the foreign powers. In the early decades of the nineteenth century, China had posed as a great celestial empire; by the end of the same century she had become a frustrated nation which survived only at the mercy of other powers. As a result, the Chinese change their sense of superiority and arrogance to one of inferiority and humiliation. The Chinese attitude toward the foreigner became a complex of feelings, which was in general a mixture of alienation, avoidance, disdain, hatred, fear, and admiration. Defeats and national humiliation always breed social discontent and dissatisfaction with the government, so the Ching Dynasty, the Manchus, received all the blame for the deplorable state of affairs that existed both in its internal and external affairs. As one looks back over those years, the ordeal of China was largely inevitable in view of the fact that China was so proud of her own culture, so grossly ignorant of the Western world, and so unprepared for war, while the Western powers were pursuing the policy of colonialism and world expansion which was backed up by industrialization and superior weapons of war.

As a result of the social discontent, revolts broke out one after another, every one of which added more disorder and further weakening of the empire. The first major revolt was the Taiping Uprising which the Ching Dynasty used to call the Taiping Rebellion and the Chinese Communists now call the Taiping Revolution. It was led by Hung Hsiu-chuan, a Christian convert in Kwangtung who succeeded in establishing a new empire, the Tai Ping Tien Kuo (the Heavenly Kingdom of Peace) which survived for 18 years from 1851 to 1868, sweeping over eleven provinces with its capital in Nanking. It was finally suppressed by the Manchu Government under the leadership of a famous Chinese scholar-general, Tseng Kuo-fan, with the support of the Chinese gentry. The second major revolt in 1911, now credited to Sun Yat-sen, succeeded, however, 40 years later. It resulted in the establishment of the Chinese Republic, of which the Chinese Government under Chiang Kai-shek is still the legacy, with the celebration of its 55th anniversary on 10 October 1966.

To be fair, the Ching Dynasty was not entirely without the desire to reform. As early as 1862, realizing the futility of shutting their eyes to the Western world and the necessity of learning the languages and technologies of the West, the Imperial Government established in Peking the first Language Institute, the *Tung Wen Kuan*, which was later developed into the famous University of Peking. Again, in the years 1872–5, as a result of Yung Wing's proposal to Tseng Kuo-fan, four groups of 120 bright teenage boys in all were sent to the United States to study. They were the first groups of Chinese students to study abroad. In spite of the fact that these students were recalled before they completed their studies, many of them played significant roles in China's modernization after their return.

Another gesture for reform was the famour 1898 Reform, which, because of its short life of a hundred days, is often called by the West the Hundred-day Reform. Its programme for modernization and preparation for constitutional monarchy was proclaimed by Emperor Kuang Sui, advised by one of the greatest Chinese scholars, Kang Yu-wei. The reform was brought to an end by the *coup d'état* of Empress Dowager Tzu Hsi, who executed six great scholars in Kang's group and imprisoned Emperor Kuang Sui, who remained in confinement until he died in 1908, also the year of Tzu Hsi's death.

There was reaction to every measure for reform, as was to be expected in a country which was so well established in traditions, particularly when reforms always upset vested interests. The most notorious incident was the so-called Boxer Rebellion of 1900, which the Chinese Communists insist in calling the I-Ho-Tuen Uprising. To many, the rebellion or uprising or whatever one calls it, was sheer ignorance and blind xenophobia which proved to be most disastrous for China. It became the last measure of resistance.

China's defeat in 1895 by Japan, a small but recently modernized neighbour, taught China a good lesson; the fatal blow of 1900 taught her another lesson. Then the victory of Japan over Russia in 1905 taught her the most convincing lesson that anything could have done. Thus we see that beginning from 1905 the movement for reform launched forward without hesitation and reservation. In the year 1905 alone, 15,000 Chinese students flocked to Japan to study. It was also in 1905 that the thousand-year-old examination system was abolished and in its place the school system of the modern world was adopted. The enthusiasm of the Ching Government for reform since 1905 was most surprising, but it was too late to save the dynasty. The Manchus had been in a great dilemma. They were aware that permitting the country to undergo modernization might result in its final overthrow. Their fear was justified, as it turned out. The measures of reform accelerated its downfall.

## FROM THE BIRTH OF THE CHINESE REPUBLIC UP TO THE BIRTH OF THE CHINESE PEOPLE'S REPUBLIC

The four decades from the birth of the Chinese Republic in 1911 to the birth of the Chinese People's Republic in 1949 constituted a very eventful period in modern Chinese history. Two world wars took place in this period. If wars have always been considered as the most vital sort of human experience, the two world wars have certainly brought unprecedented national experiences to the Chinese people. World War I saw the rise of the Chinese Renaissance followed by the famous Student Movement of 1919, the formation of the Chinese Communist Party in 1921, the first co-operation between the Chinese Communists and the Nationalists, and two decades of the Nationalist régime. World War II brought about the second co-operation between the Nationalists and the Communists which lasted for 8 years; then they were at civil war again, as a result of which the Nationalists were driven to the island of Taiwan, while the Communists established the new régime of the People's Republic on the mainland.

## Early Years of the Republic

Going back to the early days of the Chinese Republic, it was probably the most enthusiastic and optimistic period of Chinese history for many centuries. That enthusiasm for the republican form of government and that optimism in China's future, as we review it today, were as naïve and illusory as unwarranted. With the exception of the Manchus and the monarchists who were the losers, the outburst of enthusiasm among the Chinese was most spectacular in every aspect of life. They acted in the belief that the evils of the past would thereafter be swept overboard, and all blessings were in store for them in their future. The enthusiasm was similar to that of a Chinese boy who goes to school for the first time in his life. The popular thinking at that time was that it was monarchy that brought China its weaknesses and humiliation, and it was monarchy that had alienated China from the family of nations. It was not republicanism, supposedly the most modern form of government, which would dispel all evils, heal all wounds, and bring China to the harmonious family of nations. In the school textbooks we found that George Washington stood out as the champion of republicanism;

his boyhood story of felling the cherry tree was the best example of honesty that could be taught to the Chinese children. Abraham Lincoln, the emancipator of American Negro slaves, appeared to them their own emancipator. The faith and enthusiasm of the Chinese in republicanism were largely accounted for by their disgust over the absolute monarchy of the Ching Dynasty, and were further aggrvated by their gross ignorance of what republicanism involved and its many limitations and conditions of success. It did not take long for such fancies to disperse in the presence of hard realities, of internal and international confrontations.

It may be that the Republic was too easily attained. It was largely the result of insurrections sponsored by local leaders throughout the country, where little blood was shed, and also the result of the voluntary abdication of the boy Emperor Hsuen Tung on the advice of his court. In order to reach a quicker solution in the formation of the Republic without the use of force, Sun Yat-sen, the provisional president, stepped down from his presidency and offered it to Yuan Shih-kai, who was controlling North China, in exchange for his pledge to the Republic. Sun did it in the spirit of the earliest emperors in Chinese history as exemplified by Emperors Yao who offered the throne to Shun, and Shun to Yu, but because of real differences of ideas and policies and because of personal greed, civil war broke out in 1914; at first as a protest against Yuan Shih-kai's attempt to become emperor, and later as a struggle for power among the different political cliques and military leaders who have been termed warlords. Civil war lasted for about 14 years until the country was unified by the Chinese Nationalist Party, the Kuomintang, in 1928, under the leadership of Chiang Kai-shek.

## World War I

The Chinese Republic was less than 3 years old when World War I broke out in 1914. China did not take either side until

1917 when it declared war against Germany. The war was never fought in its territory. China's main contribution to the battle-front was the sending of Chinese labourers to France to dig the trenches. In the past decades since the Opium War, the foreigners had always stood together in their confrontations with China, notably in their defence of the special rights and privileges, of which the extraterritorial rights and control of the Customs were the most outstanding. Even in private affairs the white men who came to China often refrained from speaking unfavourably of another white man before the Chinese. To the masses of the Chinese people, the Westerners had common interests and worked in harmony. In religion it was thought they were all Christians worshipping the same god. Thus one of the first things which shocked the Chinese was the graphic propaganda material circulated in China by Britain and Germany, each accusing and condemning the other; each claimed that it was fighting the other for the sake of justice, and each claimed that it had a superior fighting force. This happened as soon as World War I broke out in 1914, before China joined the war, when both Britain and Germany had concessions in China from which to operate their propaganda campaign. Then, in 1917, the October Revolution of Russia brought about a different approach to the problems of government and of international affairs. The Chinese began to see that Westerners differ greatly. Republicanism and democracy began to appear as different things to different people according to individual conceptions of values which we now call ideology.

We shall not discuss the war nor how China entered. But when Germany was finally defeated, China did not get its share of the reward as a participant on the side of the allies. Instead, it suffered humiliation. The Japanese delegation at the Peace Conference in Paris demanded the transfer of the German concessions in China to Japan, which had been prearranged by secret diplomacy. Liang Chi-chao, a Chinese delegate at Paris and a great Chinese scholar in his own right, telegraphed the Chinese people of the impending national humiliation. The famous Student Movement under the leadership of the students in Peking broke out on 4 May 1919 in protest against the signing of the Treaty of Versailles; many university professors also participated. In a few days' time, the movement spread through all the cities in China, arousing unprecedented national indignation which later gave rise to the development of strong nationalism in the decades to follow. The illusion of republicanism, of human justice, and of membership in the family of nations was shattered.

## The Chinese Renaissance and the Student Movement

The Chinese Renaissance is an important movement in the history of modern China. It had a great bearing not only on the immediate Student Movement but also on the events which followed.

To trace the origin of the Renaissance Movement, which the Chinese call Hsin Wen Hua Yun Tung, the New Culture Movement, credit should be given to the publication of the *Hsin Ching Nien*,[7] *La Jeunesse* or *New Youth* magazine, which was first published on 15 September 1915 under the editorship of Chen Tu-hsiu, who later founded the Chinese Communist Party in 1921 and was its first chairman for many years.[8] The magazine was the banner of this rejuvenating movement for a new culture in the name of science and democracy. It stood for the principles of liberty and equality and thus advocated the defence of human rights, the emancipation of women, the scientific spirit of inquiry, and the liberation of language and literature. It denounced feudalism of all kinds and was thus very critical of the Chinese traditional culture.

Chen Tu-hsiu was the Dean of the Faculty of Arts in the University of Peking. The Chancellor of the University of Peking

[7] Its original name in Chinese was *Ching Nien Tsah Chih* (*The Youth Magazine*) which was changed to this name beginning from its second volume on 1 September 1916.

[8] Chen Tu-hsiu remained its chairman until 1927. He was purged in 1929.

was Tsai Yuan-pei, whose magnanimity enabled the assemblage in his university of noted Chinese scholars of all schools of thought. They ranged from conservatism to radicalism, from romanticism to classicism, from anarchism to nationalism, and from individualism to socialism. Thus the University assumed the intellectual leadership of the country. With the fervent spirit of youth manifested in the articles in the magazine, which were contributed by China's pioneer thinkers, many of whom were professors from the University of Peking, the magazine gained more prestige for the University. This explains the outburst of the Student Movement on 4 May 1919 by the students of the Peking University, and the ready response throughout the country almost overnight.

The Chinese Renaissance started off as a literary, cultural, and thought movement. But as a cradle of new ideas it ended up with many kinds of revolutions, including social revolution and political revolution. One may very properly say today that the Chinese Communist Party was conceived in this movement, if we call to our minds some of the outstanding figures of the renaissance and the events which took place at that time. Besides Chen Tu-hsiu, there was another Communist leader, Li Ta-chao, whom Mao Tse-tung praised as one of the greatest Chinese thinkers of communism. When Li Ta-chao was librarian of the University of Peking, Mao Tse-tung worked under him as a library assistant. In the special number of the *Hsin Ching Nien*, "Studies on Marxism", published in May 1919, Li wrote an article entitled "My Views on Marxism". The success of the Russian Revolution under the dictatorship of the proletariat as the first state of its kind gave the impetus which the revolutionaries needed.

A word may be in place at this juncture regarding Hu Shih and the Chinese Renaissance. In the past when the Communist Party was banned from China by the Nationalists, the contribution of the scholars to the Renaissance who later became Communists was minimized. In the Western world, the Chinese Renaissance was identified with Hu Shih, an American-trained scholar who was a spokesman for Western democracy. It is true that Hu Shih played a very prominent role in the Renaissance, but however prominent it may be, he cannot be called "the father of the Chinese Renaissance". One may recall that when the *Hsin Ching Nien* was published in Peking in 1915, Hu Shih was still a student in America and had no connection with it whatsoever. Although a few of his minor articles were accepted by the magazine, he was not connected with its operation until he returned to China in summer 1917. The Chinese New Cultural Movement is too important in modern Chinese history for the Communists to give up their claim of leadership. They have good grounds on which to build their case. However, to credit the Ranaissance to Hu Shih's initiation is historically incorrect. The Renaissance was a movement of liberalism and was not committed to any side of thought, except the side of liberalism. It may be safely said in passing that most leaders in Chinese political, social, and cultural life of the last 40 years have been connected with or influenced by the New Culture Movement one way or another.

## The Founding of the Chinese Communist Party

It was a small event in 1921 when the Chinese Communist Party was formed in Shanghai with a small group of thirteen delegates, representing a total membership of 59,[9] to constitute the first congress of the party. Chen Tu-hsiu, a leader of the Chinese New Culture Movement, was elected the first chairman as we have said. The founding of the Chinese Communist Party was an event considered so insignificant by non-Communist Chinese writers that it had never been captioned as a significant event in modern Chinese history. But as we look at modern Chinese history now, it should be considered as a very significant event and deserves special mention. Since this whole study is on

[9] According to Chang Kuo-tao, one of the founders of the Chinese Communist Party (see Chang Kuo-tao, *My Memoir*, Chapter 6; *Ming Pao Monthly*, Vol. 1, No. 6, Hong Kong, June 1966).

contemporary China, we do not need to say here that which will be covered in later pages. It may be worth noting here that it was World War I which gave birth to the Chinese Communist Party, and it was World War II which gave birth to the Chinese Communist Party's Régime, the People's Republic, 28 years after the party's formation. This is a matter of great magnitude which deserves attention.

*Two Decades of the Nationalist Régime*

By the Chinese Nationalist régime we mean the government under the control of the Chinese Nationalist Party or the Kuomintang. The Government was formed in Canton in 1925 as a revolutionary government contesting the government of the Chinese Republic in Peking. In 1927 it became the National Government of the whole of China when its northern expeditionary forces under the command of Chiang Kai-shek captured Peking and established its capital in Nanking. Since then it has often been referred to as the Nanking Government. In 1937 Nanking was captured by the Japanese army and the seat of government was moved to Chungking. In 1946, after the surrender of the Japanese, the Government moved back to Nanking. In early 1949 it was captured by the Communists and the seat of government was moved to Canton and then to Taiwan.

This Nationalist Movement and the New Culture Movement may be said to be of different origins. While the New Culture Movement was an intellectual movement started in the north and based in Peking, the Nationalist Movement was a political movement started in the south and based in Canton. The Nationalist Movement was under the leadership of Sun Yat-sen who advocated his political theory of the "Three Principles of the People"—The Principles of Democracy, Nationalism, and Livelihood—as the basis of government. It is not necessary to go into the details of the developments of the Nationalist Government in Canton. In 1924, under Russian influence and with Russian aid, Sun Yat-sen admitted members of the Chinese

Communist Party into the Kuomintang in order to inject new blood into his party and to adopt Communist propaganda techniques. Sun Yat-sen and his party adopted the so-called three great policies : Alliance with Russia, Admission of Communists, and the Strengthening of the Labour Movement. After Sun Yat-sen's death in March 1925, the Nationalist Party and the Communist Party worked hand in hand. As the Communists were getting more powerful and aggressive, a surprise purge of the Communists by the Nationalists took place in March 1927 in which many Communists were killed. This ended the first co-operation between the Communists and the Nationalists. The split lasted for 10 years. In 1937, when the Sino–Japanese War broke out, they co-operated again in a united front against the common enemy—Japan. It seems strange that the Communists have been able to sap the blood of the Nationalists whether the two parties were in alliance or in hostility.

To those who are specially interested in education, the two decades of education under the Nationalist régime were a period of nationalization and nationalism. Authority was centralized in the National Government. The school system from the kindergarten to the university was made uniform. Private schools must be registered with the Government. All mission schools and universities which had enjoyed institutional autonomy had not only to register, but also to have a Chinese as their chief executive. Curricula and syllabuses were standardized and all textbooks had first to be approved by the educational authorities. For many years private schools and universities were not allowed to undertake teacher training. San Min Chu I, the Three Principles of the People, was required to be taught in all schools and military training was required in secondary and higher schools. Student councillors of all schools had to be approved by the Kuomintang, and officers in charge of military training were appointed by the Government. In every university there was a cell of Kuomintang to look after the interests of the party. Even when the Nationalist Party was collaborating with the Communist Party in the war with Japan, it was a crime in the

Nationalist territories to preach communism or to be a member of the Communist Party.

That was the state of affairs in education in the Nationalist Government in those years. We should bear in mind that in the Communist areas, in the synchronous period, another set of conditions were in progress. Although they were minor areas, and conditions there were less stable, they too had their own system of government and system of education which were the embryos of the administrative and educational systems we find in China today. To the Communists, the reforms in the territories they later occupied were largely extensions of what they had been doing all along in their home bases. We shall take note of this fact when we discuss the social institutions and the schools in later chapters.

## World War II

World War II affected the outlook of the Chinese people as did the first one. As far as the Chinese are concerned, World War II broke out on 7 July 1937 when China declared war on Japan. It lasted 8 years, and was therefore longer than for any of her allies.

One cannot very well call this simply the Sino–Japanese War, as there was an earlier one in 1895. Future historians will probably call it the Second Sino–Japanese War. The outbreak of the war occurred in 1937 at the Marco Polo Bridge in the outskirts of Peking on 7 July, and is often referred to by the Chinese as the 7–7 Incident. It was not an isolated incidence of conflict. One should remember the 18 September Mukden Affair of 1931, which the Chinese call the 9–1–8 Incident, and the 28 January Shanghai Incident of 1932 which the Chinese call the 1–2–8 Incident, both of which had brought about national tension in China. Within a short time after the war started in 1937, China's sea coast and almost all of its cities on the eastern part of the territory from Peking to Canton were under Japanese occupation. For the first 4 years of the war, that is, before Japan's attack on Pearl Harbour in December 1941, China was fighting Japan alone. After America entered the war, China's faith in their final defeat of Japan was assured. If one asks what that war has done to China, we may say that as far as our discussion is concerned, there are significant results. First, the war brought about a great national awakening, greater than any event past. Therefore it was in a very real sense a national war in which almost everybody everywhere was affected. The area occupied by the Japanese was almost half of China's territory and the time stretched out to 8 years. In the course of the war, whether it was a regional victory or whether it was a regional defeat, nationalism was instigated in any case. Secondly, it brought about a greater unity of the Chinese people. It brought about a unity of purpose in an anti-aggression war. It also brought the people from all parts of China into the interior, giving the people in the interior, who used to be more or less secluded, a wider contact with the people of the coastal provinces as well as giving the coastal people a real glimpse of the vast dominion and its people. The language barrier gave way to the national tongue which became as necessary as it was popular. Associations of all kinds developed among people from different provinces and localities on a much greater scale than ever before. Thirdly, it developed a greater social and political consciousness among the people. There was less regard for the *status quo* as everything was undergoing change. Standards of value were changing from day to day and from place to place. With the great destruction of property and life, the idea of property and life changed. With the mobility of the population, the standard of values, of clothing, food, shelter, and transportation changed. What had been thought to be the correct thing to do in the social or the political realms became less certain. People began to re-evaluate the promises of divergent political ideologies. Coupled with this reappraisal was general discontent over the existing political régime of the Kuomintang and the allurement of promises of a new system with Communist participation. It led the Chinese people to feel that not only was communism not dangerous but also quite desirable as an agent of better government. So in a real sense the war with Japan paved the way for communism, through the spread of ideas in the great reshuffling of the population which was, indeed, a most dynamic form of mass communication.


## CHINA IN THE LAST TWO DECADES

There is an interim period of about 4 years between the close of World War II at the Surrender of Japan in August 1945 and the establishment of the Chinese People's Republic in October 1949. This period may be looked upon as a prelude to the Communist régime. Communist rule over China actually began earlier than October 1949 if we start with Communist capture of Nanking, of Peking, or of Mukden.

When the anti-Japanese war was going on, the Chinese Nationalist Party and the Chinese Communist Party were working in collaboration for a common front. They were lesser enemies when they had a greater enemy in common; but, during the later stage of the war, as soon as victory was anticipated, the two parties began to plan their own future after the war. Mutual suspicion and distrust grew as days went by. The Communists, who chose guerrilla tactics all along, had their men scattered in and around the Japanese occupied territories. These territories were administered under the puppet government of Wang Ching-wei, a defector of the Kuomintang who had no army. The situation was clear : that as soon as the Japanese surrendered, the Communists would be ahead of the Nationalists in the occupation of those territories. This worried the Nationalists. The Nationalists, however, held a strong army in reserve in China's west and north-west, behind the Communists, which they did not throw into the anti-Japanese war theatre. This worried the Communists who accused the Nationalists of threatening their rear and preparing for war against them. The rivalry between the two parties for power over China was apparent and civil war was imminent.

We shall not go into the details of their military manœuvres. The Nationalists gained the upper hand at first by reoccupying practically all of the territories formerly occupied by the Japanese army. They were able to take over Manchuria which had been in Japanese hands and, for a brief period, Russian hands, by transporting the American-trained and most modernly equipped Chinese New First Army all the way from Burma to China's north-eastern provinces via Canton and the coast. The Communists took their time. They withdrew and consolidated their forces at first, and with superior tactics and morale were able to defeat the Nationalists and take over all their mainland territory in 3 years.

For a time, at the close of World War II, there were efforts to avert a civil war in China by bringing about a coalition government of some kind. General George C. Marshall, a special envoy of the United States, tried to mediate. There was, at first, the Committee of Three, with one member representing the Chinese Nationalist Party, one representing the Chinese Communist Party, and the other being General Marshall who was the chairman. It met at Chungking, in January 1946, in an attempt to settle the differences. Then followed the Political Consultative Conference (PCC) which was composed of representatives of the Kuomintang, the Chinese Communist Party, the Democratic League, the Youth Party, and some non-party delegates. But whatever was agreed upon regarding a cease-fire, it was not observed. The Nationalists and the Communists accused each other of violation. General Marshall withdrew from the mediatorship. The two parties finally resorted to war to settle their differences.

As a result, the Communist army, which the Communists call the People's Liberation Army, was able in 1948 and early 1949 to take over not only Manchuria but also North China, including the old capital of Peking. By the end of 1949 the whole of China's mainland was in Communist hands, while Chiang Kai-shek with his army and government was driven to the island of Taiwan which was returned to China by the Japanese as a condition of peace, and which has since been the Nationalists' refuge under the protection of the Seventh Fleet of the United States.

Inferior military strength was not the only cause of the collapse of the Nationalist Government; in fact, in number, the Nationalist army far exceeded that of the Communist army, and in equipment it was far superior. To begin with they were of the same stock of Chinese soldiers. What caused the Nationalist collapse was chiefly the corruption of Chiang's Government. Corruption demoralized the army and made it an incompetent fighting unit. When there was no worthy cause to die for and when graft had rotted the rank and file, no soldier would die for a few dollars and cents in a fast depreciating currency. Corruption also demoralized the Government at all levels. The Nationalist régime was rotten to the core, so much so that even the capitalists and industrialists, the bourgeoisie, and petite-bourgeoisie, who would usually be the mainstay of an anti-Communist government, were opposed to the Government. They were given no choice except to believe that no government could be worse and any would be better. The book by Chen Pa-ta, a Communist theorist, on "China's Four Big Clans", referring to the families of Chiang (Kai-shek), (H. H.) Kung, (T. V.) Soong, and Chen (Li Fu and Kuo Fu, known as two Chens or C.C.) did a lot of damage to the Nationalist Government, accusing them of transferring national wealth to their family fortunes. The hardship of the people increased in spite of having won a war. The Government was too inefficient to cope with the situation, in fact it had accelerated the disintegration and the deterioration. The deplorable conditions were further aggravated by Communist infiltration and agitated by Communist propaganda, which made it a fatal case for the Nationalists. It was under those circumstances that the Liberation Army was able to make its onslaught from north to south and from east to west at a much quicker speed than even the Communists themselves had anticipated. This reflects the truth of the thesis : that it was not communism which the Chinese people were fond of, but it was the Nationalist Government with which they were completely disgusted.

As to the major events in China's development in the last 17 years, they may be summarized as follows.

## The Chinese People's Political Consultative Conference

The first major event in the history of the Chinese People's Republic was the convening of the Chinese People's Political Consultative Conference (CPPCC) in Peking on 21 September 1949. There had been a Political Consultative Conference (PCC) in 1946, as we have mentioned a little earlier, but it soon collapsed. In 1947, when the prospects of establishing a new Coalition Government to replace Chiang Kai-shek's Government were growing, the Chinese Communist Party advocated the convening of a new PCC under their direction to fulfil what they said the Nationalists had failed to do. By the autumn of 1949, when the Liberation army was so successful, the formation of a new nationwide government looked so feasible, that when the conference met in September it took the name of the Chinese People's Political Consultative Conference (CPPCC) to assume the duties of a provisional parliament. The representation was much wider and membership greatly increased. The participants included 14 political party units, 9 area units, 6 Liberation Army units, 16 national organization units, and a special invitation group. There were 662 delegates in all, with 585 voting members and 77 non-voting alternate members in the CPPCC when it was convened.

The conference lasted for 10 days. Some of the major decisions of the Conference were : (1) The declaration of the establishment of the Chinese People's Republic; (2) the proclamation of the Common Programme as the basis of government; (3) the adoption of the Statute of the Central People's Government; (4) the election of Mao Tse-tung as the Chairman of the Central Government and Chou En-lai as the Premier of the State Council. Some of the minor decisions were : (1) the establishment of the capital in Peking;[10] (2) the adoption of the five-star red flag as the national flag; (3) the adoption of the Christian era as the Chinese era; and (4) the adoption of the *Volunteer's March Song* as the provisional national anthem.[11] On 1 October 1949, the day immediately following the close of the Conference, Mao Tse-tung declared the inauguration of his government at the Gate Tower of Tien An Men (the Gate of Heavenly Peace), the entrance gate to the ancient Imperial Forbidden City of glamorous splendour. The Gate Tower of Tien An Men was made the coat-of-arms of the Chinese People's Republic, identified with the political prestige and authority which had taken centuries of imperial central government to foster.

## Mao Tse-tung's Visit to Moscow

Mao Tse-tung visited Moscow in December 1949 to attend Stalin's 70th birthday celebration and to negotiate various Sino–Soviet agreements, including the Sino–Soviet Friendship Alliance and the Soviet Loan Agreement with China, which were signed in February 1950. The meeting of those two Communist leaders was a great symbol of the fraternal bond between the two great Communist countries, adjacent to each other, comprising over a third of mankind. The alliance made the Chinese position in the world more secure, while the loan was a great impetus to China in the recovery of its economy in the aftermath of war. The enthusiasm over this alliance and assistance was immeasurable. It was exactly this enthusiasm that later brought almost insurmountable difficulties to the Chinese mind when the Sino–Soviet rift came into the open.

[10] Peking had been China's capital since the fifteenth century with the exception of the Nationalist period from 1927 to 1937 and from 1946 to 1948 when Nanking was the capital and Peking was called Peiping.

[11] The song was written by Tien Han to a tune by Nieh Erh. It became very popular in the Anti-Japanese War. Its motif is said to be comparable to the French *La Marseillaise*.

## The Land Reform

The purpose of the reform was to abolish the ownership of land by landlords. It was to replace the feudalistic exploitation system by one of land ownership for the peasants in order to encourage productive energy in the village, to increase agricultural productivity, and to pave the way for the industrialization of China. There had been land reform in the Communist territories long before the establishment of the People's Republic. What the reform now did was to make it nationwide and to make it thorough. The Land Reform Act was promulgated on 30 June 1950, with six chapters in forty articles. The wording and provisions were mild, but its implementation was most unjust and inhuman. As the movement was put in the hands of the masses, the sufferings inflicted on many innocent people have left a permanent scar of horror in the history of the Communist régime, whatever good one may want to say of the accomplishments of the land reform.

## The Anti-America Aid-Korea Campaign

The Anti-America Aid-Korea Compaign started in October 1950 when the Chinese fighting forces came to the assistance of northern Korea in the form of the Chinese Volunteers' Army. It was an effort to help Communist Korea to hold out, after its attempt to unify Korea in the Chinese pattern failed, and it was driven back by the southern Koreans and their American supporting forces. The campaign in China was not confined to its military nature. It was made a great patriotic movement and permeated all corners of the country and all phases of life. The stubborn resistance which the Chinese put up in face of the superior weapons of the American forces won for China a good deal of prestige. The way they succeeded in winning over numerous American prisoners of war to their side by what the Western world calls "brain-washing technique" was startling. Truce was finally transacted in June 1953 at the 38° parallel, which has since remained the dividing line between pro-Chinese North Korea and pro-American South Korea. The effect of the Anti-America Aid-Korea Campaign upon China's international prestige and conversely upon her internal economy cannot be easily calculated.

## The First Five-year Plan

After 4 years of economic recuperation, China began its reconstruction programme, following the old Soviet pattern of the five-year plans. The first five-year plan was announced in 1953 for the period from 1953 to 1957. Whatever unfavourable conditions China might have, which handicapped her economic planning, the political conditions were certainly favourable, as the government was highly centralized and central authority accepted without dispute. Whether or not one believes in the success of the first five-year plan (as the Chinese Government had claimed), the experience in such a large-scale economic planning, in its execution, management, co-ordination, and supervision, was certainly invaluable to the Chinese people who are novices at this game. The second five-year plan was launched in 1958 for the period from 1958 to 1962. Then, because of China's economic failures in those years, which were due to natural calamity, human failure, and the withdrawal of Soviet assistance, the third five-year plan was not announced until late in 1965 for the years 1966–70. There were three interim years, as we notice, between the second and the third plans.

## The National People's Assembly

The National People's Assembly met for the first time in September 1954, 5 years after the establishment of the People's Republic. This Assembly was composed of delegates elected by the electorate as distinct from the delegates in the CPPCC who were selected by political consultation. In this Assembly, the Constitution of the Chinese People's Republic was adopted to replace the Common Programme passed by the CPPCC in 1949. This Assembly again elected Mao Tse-tung as the Chairman of the People's Central Government and Chou En-lai as the Premier, while Liu Shao-chi was elected Chairman of the Assembly. In the Second National People's Assembly, held in April 1959, Mao Tse-tung announced his unwillingness to accept the chairmanship of the Central Government and so Liu Shao-chi was elected in his place as Chief of State. From then on, when Mao Tse-tung is addressed as Chairman Mao, he is chairman *only* of the Chinese Communist Party and not of the People's Republic, though everyone knows that the Party's Chairman has final authority over all matters of the State. Chou En-lai was again elected Premier. The chairmanship of the Assembly was offered to Chu Te. Thus the line-up of the four great Communist leaders was in this order : Mao Tse-tung, Chairman of the Party; Liu Shao-chi, Chairman of the Central Government; Chou En-lai, Premier of the State Council; and Chu Te, Chairman of the National People's Assembly. Their posts have remained unchanged (*Autumn, 1966*).

### "Hundred Flowers Bloom" and "Hundred Schools Contend"

The well-known "Hundred Flowers Bloom" and "Hundred Schools Contend" campaign started in 1956 and lasted for only a year. It was a brief period during which one could see a glimpse of liberalism. People aired their opinions and voiced their criticisms, but as the situation developed to such an extent to overshadow Communist leadership, and as the authorities worried lest the 1956 Hungarian uprising might repeat itself in China, the movement was abruptly turned into a movement of persecution of the rightists. We notice that those who were vocal in the Hundred Flowers and Hundred Schools Campaign have since been silent or silenced. Although that movement has been subdued, it is doubtful whether the human urge for free expression can forever be subdued.

## *The Great Leap Forward and the Three Red Flags*

The people were called to the Great Leap Forward campaign and the establishment of the People's Communes in 1958 when the country was stunned in consequence of the persecution of the "rightists" and the withdrawal of Soviet assistance. One of the most spectacular features of the Great Leap was the establishment of simple furnaces everywhere to cast iron and steel. Workers and housewives, young and old, boys and girls all participated in what Westerners call "back-yard furnaces". It was a drive for harder work and austerity throughout the land. The Great Leap generally applied to the industries in the cities, while the People's Communes applied to agriculture in the countryside. In the short period of a few months, People's Communes were established by hundreds of thousands through the merger of the rural co-operatives into production teams and brigades. Today the furnaces are no longer in operation, but the Communes have remained as the chief form of social and economic structure in rural areas. The Three Red Flags are the Flag of the Great Leap Forward, the Flag of the People's Communes, and the Flag of the Socialistic Main Line. It is the third flag, the Socialistic Main Line of Action, which is really the main flag. It forms the transition from the period of democratic revolution to socialistic revolution in Communist China, that is from the new democracy to socialism.

## *The Sino–Soviet Split*

The Chinese Communist split with the Soviets came into the open after the failure of Teng Hsiao-ping's delegation to the Soviet Union in 1963. The rift had begun as early as March 1953 when the Chinese and Soviet leaders were each mourning over the death of Stalin. In tribute to Stalin, Mao Tse-tung wrote an article entitled "The Most Precious Friendship" which appeared in the editorial of *Renmin Ribao (The People's Daily)* on 8 March 1953, 3 days after Stalin's death. In that article Mao said that he was in hearty support of the Soviet Union under the supreme leadership of Malenkov. His pledge of support for Malenkov, who was later deposed, was probably the source of his conflict with Khrushchev and the de-Stalinists. The Sino–Soviet strain was an undercurrent, mostly unnoticed. The open split was perhaps not much of a shock to the Chinese Communist leaders, but it was definitely a shock to the masses of the Chinese people who had been taught that the Sino–Soviet friendship was perpetual and unbreakable. It may be that the rift will be cemented in the future, but it has already done enough harm to the prestige of world communism in China.

## The Atomic Bomb Explosion

We may mention the explosion of the atomic bomb[12] in the western part of China on 16 October 1964 as one of the series of major events in contemporary China. This single act demonstrated to the world the ability of Chinese scientists as well as the Chinese Communist Government to master the nuclear device. Its production meant a lot of strain on China's economy. But it did win for China as its prize "membership in the Atomic Club". The prestige of the Chinese Communist Government is thus increased at home and abroad. It has strengthened China's hand in its bargaining for peace, though it has made China more vulnerable as a target of war. Here lie her hopes and her fears.

## The Great Proletarian Cultural Revolution

The latest development in China is the Great Proletarian Cultural Revolution which came to take this name on 18 April 1966 as announced in the editorial of the *Jiefangjun Bao* (*Liberation Army Daily*) on that day. The editorial was entitled "Hold High the Great Red Banner of Mao Tse-tung's Thought, and

---

[12] The explosion of the second atomic bomb in China took place on 14 May 1965. There were four nuclear tests by the end of 1966. See Chapter 7, section on "Nuclear explosions".

Actively Participate in the Great Socialist Cultural Revolution".
The campaign is as much a tightening of the Socialist endeavour
as it is intended to purge its party leaders of what the army leaders
call the anti-Maoist elements, who stand in line with the party's
high intellectuals and influential writers in their cultural views.
The campaign was at first directed against the so-called bourgeois
viewpoint taken by *Frontline* (a fortnightly in Peking) and the
*Peking Daily* and the *Peking Evening News*, and on the writings
of Teng To, Liao Mo-sha, and Wu Han who are grouped by the
army clique as "The Three Family Village". This campaign is
another anti-rightist campaign, where the leftists attack those who
do not fall in line with them as anti-Mao, anti-party and anti-
socialist. The Red Guards have posed themselves as vanguards of
the cultural revolution. In reality, it is a life and death struggle to
prevent the rise of revisionism within the Chinese Communist
Party.

In outlining the major events in China since 1949 it is hoped
that we have presented a general picture of China in the last
17 years. This period, though brief in Chinese history, is, nevertheless, a very eventful one. Mao Tse-tung has been the dominat-
ing spirit in this period of history; but he has advanced in years
and has already passed the climax of his vigour. He has no new
ideas and programmes to offer but only his old thoughts to be
studied (and studied they are seriously) throughout the whole
country as a nationwide campaign, as the last exercise of his
influence. It is probable that his leadership will pass on to others
in the near future. So this period which we have covered will
probably be known in Chinese history as the Mao Tse-tung era.

# CHAPTER 2

# The Present Social and Economic Complex

## COMPLEX AND "SIMPLEX"

IN ANY society, the social structure and economic structure were originally simple and unified. We may say that the social and economic were only two aspects of the societal structure. Take, for example, the family. In an early society, the family was simultaneously a social structure and an economic structure with their functions and values well integrated. But as life became more complicated and diversified, and as social change came about, within its structure and outside of it, the social and economic functions began to diverge and their values to conflict with each other. Disintegration and contradiction followed. Such a state of affairs is most seriously aggravated in the societies of the modern world which have emerged from an agrarian order to an industrial order, or which are shifted from an oriental civilization to an occidental civilization. The case of China in the modern period, particularly since the opening of the twentieth century, is a clear example. The confusion and anachronism of social and economic life in Shanghai up to 1949 or in Hong Kong today reveal, in an alarming degree, the contradictions and eccentricities which exist between one social institution and another, between one economic institution and another, and between the social institutions and the economic institutions. It seems that some kind of reshuffling and simplification is justified.

The Chinese society today, under the Communist régime, is, in a perfect sense, undergoing this process of reshuffling and simplification, of reorganization and reordering. The new régime has aimed to abolish all the social and economic structures of the past, condemning them as the remnants of feudalism, colonialism, official bureaucracy, and "compradorism". In their place, a new social and economic order is to be installed under the ideology of Marxism–Leninism. In the process of reconstruction, what has been irrational has to be changed into rational, contradictory into synthetic, and outmoded into up-to-date.

Everything must be unified and streamlined. Thus every social institution has to be remodelled to make it harmonious with other social institutions; every economic institution has to be remodelled to make it harmonious with other economic institutions; and, indeed, all social institutions and economic institutions must be remodelled in such a way that they are complementary with each other. The social and the economic structure in China today are so much bound up with each other, in such a unified manner, that the system may be likened to a net whereby in hooking any one grid, the whole net is pulled up. If a social institution has its economic implications (as surely it has) and if the economic implications are further involved (e.g. with the values of austerity, or with the cultivation of personal consideration in social relationships) then the social custom of offering a cup of tea or a cigarette to a caller, small and insignificant as it is, is brought to consciousness as behaviour which goes beyond one's legitimate expenditure, seeking favouritism in the form of bribery. Again, if an economic institution has its social implications (as surely it has) and if the social implications involve the dignity of man, the dignity of service and the dignity of the working class, then the economic institution of tips in a restaurant, small and insignificant as it is, is criticized as humiliating the waiter, degrading the genuine motive of service, and insulting the working class as a whole. We need not elaborate here. But from what seems trivial and insignificant, we may say that every single facet of life reflects the total structure. In such a sense the social–economic structure is really a social–economic *complex*. But, on the other hand, when we think of the unified character of the social and economic structure in China which eliminates

40       *Society, Schools and Progress in China*

contradictions, it becomes a social–economic *simplex*. So while the social and economic structures of the capitalistic societies may be called a social–economic complex, those in the communistic societies as seen in China today may be more properly called a social–economic *simplex*.

## THE PEOPLE'S DEMOCRATIC DICTATORSHIP

There has been a great deal of talk about the dictatorship of the proletariat in the pronouncements of the Chinese Communist Party today, but according to the Constitution of the Chinese People's Republic, the basis of the political, social, and economic structure of the People's Republic is the People's Democratic Dictatorship. How did the People's Democratic Dictatorship come about?

In 1940 Mao Tse-tung published an article "On the New Democracy".[1] He differentiated the "democracy" he favoured from the Western democracy which he opposed by calling his "the new democracy". In that article the word "dictatorship" did appear, but it was not conspicuous. In July 1949, however, as the formation of the Chinese People's Republic was in sight, Mao published the article "On the People's Democratic Dictatorship".[2] His idea there served as the basis of the new régime to be set up. Here "dictatorship" is given emphasis.

Let us first observe the term "the People's Democratic Dictatorship". This term is Mao Tse-tung's coinage. It may not sound too odd to those who are familiar with the developments in Eastern Europe after World War II, when several people's democratic republics came into existence. But to many others it does sound so. To qualify "democracy" with "people" is odd indeed. Though the term "people" and "demo" mean the same thing in English, their Chinese equivalents, *Ren-Min* and

[1] It was an article which Mao Tse-tung contributed to the *Chinese Cultural Magazine* on 19 January 1940. The original title was "The New Democracy's Politics and the New Democracy's Culture".
[2] It was written by Mao Tse-tung in commemoration of the 28th anniversary of the Chinese Communist Party on 1 July 1949.

*Min-Chu,* are slightly different. As long as the term *Ren-Min Min-Chu-Chu-I* (People's Democracy) goes well in Chinese usage, Mao was not particular how it would sound to the English-speaking peoples who go by Latin or Greek roots. Another thing in the term which is odd is the use of "democracy" as a prefix of "dictatorship". Mao evidently was not bothered by the conventional usage in the Western world. He might even enjoy the disrepute of the traditional Western concepts of government. When "people" is used to modify democracy, its purpose is to eliminate these elements in the state which are considered to be outside the definition of "people". When "dictatorship" is used in conjunction with the concept of democracy, it makes provision for the control of the Chinese Communist Party over the Government.[3]

## *The Meaning of "People"*

Since the term "people" as used in China today has great bearing on the understanding of Chinese affairs, an exploration of its meaning is in order. The Chinese Communists are very fond of using the term "people" to qualify their institutions as if the term possesses a magic power. As for their republic, they call it the "People's" Republic; their government, the "People's" Government; their court, the "People's" Court; their liberation army, the "People's" Liberation Army; their currency, the "People's" Currency; their bank, the "People's" Bank; their postal service, the "People's" Postal Service; their communes, the "People's" Communes; their major party newspaper, the "People's" Daily, etc. Instead of saying "for the service of the State", they say "for the service of the people". Certainly, the term "people" is more concrete than the term "State", and it is for the people that the State exists. When Abraham Lincoln spoke of the government of the people, by the people and for the people,

---

[3] It may be because of the inherent contradiction in the concept of "democratic dictatorship" that the Chinese Communists came out openly in 1966 to advocate "proletarian dictatorship" in China.

by "people", he meant "everybody". So Americans must be specially aware that, by "people", the Chinese Communists mean something else. In order to look the Chinese Communists straight in the eye, one must be clear what "people" does mean and what it does not mean in Communist usage.

First of all, "people", to them, does not mean "anybody". It does not mean "human beings" in general nor does it mean "citizens" or "nationals". Landlords, for instance, are Chinese citizens or Chinese nationals in the sense that their nationality is Chinese, but they are not in the category of "Chinese people". Indeed, they are considered enemies to the Chinese "people". They are "anti-people". As we see it now, which few Chinese saw even at the time of the formation of the Chinese People's Republic, "people" are primarily the workers, peasants, soldiers, and the masses who share the ideology of the Chinese Communists. The bourgeoisie (*petite* or *grande*) are not in the "people" category *per se*; but in so far as they are willing to forsake their own class and submit themselves to the interest of the working class and their revolutionary cause, they could be admitted into the "people" category. So when the Chinese Communists say that the fundamental interests of the Chinese people and the American people are the same, they do not mean that the fundamental interests of the Chinese nationals and American nationals are the same. What they mean is that the fundamental interests of the working class in China and those of the working class in America who share the Chinese Communists' view of world revolution are the same. The American president, for instance, does not belong to the "people" category, nor do the American senators and representatives. They are said to be "anti-people", as they do not represent that fraction of the working class in America who subscribe to the Communist revolutionary lines.

For that matter, the Soviet leaders of recent years such as Khrushchev, Kosygin, and Brezhnev, who pursue a different line of Communist revolution which the Chinese call "revisionism", are also "anti-people". The word "people", common as it is and pleasant as it sounds, means different things to the Communists and to the non-Communists, and means even different things among Communists of varying fields of thought. Unless one is constantly aware of the fundamental difference in the employment of the term in the two totally different worlds, he is sunk in his own illusion of the traditional humanitarian concept of "people" among whom he is included. Unless this awareness is alert, one's hope of understanding the tactics and the propaganda of communism is small.

The reason why many Chinese patriots who joined the Chinese Communist régime were later disappointed and persecuted is that they had failed to understand that "people" meant different things to them and to the Communists. By the time they realized the difference it was already too late. So either the so-called "democratic elements" have to admit their negligence in failing to understand the different meanings of the term "people" when they joined the Coalition Government, or else the Communists have to be accused of breach of promise in failing to live up to their word when they asked the democratic elements to come to their alliance.

## *The Provisions in the Common Programme*

The People's Democratic Dictatorship was installed when the Chinese People's Republic was established on 1 October 1949. Its declaration was based on the platform of the Chinese People's Political Consultative Conference (CPPCC) which is known as the Common Programme. Since the Preamble of the Common Programme[4] sums up the main theme of the programme and the nature of this People's Democratic Dictatorship, it may be worthwhile to quote it in full :

> The great victory of the war of liberation of the Chinese people and the people's revolution has declared the termination of the

---

[4] The Constitution of the Chinese People's Republic of 1954 which replaced the Common Programme also reaffirms this People's Democratic Dictatorship in its Preamble. See Chapter 3, The Broad Outline of the Political and Administrative Structure.

period of feudalistic, bureaucratic and capitalistic rule in China. The Chinese people have changed their role of the oppressed to that of the masters of a new society and a new state, with the republic of the people's democratic dictatorship to replace the reactionary rule of feudalistic, compradoristic, fascistic dictatorship of the Kuomintang. The Chinese people's democratic dictatorship is the assumption of political power by the People's Democratic United Front composed of the working class, the peasant class, the small-bourgeoisie class, the national bourgeoisie class and other patriotic democratic elements of China, which is based on the workers' and peasants' alliance and the leadership of the working class. The Chinese People's Political Consultative Conference is composed of delegates from the Chinese Communist Party, the various democratic parties, the people's organizations, the various areas, the Chinese People's Liberation Army, the various national minorities, overseas Chinese, and other patriotic democratic elements, and is the structural form of the People's Democratic United Front. The Chinese People's Political Consultative Conference, representing the will of the people of the whole of the country, declares the establishment of the Chinese People's Republic and organizes the Central Government of the people themselves. The Chinese People's Political Consultative Conference unanimously agrees to accept the New Democracy, that is, the People's Democracy, as the political foundation for national construction of the Chinese People's Republic, and has worked out the following Common Programme by which all participating units of the Chinese People's Political Consultative Conference, all levels of the People's Government, and all people throughout the country must mutually abide.

Now that we have presented the concept of the People's Democracy and the nature of this dictatorship, we shall proceed to an analysis of the implications on the social and economic structure in the early days of the Chinese People's Republic and the problems involved. Let us first examine the platforms of the two régimes—the Nationalists and the Communists. As far as national goals are concerned, the Nationalists are no different from the Communists in their aim of building a China which has to be independent, democratic, unified, peaceful, and prosperous. Regarding the objects of struggle, the Nationalists subscribe to only half of the Communists' cause. The Nationalists are as opposed to imperialism as the Communists, but when it comes to fighting feudalism, the Nationalists are not so definite. Among the Nationalists, some are strongly opposed to feudalism while others are not. As to bureaucratic capitalism, the Nationalists not only favour but are themselves its main stem and support.

One should bear in mind, as an historical fact, that the People's Democratic Dictatorship as declared in October 1949 was not the dictatorship of the proletariat. It did not go so far. Although the working class was to assume the leadership, the peasants' class was given its role as specified in the workers' and peasants' alliance. Besides, the "democratic classes" were also given a place in the political power structure, which included the petty bourgeoisie class and the "national bourgeoisie" class. These provisions make the People's Democratic Dictatorship different from the Dictatorship of the Proletariat which in turn determined the social–economic structure of the Chinese society, at least for the first few years of the Chinese People's Republic.

It is of special significance to note that at the formation of the Chinese People's Republic, the People's Democracy was not meant to be socialism and much less to be communism. In the Common Programme the term "socialism" did not appear at all. It did not appear in the preamble nor in any of its sixty articles. This was not an accidental omission—it was intentional. In one of the first sessions of the CPPCC, Liu Shao-chi delivered the major speech on behalf of the Chinese Communist Party delegation in which he said definitely that although it had been suggested to them that socialism as a future development be included in the Common Programme, they, the Communists, considered it too distant a future to mention it. He said :

> In the process of consultation, some delegates proposed that the prospects of socialism in China be mentioned in the Common Programme, but *we* consider it still improper. . . . Without doubt, China in the future will have to proceed to socialism and communism. . . . But that is something very far off from now. . . . The adoption of socialism in China must be based on practical needs in the development of Chinese society and its economy, and the demands of the great majority of the Chinese people.

In order to see, from another angle, the implication of the social and economic basis of the People's Democratic Dictatorship at the formation of the Chinese People's Republic, let us look at its national flag, commonly known as the five-star red flag.[5] Red was to symbolize revolutionary struggle, the big star was to symbolize the leadership of the Communist Party, and the four small stars the solidarity of the four classes consisting of the working class, the peasants class, the small-bourgeoisie class, and the national bourgeoisie class. Such was the meaning of the stars and such was the spirit of the People's Republic as it was founded.

## The Four Democratic Classes

Since the development of communism, the class concept has been very much played up. Class stratification and class consciousness have been underlined and exploited. It is by this means that class alienation and hatred are bred and the class struggle of the proletariat find its basis. The free world must be

---

[5] How the five-star flag was chosen is interesting. In the agenda of the CPPCC in September 1949 was an item on the decision of the national flag. Out of 2992 proposed designs contributed throughout the country, 38 were short-listed and printed in colour in a booklet and submitted to the delegates for consideration. The delegates in their preliminary discussion groups selected three designs but could not agree on which was the best. As the day for the declaration of the People's Republic was approaching, on which the National Flag had to be hoisted, there could be no further delay. It was decided that Mao Tse-tung be asked to make the choice. But to everybody's surprise, Mao did not choose from the three which the delegates had selected. He selected this five-star red flag which was No. 32 on the list in the booklet. It was a dark horse, indeed. After Mao had made the choice, all the delegates concurred that it was really the most beautiful flag. The delegates of bourgeois affiliation were particularly happy to have the assurance that their classes were given a prominent place and a permanent recognition, an assurance they had wanted to have but had no courage to request. According to the words of the designer, Tseng Luen-sung: "Red represents revolution and struggle; the big star represents the leadership of the Communist Party and the People's Liberation Army; the four small stars represent the alliance of the four classes in the new democracy; and yellow represents the yellow race of the Chinese." While the flag is still waving bright and high, the bourgeoisie classes are now being persecuted and liquidated. So by those who have always been sceptical of the Communists' words of faith, the five-star red flag is looked upon as the greatest political mockery in modern times.

aware that the prominence given to the class concept in sociological study today is very favourable to the furtherance of communism.

Before we speak of the four classes separately, let us take a look at the four classes as a whole.

*The four "classes" in traditional China.*   While the Chinese Communists speak of the four democratic classes in the People's Democratic Dictatorship today, the Chinese people have for ages spoken of their society as composed of four "classes". We use quotation marks for "classes" here because they mean the four occupations which are sometimes called the four peoples, or four types of people as marked by the nature of their occupation. They are the scholars, the farmers, the artisans, and the traders. So the four "classes" represented the four occupational arts rather than four social strata. The "classes" were interwoven and integrated. For instance a family may have its members involved in all the four occupations.

In Chinese society, for thousands of years, the scholar has been the most respected and the trader the least. The Chinese intellectuals have always played a major role in Chinese affairs and are still playing a major role in Chinese affairs today. As to the traders or merchants, since their motive is mercenary, a motive much attacked by Mencius among other sages, they have generally been looked down upon. According to Chinese traditions, no matter how much wealth a merchant might have acquired, he was not eligible for the "Village Honour Roll of the Virtuous" or the "Village Hall of Fame". So while people in the capitalistic countries, particularly people in the United States, are apt to think of the bankers, financiers, and business magnates as the top of the scale in their society, they should not be too surprised to find such a group of people placed in the bottom of the Chinese social scale.

*The four new classes.*   The four classes are sometimes called the four democratic classes or the four revolutionary classes.

They are the workers, peasants, petits-bourgeoisie and the "national bourgeoisie". We can well understand why the workers and peasants are included and placed at the top in a revolutionary régime. They constitute the largest bulk of the population and bear the chief burdens of production; but at the same time they have been most underprivileged. The scholars, those who handle ideas, are not grouped as a class. Yet the bourgeoisie, oddly enough, are not only included in this new régime but occupy two out of the four classes. This is of special intent and significance.

The bourgeoisie were included for practical and tactical reasons. It was practical at that time, when the People's Republic was under organization, though it might not be so now if the 1949 CPPCC were held today. If the Chinese People's Republic had been declared to be exclusively under the dictatorship of the workers and peasants, it could not have attained its success. The political, social, and economic power of the non-worker and non-peasant population was so great that even the most radical Communists would not have dared to ignore it. It was tactical because it was by admitting the bourgeoisie, they thought, that they could reduce the antagonism of the bourgeoisie at home as well as abroad. This is the policy and meaning of the United Front, as a modified method of world revolution. It was only by such an admission that their advocacy of a coalition government had any future.

But how can the bourgeoisie as a class be represented? It would be ridiculous to say that the Communist Party, which is avowed to stand for the interests of the workers and peasants, also represents the interests of the bourgeoisie. As a matter of fact, some Communists considered it an insult to be associated with the bourgeoisie. So the Communist Party took advantage of the non-Communist parties which participated in the CPPCC (such as the Revolutionary Committee of the Kuomintang, the Chinese Democratic League, and the Chinese Democratic National Reconstruction Association) and assigned them a role as the representative bodies of those particular groups. They proclaimed them as such in spite of the fact that those parties were unwilling to be so narrowly identified as they themselves had claimed to represent all classes of the people. No party other than the Communist Party could thereafter[6] claim to represent the peasants and workers. The Communist Party claims to be their exclusive representative.

*The workers' and peasants' alliance.* Some Western writers on Chinese affairs in the 1940's used to call the Chinese Communist Movement an agrarian reform. As every one would see it now, that is not the case. It is true that the peasants constitute the bulk of the population and from them the Liberation Army has been recruited. It is also true that the class struggle was most severe in the rural areas between the peasants and the landlords, and that it is on agriculture that China's economic revival must first depend. But the industrial workers as a class assume a very important role in the Communist revolution. Thus the dictatorship must be based on the alliance of the workers and peasants. So it is far from being just an agrarian movement.

*The leadership of the working class.* More than that, this workers' and peasants' alliance is to be under the leadership of the working class. The reasons for the assumption of leadership by the working class and not by the peasants' class may be explained in this way. First, in the Communist revolution, the workers, in the sense that they are the proletariat, are considered to be more reliable than the peasants. Unlike the peasants, they do not own the tools of production or property such as land; they are thus more susceptible to the class consciousness and ideology of the propertyless class. Second, in the drastic indus-

---

[6] There was a minor party, the Chinese Workers and Peasants Democratic Party, which participated in the CPPCC in 1949. It was founded by Teng Yen-ta in 1930 and followed up by a small group of political aspirants which had been orbiting around the Communist Party in the non-Communist territory. It now exists in name only and has no functions whatsoever.

trialization of the country, the vitality and enthusiasm of the industrial workers must be summoned to the utmost degree. If accorded this status as the spearhead of the revolution, they can be rallied for support.

Strictly speaking, by the worker is meant the proletariat working with machinery and industrial installations such as factories, railways, mines, etc.; they cannot produce without those tools and facilities, and yet they do not own them. The term "worker" is used rather loosely in China today to include even street cleaners and sweepers, nurses in the hospitals, the waiters in the hotels, the clerks in the offices and stores, the teachers in the schools, and the researchers in the laboratories. Enlarging its scope boosts the numerical strength of the working class in an underdeveloped industral society; including intellectuals increases the prestige of the working class. Another departure from the Marxian concept of the worker as one without a fatherland is that in China the worker is also appealed to through his patriotism so as to make China a strong nation and to surpass other countries.

*The bourgeoisie.*  This French word meant the class of people of the towns who are shopkeepers or small businessmen. They constitute the backbone of the middle class, a class of people between the gentry and the peasants. The population in this class is small, but it is a very dynamic one. In China the characteristic of this class is that they are closely related to the merchant class either by family origin or by association. These people are more sensitive to public issues and affairs. They are the literate, not the illiterate, of the country. It is from them that most of the intellectuals came and, indeed, from them practically all Chinese Communist leaders today have come. They form the brain of society and assume the place of leadership among the people, as shown in the 1911 revolution, the various patriotic movements, and particularly in the Student Movement of 1919 when townspeople and shopkeepers throughout the country used boycotts and strikes as their instruments in protest against the signing of the Versailles Treaty. It was the inherent power of the city bourgeoisie which the Chinese Communists respected and feared.

Small as the bourgeoisie is, it is further subdivided as the "small bourgeoisie" (or petty bourgeoisie) and the "national bourgeoisie"; these groups are thus represented by two stars on the flag, which seems to accord the bourgeoisie special honour. The Communists, however, by giving the bourgeoisies two places intended to weaken the constituents through the process of division. By wooing the non-workers and non-peasants and the bourgeoisie to their side, the Communists could then split them, subjugate them, struggle with them, reform them, persecute them, and finally liquidate them and prevent them from revival as a class.

The number in the bourgeoisie as a whole was small, as we have said. The number in the "national bourgeoisie" was even negligible. They were the industrialists, capitalists, bankers, financiers, and big business men, who were few in China. And when those who had the status or connections with the status of landlordism, of civil and military officialdom, of imperialism, of colonialism, of compradorism (i.e. agency of foreign business firm), or of illegitimate business, are further subtracted from this class because of their anti-people nature, the numbers of the "national bourgeoisie" were further reduced to what one may count on his fingers.

One of the reasons why the vast territory which was in the Nationalists' hands fell so quickly to the Communists without local opposition, was that the Communists had advocated a coalition government of all democratic classes, and announced their economic policy of *Kung Szu Chien Ku* (Assistance both to Public and Private Business), and *Lao Tzu Liang Li* (Mutual Profit for Labourers and Capitalists). Those were good tactics because they implied a mild form of economic control similar to what Sun Yat-sen had advocated as regulated capital.

If one were to infer the state of affairs to be found in China in the People's régime simply from the promises of the Chinese Communist leaders, the concept of a coalition government, and the symbol of the five-star flag which still flies, one would expect a society of the workers, peasants, and small and big businessmen working harmoniously and hand in hand as respectable members of a common society. One would expect their respective activities to flourish with the blessings of the Communist Party and, when differences arise, to have them ironed out under Communist paternal supervision. He would expect the tillers to own their farms, the workers to have shorter hours, higher wages, better terms of employment, and to be protected from exploitation. One would expect the petty bourgeoisie to run their own business, employ workers, to be allowed reasonable profit, and the big industrialists and big business men to be able to employ their resources and use their talents to develop their enterprises as their contribution to the nation's economy. To many, such expectations were as logical as they were legitimate; it was only in that way that the admission of the bourgeoisie, the solidarity of the four classes, the five-star flag, and the statement of Liu Shao-chi of the impropriety of mentioning socialism in the Common Programme could make any sense.

But this is not the case in China today. All visitors in China can testify that the peasant does not own his own farm, the worker can make no wage demand. There is no such thing as private business or private industry. A great change from earlier picture has taken place in China; but what accounts for this change, and particularly what accounts for the forfeiture of the bourgeoisie?

To those who see only evils in communism, the explanation is simple. They consider every Communist promise a lie. What the Communists had promised was meant to allure and to deceive. Such a view and such an explanation are not without grounds.

But if one wants to go further into the inquiry, he might make these observations. In the first place, there are probably, at any time, two contesting groups within the Communist Party as within the Communist camp : one is for a more moderate policy and the other for a more drastic policy. All the latter group were most dissatisfied to see the bourgeoisie still swaggering in the new régime—in the high offices of the Government, in national and local public functions, and in social and economic life. They wanted to contrive a show-down as soon as the security of the Government was ascertained. For them there is a minimum programme and a maximum programme. The admission of the bourgeoisie and the solidarity of the four classes was definitely their minimum programme. Such a compromise was a sacrifice of their ideals in face of social realities. But they must move toward the maximum programme as soon as they can; and the earlier the better. In the second place, after the People's Government was established, the significance of the bourgeoisie was lost. It was no longer necessary to recognize them as a partner and play the tedious game of consultation. Besides, in the dismantling of the bourgeoisie class structure in the various social reforms in the early years of the People's Republic, the opposition from the ranks of the bourgeoisie was so negligible that the Communists came to realize that they could shorten their timetable. The Communists accept a dynamic view of society and do not feel they are the type of people to be bound by past pledges. In the third place, the idea of the solidarity of the four classes sounds good; but in practice it is difficult to operate. When the working class really takes up the leadership, it is inconceivable that the employer who belongs to the bourgeoisie and is lower in social and political status could dictate to his employee, a working man, what to do. A household cannot continue long in a scheme where the master is master in role but servant in status, while the servant is master in status but servant in role. The concept itself invites irreconcilable contradictions.

Now that the bourgeoisie, either as petty bourgeoisie or as national bourgeoisie, are out of the picture in the political and power structure, the Chinese Communists should be able to sleep well. But what is more fatal to them now is not the "body" of the bourgeoisie, which they can extinguish if necessary, but the "soul" of the bourgeoisie which is invisible. The values and value systems of the long-established bourgeois culture or the ideology of the bourgeoisie are still bothering the Communists, not only among the common people but also within their party, among their party leaders, and even among their party's leading theorists. The ghost of the bourgeoisie seems to be haunting them. When things do not go the way they want them to go, they blame it on the obstruction of bourgeois ideology or the revival of bourgeois thinking. It seems difficult to build a proletarian order with people who came originally from what they call a bourgeois home, including all their leaders today. The biographies of Liu Shao-chi, Chou En-lai, Chu Te, Teng Hsiao-ping, Lu Ting-yi, Peng Chen, and the whole list of the Party Central Committee members will tell the story. The softness of Mao Tse-tung's hand which many people have shaken, cannot fail to impress one that it had neither tilled nor toiled. But it is claimed that Mao Tse-tung's thinking is entirely free from bourgeois ideology—that of a Communist saint whose mind is supposed not to have been adulterated by the circumstances of the culture in which he was brought up.

## THE LAND REFORM

Land reform was one of the major themes of the Chinese Communist Revolution. The Chinese Communists advocated it from the very beginning. As early as 1923 it had appeared to Mao Tse-tung that the peasantry in China was good capital for Communist power and good material for the Communist Movement. This line of thought is sound, since it is the discontented and the destitute that are most susceptible to the call of revolution. They too are the people who have nothing to lose. Among the peasants in China there have always been complaints of great magnitude and from them an unlimited number of ardent supporters can come forth. In order to train leaders to undertake the promotion of the Peasants' Movement, Mao set up the Peasants' Movement Training Institute in Canton in 1924 as a licensed organization of the Nationalist Government during the period of the first collaboration of the Chinese Communist Party and the Kuomintang. Mao was the director of the Institute. The first piece of writing by him which attracted attention was his report on the work of organizing the peasants in Hunan, which was entitled "An Investigation into the Peasant Movement in Hunan", published in 1927.

Looking back over modern Chinese history, when the Chinese revolutionaries, whether Nationalists or Communists, first advocated land reform, we see that they approached the problem chiefly from the social aspect, namely from the standpoint of humanity and social justice. Sun Yat-sen's revolutionary programme which he advocated as early as 1912 included land reform. His slogan, as indicated in the title of the public address he made in that year, was : "The Equalization of Land Ownership."[7] In 1924 he made a speech at the graduation ceremony of the first batch of the short-course graduates in Mao's Peasants' Movement Training Institute. His topic was "To the Tiller, His Field", which also became a revolutionary slogan. Sun saw the need to remove the sufferings of the peasants, but he had no definite programme. He only pointed out at that time the need for the peasants to organize themselves as the immediate first step.

However, the Communists gave the matter further thought. They reinforced it with the economic side of their reforms, as a means of releasing human energy for greater productivity. Later, they made out a programme of their own and devised tactics of approach. Their tactics were first to divide the peasants into various categories, then win over certain groups to the Communist side and unite them, then isolate certain groups and mobilize certain others to attack the isolated ones. The war of land reform has been won in China by this strategy.

In the Land Reform Law which we shall mention later, rural society is classified into five main categories for the purpose of the class struggle. They are : the landlords, the rich peasants, the middle peasants, the poor peasants, and the employed peasants. In the land reform, in the persecution of landlords which they call "the struggle with the landlords", the tactics were to unite

[7] See Sun Yat-sen's Address to the Assembly Delegates and Newspaper Reporters in Canton, dated 9 June 1912.

the poor peasants and employed peasants, win over the middle peasants to their side, and isolate the rich peasants. One should bear in mind that in China such rural classes were not socially hereditary as they were in the West in the days of serfdom. Their status was in constant mobility. A poor peasant by working hard or by his ingenuity or by acquiring wealth elsewhere or by becoming a scholar and official, would have the means to acquire land and became a landlord, while landlords and their descendants, because of inability, laziness, indulgence, and crime might lose what they or their ancestors had acquired and become poor peasants. It may be of interest to note that landlords in China who were persecuted in the land reform often owned much less land than an ordinary farmer in America.

Village life in China has been painted by Western missionaries and travellers all along as a very peaceful and amiable one. True as it might be, there was a gloomy side which they seldom portrayed, apart from the superstitions and lack of hygiene which they did expose. That was the injustice and suffering, both social and economic, of the poor peasants who did not own land or who owned insufficient land to make a living and who had to pay high rent to the landlords. In cases where they had to borrow money from the landlords to tide them over the seasons, they had to pay extortionate rates of interest. The landlords were the only financiers in the rural areas.

There were very few big landlords in China who owned large tracts of land or who owned land outside their native place. Most of the landlords were small landlords who owned only the local land. Since small landlords are less magnanimous and are more exacting in dealings with their tenants, the peasants had unusual suffering. As Sun Yat-sen had said, it was because the landlords were mostly small landlords that the peasants in China suffered more than the peasants in Russia who suffered at the hands of imperial Kukahs. It would be too long a tale to describe the sufferings of the Chinese peasants from the established and abused system of landlordism. Dramas on the stage, museum exhibitions, and movies on the screen in Communist China today are full of stories of such tragedies. The accusations of the peasants against the landlords in the public trials during China's land reform would fill volumes and volumes of such accounts, some of which were true and some only alleged. Though containing much exaggeration and fabrication, they represented the general nature of things as they existed under the landlord system, especially when it was at its worst. Besides high rent and high rates of interest, the landlords exacted labour from the peasants without compensation, required tributes from their peasants, forced the tenants to sell their daughters to be their slaves and concubines, punished and imprisoned the poor peasants for offences in the landlords' area of influence, restricting the liberty of the tenants, persecuting them and poor peasants in case of resistance. There were all kinds of ill-treatment and humiliation. Those who have lived in Chinese villages for any length of time, and have seen those things with their own eyes, are of one accord on the need for reform as a redress for the wrongs inflicted upon the peasants and as a measure for a more humane rural order.

The land reform was vigorously carried out in the years 1950–3. Now it is all over and is something of the past. The reform was complete and thorough. It was really one of the greatest events in Chinese history, involving at least 80 per cent of the population of over 600 million in number. As the reform under Communist hands aimed at drastic demolition of the time-honoured system of land ownership and not at maintaining individual justice, the suffering brought to the people classified as landlords was unspeakable. More often than not, greater injustice and inhumanity were inflicted upon the landlords than they had ever inflicted on the peasants, unless it was intended that the landlords of this unfortunate generation had to pay once and for all, the wrongs which their ancestors and the landlords of generations and generations had done. There were many, many tragedies in the persecution, leaving in the minds of the Chinese people, including the persecutors themselves, unforgettable scenes of horror, more horrible than any revolution's quick bloodshed. It was the deliberate design of the manipulators of the reform to make it so horrible that there would be no roots left for the revival of the landlord class, and no one would ever dare to entertain the idea of re-establishing landlordism in the future.[8] The people were taught a lesson on the meaning of the class struggle, of drawing the line between the classes and of knowing on which side they should claim to be, forsaking the human feeling of tender-heartedness.

Before the Communists took over the Nationalist territory, they had a programme of land reform in their so-called "liberated areas". After the People's Republic was established and when the conditions, particularly the economic conditions, were under their control, they launched the nationwide programme of land reform. The land reform was based legally on the Chinese People's Republic Land Reform Law which was enacted in the CPPCC and promulgated by the Central Government on 30 June 1950. When the law was brought before the CPPCC in its Second Session on 14 June 1950, Liu Shao-chi introduced it with a report entitled "The Problems of the Land Reform". From his report as well as from the law itself, the impression one got was that the reform was to be carried out in a reasonable, mild, and humane manner. But, as everyone knows, it was carried out with much injustice and cruelty, costing the lives of millions of people in spite of the fact that there was practically no organized or violent opposition on the part of the people whom they classified as landlords and rich peasants. Granted that the reform did bring about a better social and economic system for the future generations, the price was much too costly for those who had to pay it in this generation. The land reform has left a very dark page in Chinese history. Future historians will surely not overlook its verdict and curses. It is not our business now to discuss it here.

What concerns us now is rather the social and economic structure in the countryside as a consequence of the land reform. The

[8] After the land reform was over and things in the villages became calm, a peasant was thinking of buying a young pig to raise. His wife rebuked him and said: "What is the big idea? Have you not learned enough? Do you want to become a landlord?"

old social and economic structure of the Chinese village which was the core of Chinese society was destroyed. On the social side, while the evils were removed, the leadership provided by the landowners and well-to-do farmers, who were the intellectuals and the gentry of the community, was also removed. The time-honoured respect for the village elders was gone. The traditional function of the family and the clan in binding the community together was dissolved; so the concept of kinship and the feeling of belonging together was destroyed.

On the economic side, while the peasants' energies were released through the emancipation of labour, the economic benefit of oversight in farming from the experienced landlords was then unavailable. The supply of capital as well as large-scale irrigation and soil improvement was interrupted. As we recall, in order to keep production from being disrupted, even the Communists took very cautious measures in the launching of the land reform. They took care that the persecution of the landlords in the villages was timed after harvest and that the landlords were heavily watched so that they had no opportunity to remove their capital, destroy their property, or damage the implements and animals of production.

For the first few years after the land reform and before the People's Communes came into being, the poor peasants who had no land or very little land were given some land. This was the sort of idea which Sun Yat-sen had advocated, "To the tiller, his field". It did satisfy a longstanding wish and fulfil a promise, but individualized farming had its difficulties in actual operation. There was the question of credit for seeds and fertilizers, the disputes over the use and upkeep of implements and draft animals confiscated from the landlords, the supply and mainten-ance of irrigation, inequality in the division of the landlord's property, the supply of provisions and the disposal of products, etc. So as a social and economic system, the individualization of farm lots brought in conflicts and difficulties, which resulted in a decrease in production. This led to a further change in the structure of the Chinese farm.

THE PEOPLE'S COMMUNE

The type of social and economic structure in China's rural areas since 1958 has been known as the "People's Commune". Its development deserves a few words of description. Before the People's Communes came into being—that is a socialistic type of structure—two preliminary types had evolved. The earlier type was the Mutual Assistance Production Group which was the simplest form of social organization to remedy the shortcomings of individual farming immediately after the land reform, in which productive resources could not be consolidated for effective use. The more advanced type which followed was that of agricultural co-operatives which were organized by taking shares in terms of the land, implements and finance contributed by the participants in the joint operation. Since membership was voluntary and profits shared among the members, they were called a semi-socialistic system on a small scale. The co-operative, as a matter of fact, had been in existence in the Communist areas all along, as the system eliminates the element of exploitation. It is reported that there were some 300 agricultural co-operatives in China in December 1951 when the Chinese Communist Party Central Committee instructed their local party organs to extend the movement. By December 1953, when the Central Committee took a further step in formally promulgating their resolution for the promotion of Agricultural Productive Co-operatives, the number had been increased to over 14,000. By June 1955 the number had reached 650,000 with a total of 16,900,000 households, having an average of twenty-six households to a co-operative.

It was Mao Tse-tung's idea in 1955 that in a year's time, that was by 1956, the number of co-operatives would be doubled to about 1,300,000, so that among a total of about 200,000 *hsiangs*[9]

[9] The *hsiang* is a local administration unit formerly composed of a number of villages. It was a subdivision of a *chu* (district) which in turn is the subdivision of a *hsien*. For *hsien*, see Chapter 3, "The Broad Outline of the Political and Administrative Structure".

(rural sub-districts) in China, there would be one or more semi-socialistic agricultural productive co-operatives in each. According to Mao, by spring 1958, that was, at the juncture between the end of the first five-year plan and the beginning of the second five-year plan,[10] there would be about 55 million households participating in this semi-socialistic co-operative scheme. With an average of $4\frac{1}{2}$ persons for each household, it would involve a population of about 250 million.[11] It was Mao's calculation in 1955 that by 1960 the other half of China's rural population would also have entered into these semi-socialistic co-operatives while the earlier half would be transformed into fully socialistic co-operatives.

Surprisingly, in the summer of 1958 it was suddenly announced that the People's Communes had spontaneously and unexpectedly swept over China. By the end of that year they were said to have comprised 120 million households or 99 per cent of the peasant population. It was said that the rise of the communes was so rapid that it even took Mao Tse-tung by surprise.

The fact that the announcement of the rapid rise of the communes and the proclamation of the Communization Programme came in 1958 has its special significance. It was reported that resentment was prevalent among the peasants when they were forced to communization. Within the Communist Party there were dissenting opinions which regarded China's condition as not yet ready for communization. If one recalls the year preceding it (that was 1957) in which the "Hundred Flowers Bloom and Hundred Schools Contend" Movement waxed a little while and soon waned, followed by the severe anti-rightist movement, he will find the clue to the sudden communization. For one thing, the Communist left-wing predominated in the party; and for another, party leaders needed another drastic movement to keep the people busy with something else.

[10] The five-year plans will be discussed in a later chapter.
[11] According to Mao Tse-tung's report on "Problems Concerning Agricultural Cooperatives" at the meeting of the Provincial, Municipal, and District Party Secretaries on 31 July 1955.

As a first step, the formation of the People's Communes began with the amalgamation of the agricultural productive co-operatives wherever they existed. According to the direction of the Communist Party, each commune normally consisted of from 1000 to 2000 households. Communes of over 10,000 households were also permitted. It was considered normal to have a commune in each *hsiang*, though several *hsiangs* could combine to form a commune. After the commune was formed, what were formerly the administrative functions of the *hsiang* or the locality were taken up by the commune. The party secretary of the *hsiang* was simultaneously party secretary of the commune. This is what they called "political and communal unity" by means of which they expected the communes to be the foundation units of a Communist society. One must be aware that the term "commune" as used in China is not quite the same as that used in Western history. The Chinese commune assumes economic and social as well as political and military functions. On the economic side it is engaged in agriculture, forestry, animal husbandry, fishery, industry, transportation, and commerce. It runs the local branches of the State bank and State trade and looks after taxation. On the social side it runs schools, nurseries, theatres, sports, recreational activities, old people's homes, and health and medical services. It does not only look after the administrative and political affairs of the locality, but also its military affairs in the form of local militia. Its structure combines into a single body, workers, peasants, traders, scholars, and the militia; all under the control of the party cadres appointed by the party, who do not have to be natives of the locality. Most of them are not, nor have even lived there before.

In every commune there is the Communal Committee, which is the centre of administration and control. It is the Communal Committee that the party, the Government, and the People's Liberation Army rely on. It is they who are supposed to know party policies and how to interpret the policies and the directives. It is they who have the status of negotiating with other departments and agencies vertically as well as horizontally. One should realize that the main purpose of the People's Commune is political. Mao Tse-tung said in the first five-year plan that agricultural social reform must precede technological reform, and political reform is the essence of social reform. So long as they have as many reliable party cadres for each commune as they have communes, the political situation is well in their hands. When they put rationing of rice into operation it was not the economic aspect that was their chief concern. It was the political control of the people, that is of their persons and movements. With the production and distribution of rice in the hands of the Government from whom every single grain has to be obtained by each person once every month, on presentation of his ration card which is only valid in that commune, the movements of the people are thus restricted to the limit. Furthermore, there is no chance of anyone hiding out or any anti-Communist agent sneaking in from outside.

Under the Communal Committee are the Production Brigades, which are again subdivided into production teams. In the smaller communes there are only production teams without the super-structure of production brigades. To these brigades and teams are assigned the various productive activities, which may be agriculture, forestry, stock-raising, fishery, or industry, depending on the productive opportunities of that locality. Sometimes the communes accept contracts from the purchasing departments of the Government to produce local products of specified quantity and quality. The key persons for control in the committees, brigades, and teams are the watchdogs of the party who see to it that loyalty is shown and the programmes are kept to schedule. In order to keep these persons properly informed, directives are sent from their higher authorities from time to time, and officials are called to conferences to hear reports given by the superiors. They then pass on to the commune members the policies of the party and the Government. Thus the whole population is geared to the national drive for socialization and production. By this means the progress and attainments of the agriculture programme of the five-year plans can be largely ascertained.

How are the peasants paid for their labour in the communes? Generally speaking, the slogan is : "Partly in provisions and partly in wages." What is paid in provisions is very meagre and what is paid in wages is even more insignificant. In provisions, one has shelter, 3 yards of cloth per person for clothing per year, and enough staple food to keep one going. For a time, meals were served in the communal dining halls and no private kitchen was allowed. But now people do most of their own cooking. As to wages, even with the little they are paid, there is not much to buy in the communes anyway. The great variety of fine Chinese products which one finds in Hong Kong Communist stores are only for export purposes and are not seen in the stores in the communes.

According to the Chinese Communist programme, the present stage of development in China is still confined to the stage of socialism, of which the motto is : "From each according to his ability, to each according to his labour (his work or his worth)." It is far away from the stage of communism where the second part of the motto is to be : "To each according to his needs." Whatever the motto is, the fact remains that the Chinese peasants today are required to give much work and long hours, in return for little reward. Since there is insufficient incentive to work, except for the handful who aspire to be labour heroes, in which case they could have certain special privileges, production is achieved by political drives and by the spur of the cadres, using means of mass pressure and impending persecution. For a time, farm produce derived from small lots of land around the peasants' dwellings which the peasants cultivated individually was required to be turned over to the commune. But since such produce showed a marked decrease, peasants have now been allowed to retain such lots and their yields. With this change, small as it is, vegetables, poultry, eggs, and other minor food stuffs again increased. The peasants can have them for their own consumption or for sale in the free markets in the towns. This reflects in a way the place of private ownership and profit motive in agricultural production, especially in small-scale manual farming.

When communism was new to the Chinese, especially when it was suppressed by the Nationalists, there was a popular rumour in China that communism was a system that practised "common property and common wives". In Communist China today, although there is common ownership of property, there is no such licence of common sharing of wives or promiscuity. Even the surrendering of children for public rearing is not practised, though, of course, there are nurseries to look after the young when parents go to work. The family is preserved and is protected by the marriage law of which we shall speak further in a later chapter. In the communes the old people are assigned work according to their ability. In rural communities with so little mechanization, old people and children have their respective contributions to make in the productive process. The success of the commune varies from commune to commune and from province to province. To take Kwangtung Province as an example : out of 1500 communes there is no doubt that there are some which are very successful, as some foreign visitors have reported. But to say that such cases are the rule rather than the exception is another story.

Spokesmen for the People's Commune have said with pride that the communes excel in these virtues : they are army-like in organization, combatant in action, collective in daily life, and democratic in management. How democratic their management is, all depends on what "democratic" means. There is, however, no doubt that the military atmosphere is strong and the fighting spirit is dominant. One should remember that the People's Liberation Army was mainly recruited from the rural areas. Now that many of them are retired and rehabilitated, including those who had been disabled during the war, they are naturally appointed, whenever possible, as cadres in the villages and communes. With the Liberation Army background one can readily see how militaristic, disciplinary, and, indeed, how demanding, coercive, and harsh the life in the communes can be. When the system has to depend on external force in order to operate, one has a right to suspect that it has no root in the life of the people.

In the commune, where life is marked by work, regimentation, discipline, and study, it may be looked upon as the amalgamation of agriculture production, army corps, concentration camp, and school all in one. The Chinese peasant is no more the ignorant and isolated villager he used to be. He is now taught to be alert about the relationship of his work to the political, social, and economic programme and problems of his country in the light of the international scene. He is also schooled in the discipline of socialistic living. Whatever one may say in favour of the People's Commune, there is also the other side of the picture. It may be anything but happy living. Life in the commune is full of both tension and drudgery. There is an absence of personal freedom, individual expression, voluntary endeavour, cultivation of private relationships, or leisurely enjoyment of living. One has no reason to believe that life in the People's Commune is superior to that found in Chinese villages under the old régime.

In the field of agricultural production, besides the communes, there are also State farms in various parts of the country. The major difference between the State farms and the People's Communes, aside from the fact that the State farms are State owned and operated while the communes are not, is that the constituent members of the State farms are not the original inhabitants of the place. They are usually mobilized from different parts of the country.

### INDUSTRIAL AND URBAN SOCIETY

The People's Communes comprise about 80 per cent of the population. They are all in rural areas, transformed by the combination of villages. Outside the rural areas are the industrial areas and the urban areas. The population in the industrial and urban areas is much more diversified, and so are their activities. Though this population is less than a quarter of the rural, it is a very dynamic group whether one looks at it from the economic, the political, the social, or the cultural standpoint. It is in this group that most of the so-called middle-class people concentrate, and it is in this group we find the industrial workers and the intellectuals in China today.

The industrial workers bear the chief burden of industrial development and upon them China's aspiration for world power and its military build-up depends. They are the proletariat in the truest sense of the term, who are supposedly most susceptible to the ideology of the working class and the class struggle. They are the people who, among the other classes of the "people", are to assume the leadership in the people's régime.

The intellectuals, though naturally very few in number, have always played an exceedingly important role in Chinese society. Their role is no less significant in Communist China today. They come principally from the middle class or the bourgeoisie and certainly have to unlearn and relearn in order to be useful to the new society. They constitute the main body of the staff in economic, banking, business enterprises, administrative organizations, and in all cultural and educational institutions. They include clerks, secretaries, managers, directors, executives, engineers, newspaper reporters and editors, accountants, teachers, researchers, artists, scientists, writers, playwrights, doctors, foreign and legal affairs personnel, etc. Above all, they include the exponents and interpreters of the ideology of communism, Marxism–Leninism, Maoism, and the leaders who have in their hands the formation or reformation of the party line in face of changing social and economic conditions as well as of the changing internal and international situation. Indeed, it demands high intellectual calibre to define the demarcation within the Communist ranks between what is said to be "true Marxism–Leninism" and the so-called "revisionism", between what is dogmatism and non-dogmatism, between what is leftist-infantile-sickness and non-leftist-infantile-sickness, between adventurism and non-adventurism, and, indeed, between what is "true Mao Tse-tung thinking" and what is not. Take the example of explaining to the masses the underlying differences in the Sino–Soviet ideological dispute; it is in itself a taxing intellectual engagement which cannot be undertaken by one who is not an intellectual; that is, one who is not capable of handling abstractions and ideas, of making sharp distinctions, and pointing out the significance and relationships of one philosophical position to another.

We shall speak of the education and re-education of intellectuals in various places in this book, so we shall not go into the subject here. What we want to point out here, however, is the fact that the intellectuals are essentially urban folk. It is only in the urban environment that intellectuals assemble, and only there that intellectual development finds its stimulation and nourishment. Though the proletarian régime insists on the importance of manual labour for proper intellectual development, the truth remains that those whose life is spent in the routine of farm work or factory work have to leave intellectual tasks to those who are freed from such daily drudgeries. The intellectuals, particularly the high intellectuals, whether the Communist leaders like to admit it or not, are still the manipulators of the destiny of China today in all its social, economic, political, and cultural aspects, as they have always been in Chinese society in the past, though it is now insisted that they must be "proletarianistic" intellectuals.

Of the industrial and urban population which we are now considering, first, there are those in the industries; that is, in the factories, mines, railways, transport, and economic enterprises managed by the State such as banks, stores, shops, etc. Then there are those in the governmental organizations; governmental departments of various kinds, schools and universities, hospitals, newspapers, police, the court and the prisons, the labour camps, etc. Then there is the People's Liberation Army, which is distinct in itself both in structure and character. There are few in the urban areas who do not belong to one of the industrial, economic, governmental, cultural, and military activities mentioned above. Even these few, such as the old and unemployed, the dependants in the households, must belong to the neighbourhood structure where they domicile, and that is under the constant supervision of the police outposts. That is to say, no one can keep himself aloof from the social–economic structure of the Communist régime whether he is in the town or in the country. He must belong somewhere, and wherever he belongs, he is under the close supervision of the Government and the party. In that sense, every person is counted and made to keep in step with the Communist Movement.

# CHAPTER 3

# The Broad Outline of the Political and Administrative Structure

## POLITICAL GEOGRAPHY

IN CHAPTER 1 we spoke briefly of the natural geography of China with the intention of giving the reader a glimpse of the geographical background to the economic and cultural life of the Chinese people. Here we want to give a description of the political geography of China. It is only when one has a general picture of the pattern of the territorial units in the political and administrative structure of this vast country which is as large as Europe,[1] that he can read the political accounts of China intelligently. Again, it is only when one is aware of the long history of the Chinese system of political and governmental divisions that he can understand the authority of the Central Government over its various levels of administration, a phenomenon which is not found in other countries, particularly in the countries of the Western world.

Bearing in mind the subject of education which is our chief concern, we shall speak of the political and administrative structure in so far as it has special bearing on that subject. Those who are interested in the political and governmental structure of

[1] China: area 9,597,000 sq. km. (3,705,405 sq. miles), population 656,630,000, according to *People's Handbook*, 1965, Ta Kung Pao, Peking. Europe: area 10,334,100 sq. km. (3,990,000 sq. miles), population 587,723,234, according to *Encyclopaedia Britannica*, 1964.

China from the standpoint of politics and government will have to turn to other sources for information.

There are two basic territorial units in political and governmental administration in China. One is the *sheng* (province) and the other the *hsien* (often translated as "county").[2] They are the basic units but definitely not the only ones. There are political and administrative units bigger than provinces,[3] units smaller than *hsiens*,[4] and units between the province and the *hsien*.[5] In China today there are some administrative units such as *tzu chih chu* (autonomous regions) which are similar to *shengs* in size, and the *tzu chih chou* (autonomous districts) which are similar to *hsiens* in size. Both of these are for the national minorities. There are also cities such as Peking[6] which, because of their population and importance, are classified as equivalent to the provinces in status and are directly controlled by the Central Government. There

[2] Since the word "province" is a good translation of *sheng* and has been in common use, we shall hereafter use "province" in place of *sheng*. But since "county" is not a good translation of *hsien*, we shall use *hsien* instead of "county".

[3] In the Ching Dynasty, sometimes a viceroy was entrusted with two provinces. In the early years of the Communist régime, the whole country was divided into six great administrative areas. Each area included several provinces. For example, the provinces of Kwangtung, Kwangsi, Hunan, Hupei, Honan, and Kiangsi were under the administration of the Central-south Military and Administrative Council, which was further under the supervision of the Central-south Bureau of the Communist Party. Now the great administrative areas and their military and administrative councils do not exist, but the party bureaux of the respective areas are still retained.

[4] A *hsien* is subdivided into *chu*, or *hsien* districts, each of which includes a group of *hsiangs*, and each *hsiang* includes a group of villages.

[5] The intermediate unit between the province and the *hsien* is the commissioner's district. Every commissioner's district is under a commissioner with a large staff who supervises a group of *hsiens*.

[6] The city of Peking has under its jurisdiction nine *hsiens*. It is directly under the control of the Central Government in spite of the fact that Peking is in Hopei Province. The city of Shanghai has under its jurisdiction ten *hsiens*. It is directly under the control of the Central Government in spite of the fact that Shanghai is in Kiangsu Province. They are like the District of Columbia in the United States which, though situated in the State of Maryland, is under the direct control of the Federal Government.

are also some cities such as Canton,[7] which are equivalent to commissioner's districts in status and directly controlled by the Provincial Government. We shall not complicate matters by mentioning another category of cities which are under the *hsien* government. Anyway, autonomous areas are out of the ordinary, and cities are few. So province and *hsien* remain the basic territorial administrative units. Now let us give the province and the *hsien* a further word of description.

The province is a well-established unit of administration. Ever since the first unification of China by Chin Shih Huang in 221 B.C. the whole country was divided into provinces. In place of the feudal states which he abolished, Chin Shih Huang divided the whole country into thirty-six provinces for the convenience of unified administration. Although the term *chun*, and not *sheng*, was used at that time, and the size was slightly smaller, yet it is generally considered as the origin of the unit of *sheng*. The term *sheng* has been in use since the Yuan Dynasty. The names of the *shengs* and their boundaries may alter from time to time for political and other reasons, but the framework of provincial administration has remained. At present there are twenty-one provinces in China excluding Taiwan.[8] Besides, there are five national (minority) autonomous regions which are as big as provinces, many of which were originally called provinces before the Communist régime.[9]

---

[7] The city of Canton has under its jurisdiction ten *hsiens* and,

[8] The twenty-one provinces are: *North-eastern Region*: Heilung- although it is situated in the juncture of the Nan Hai *Hsien* and Pan Yu *Hsien*, which are under the Commissioner's District of Fatshan, is directly controlled by the Provincial Government of Kwangtung.

kiang, Kirin, Liaoning. *Northern Region*: Hopei (Hopeh), Shansi. *Eastern Region*: Shantung, Kiangsu, Anhwei, Chekiang, Fukien. *Central-southern Region*: Honan, Hupei (Hupeh), Hunan, Kiangsi, Kwangtung. *South-western Region*: Szechwan, Kweichow, Yunnan. *North-western Region*: Shensi, Kansu, Chinghai (Tsinghai) (see also *Statesman's Yearbook, 1965–6*).

[9] The autonomous areas are: Inner Mongolian; Ning-Hsia Moslem; Sinkiang; Tibet. Kwangsi was originally a province. But it is now called the Chuang Nationality Autonomous Area of Kwangsi.

The area of the provinces vary. For example, Szechwan, the largest, has an area of 569,000 sq. km. (219,691 sq. miles), while Chekiang, the smallest, has an area of only 101,800 sq. km. (39,305 sq. miles). The provinces also vary in population, resources, economic, and cultural development which we shall not go into here. Their boundaries are formed by natural geographic barriers; usually by watersheds in mountain ranges.

In each province now there are a governor and a number of vice-governors, ranging from 5 to 13 in number, all of whom are nominally elected by the Provincial People's Congress. In the earlier days of the People's Republic a few governors and a number of vice-governors were non-Communists. They were public leaders who had certain prestige in the former régime and who pledged their loyalty to Communist leadership, but as time went on and as new Communist leaders had become familiar in the eyes of the public, the need to count on such old figures for the support of the Government gradually declined.

The *hsien* is the real basic unit of governmental administration. Each province is composed of a large number of *hsiens*, which are similar to the larger counties in the United States and in England. Roughly speaking, there are about 2000 *hsiens* in the whole of China. To be exact, there are 2007 *hsiens* in China excluding Taiwan, listed in the *People's Handbook* of 1965. There have been minor changes in the number of *hsiens* all along as a result of merger or of subdivision; but, by and large, the *hsien* units are very stable and intact. The origin of the *hsien* was much earlier even than that of the provinces. It is traced back to the Chou Dynasty, as early as 627 B.C., when this system of territorial division was first inaugurated in the Dukedom of Lu. The *hsien* is unique because it is neither too large for its administrator, the magistrate, to be familiar with its social, cultural, economic, and administrative needs and problems, nor too small for it to be insignificant and incapable of self-support. They each have their natural boundaries and, through the ages, have built up their own history, tradition, characteristics, specialities, local culture, and local pride. Many of the *hsiens* have their own *hsien chi* or *hsien* records[10] which are compiled by their own scholars of repute and supplemented from time to time. From these records one can learn the history, geography, and the economic, social, political, and cultural life of the place, as well as the well-known scenic spots, and famous men and women who were born there or who lived there.

Those who are familiar with Chinese traditions will know that the Chinese people like to identify themselves with their native *hsiens*. In the past when two gentlemen met, after inquiry into each other's names, they inquired about each other's *hsien* as a birth-place. One's identity was reinforced by the *hsien* to which he belonged.

The number of *hsiens* also varies from province to province. There are as many as 184 *hsiens* in Szechwan Province while there are as few as only 63 in Chekiang Province. The number of *hsiens* in Kwantung Province is 101, which is slightly above the average. As to the subdivisions within the *hsien*, they have been explained in a previous footnote (p. 71). Regarding the area of the *hsiens*, the norm is about 1000 sq. km. (386 sq. miles). In order to give a more concrete idea of the size of a *hsien*, let us take the areas of Hong Kong and Macao with which many people are more familiar. Hong Kong and Macao are on the coast of the Province of Kwantung at the two sides of the Pearl River estuary. They are under the jurisdiction of Great Britain and Portugal respectively. Roughly speaking, the area of Hong Kong, including the New Territories and the sea, is about 1031 sq. km. (398 sq. miles). It is situated in a peninsula of Pao An (Po On) *Hsien*. Hong Kong is nearly half of its *hsien* area, which is 2200 sq. km. (1089 sq. miles). The land area of Macao is about 16 sq. km. (6 sq. miles). It is situated in a peninsula of Chung Shan *Hsien*, which is 1/180th of its *hsien's* land area of 2876 sq. km. (1110 sq. miles).

[10] Many oriental libraries in the United States have good collections of such *hsien chi*, sometimes called *fang chi*, meaning "local records", the most outstanding of which are Columbia University Library, the Harvard Yenching Institute Library, and the Congressional Library.

One word more about the *hsien*. During the Republican era, that is, before the Communist régime, there were some civic and public leaders who believed that the best way to achieve national reconstruction in China was to go by the *hsien* as a unit of reconstruction. According to their view, if there were 2000 good *hsiens*, the reconstruction of China would be getting under way. And if they could get 2000 good magistrates, which was not too great an expectation, the reconstruction of China would be assured. To study how the problems of *hsien* reconstruction should be attacked, experiments on *hsien* administration were conducted, the most famous of which were the Ting *Hsien* experiment in Hopei Province under the leadership of Jimmy Yen[11] and the Chou Ping *Hsien* experiment in Shantung Province under the leadership of Liang Shu-ming.[12]

We have dwelled in some length on the *hsien* because it is a conceptual unit of local government well established in the mind of the Chinese people. The Communist régime, though pledged to break down all institutions of the past, has kept intact the *hsien* as a political institution of governmental administration.

## THE CONSTITUTION AND THE GOVERNMENT

### The Constitution

Theoretically and legally, the basis of the Chinese People's Republic and its Government rests upon the Constitution of the Chinese People's Republic passed by the First National People's Congress in September 1954. This Constitution replaced the Common Programme enacted by the Chinese People's Political Consultation Conference (CPPCC) in September 1949. Although the CPPCC still exists as an organization, it lost its legislative power after the First People's National Congress was convened and has been losing more and more of its political and social

[11] A Yale University graduate and a well-known mass education pioneer in China.
[12] A well-known Chinese philosopher who was for many years professor of philosophy in the University of Peking.

role as the years go by. Except for such united front functions as the welcoming of Li Tsung-jen, once Acting President of the Chinese Nationalist Government, who returned to China from the United States in 1965, and the reception of the delegation of Asian and African writers in the summer of 1966, etc., the CPPCC is already out of the picture in China's politics today.

It may be worth while to note here a few basic differences between the Common Programme of the CPPCC and the Constitution[13] of the Chinese People's National Congress. Such differences mark the departure of the latter from the former, which the Communists neatly call the development of the latter from the former. The differences may be seen as follows: (1) While the term "socialism" did not appear in the Common Programme, as we have previously pointed out, the Constitution nevertheless contains the term "socialism" or "socialist" as many

[13] For comparison of the Preamble of the Common Programme which we quoted in Chapter 2, we quote here part of the Preamble of the Constitution as follows: ". . . The First National People's Congress of the People's Republic of China, at its first session held in Peking, the capital, solemnly adopted the Constitution of the People's Republic of China on 20th September, 1954. This Constitution is based on the Common Programme of the Chinese People's Political Consultative Conference of 1949, and is an advance on it. It consolidates the gains of the Chinese people's revolution and the political and economic victories won since the founding of the People's Republic of China; and, moreover, it reflects the basic needs of the state in the period of transition, as well as the general desire of the people as a whole to build a socialist society. In the course of the great struggle to establish the People's Republic of China, the people of our country forged a broad people's democratic united front, composed of all democratic classes, democratic parties and groups, and popular organizations, and led by the Communist Party of China. This people's democratic united front will continue to play its part in mobilizing and rallying the whole people in common struggle to fulfil the fundamental task of the state during the transition and to oppose enemies within and without.

". . . China has already built an indestructible friendship with the great Union of Soviet Socialist Republics and the People's Democracies; and the friendship between our people and peace-loving people in all other countries is growing day by day. Such friendships will be constantly strengthened and broadened. . . ."

as fifteen times.[14] (2) In the Common Programme the term "people's democracy" was annotated thus : the new democracy is the same as the people's democracy. The People's Democratic Dictatorship is the power structure of the People's Democratic United Front, composed of the working class, the peasants' class, the petty bourgeois class, and the national bourgeois class and other patriotic democratic elements, based on the alliance of the workers and peasants under the leadership of the working class and the unity of all democratic classes and national minorities. But in the Constitution the term "people's democracy" is used without annotation. (3) The admission of the bourgeoisie class into the power structure was specified in the Common Programme; but it has no place in the Constitution except as an object of struggle. (4) The first article in the Common Programme as a statement of basic principle was :

> The Chinese People's Republic is a state of the New Democracy, that is to say, the People's Democracy. It exercises the People's Democratic Dictatorship which is based on the leadership of the working class, the alliance of workers and peasants, and unites all democratic classes and all national minorities, in opposition to imperialism, feudalism, and bureaucratic capitalism in the struggle for the independence, democracy, peace, unity and prosperity of China.

But the first article in the Constitution, also as a statement of basic principle, simply states : "The people's Republic of China is a people's democratic state led by the working class and based on the alliance of workers and peasants", and stops there, with

[14] "To build a prosperous and happy *socialist* society . . . from the formation of the People's Republic of China to the attainment of a *socialist* society is a period of transition . . . *socialist* industrialization . . . *socialist* transformation of agriculture, handicrafts, and capitalist industry and commerce . . . the necessary conditions have been created for gradual transition to *socialism* . . . to build a *socialist* society . . . in the matter of *socialist* transformation . . . an indestructible friendship with the great Union of Soviet *Socialist* Republics and the People's Democracies . . . by means of *socialist* industrialization and *socialist* transformation . . . the building of a *socialist* society . . . the state sector of the economy is a *socialist* sector . . . on which the state carries out *socialist* transformation . . . the cooperative sector of the economy is either *socialist* . . . or *semi-socialist*. . . ."

what was contained in the second part of the Common Programme curtailed.

In making the comparison here between the earlier and later
declarations of government, the purpose is not to lament over
the lost cause of those who had believed in a republic of all the
classes of people, nor to accuse the Communists of their breach of
promise. Its purpose is rather to show first, that the 1949 Common
Programme and the 1954 Constitution are basically different in
the constituency of power; that is to say, it means that the concept of power structure for the first 5 years of the People's
Republic was different from the concept for the period since
1954. Second, the Communists played a very clever game of
omitting certain items of phraseology in an inconspicuous
way, the retention of which would have given the non-Communists a continued partnership in the operation of government.
Third, the influences and functions of the non-Communist parties
and the bourgeois classes had waned and their power had been
so much subdued in a five-year period that no voice of opposition
to the wording of the Constitution would have been possible;
and, fourth, the Common Programme and the Constitution each
represented a strong but different view of China's road to
nationhood and prosperity, the one more moderate, and the other
more drastic. To win the battle in one day, as the Constitution
has done, does not necessarily mean that the victory is an ever-
lasting one. The battle for power may come again when the
present scheme does not work in face of China's realities or when
the contending side again arises. That is why the Common
Programme should not be treated as something which has passed
into oblivion. The position which is suggested here is what the
Communist leftists call revisionism.

Putting aside the criticism of the Constitution from the moderate wing, the Constitution still awaits change from the standpoint
of its defenders. We refer to the statement in the Preamble of the
Constitution in reference to Soviet Russia which says "China has
already built an indestructible friendship with the great Union
of Soviet Socialist Republics and the People's Democracies; and

the friendship between our people and peace-loving people in all other countries is growing day by day. Such friendship will be constantly strengthened and broadened." If the Chinese Communists are serious about their Constitution, the above statement in the Constitution as it stands must make them feel very awkward in the present Sino–Soviet confrontation.

## *The National People's Congress*

The highest organ of authority in the People's Republic is the National People's Congress which is, according to the Constitution, the highest legislative authority in the country. It is composed of deputies or representatives from provinces, autonomous regions, municipalities directly under the control of the central government, the armed forces, and Chinese residents abroad. Its term is for 4 years. The first congress met in September 1954. The present congress, which is the third, met in December 1964, in which Chu Te, the Veteran Communist Commander-in-chief, was again elected chairman of the National Congress. Peng Chen, the Mayor of Peking from 1949 to 1966, was elected the first vice-chairman, followed by fifteen other vice-chairmen.

## *The Central Government*

The Chairman of the People's Republic of China is elected by the National People's Congress whose term of office is also 4 years. Liu Shao-chi is the Chairman. There are now two vice-chairmen, Soong Ching-ling (Madame Sun Yat-sen) and Tung Pi-wu. The highest administrative organ of the state is the *Kuo Wu Yuan* (the State Council) which is the Central People's Government. It is composed of the premier, the vice-premiers, the ministers, the heads of commissions, and the secretary-general. Chou En-lai has been the Premier all along, not only since 1954 when the First People's National Congress met, but since 1949 when the CPPCC met. There are many vice-premiers, at present sixteen in number. Generally they each oversee a group of ministries and commissions which are of a similar nature. The ministries and commissions have been undergoing addition, abolition, and merger, since the Organic Law of the State Council was first promulgated in September 1954. The list in the State Council in 1965 contains forty ministries and several commissions.[15]

We see from the list the large number of ministries devoted to economic and productive activities. The ministries directly related to education and culture are few. They are the Ministry of Culture, Ministry of Education, Ministry of Higher Education, and Ministry of Health, all of which are under the supervision of a vice-premier, Lu Ting-yi, who for years was Chief of the Propaganda Department of the Chinese Communist Party. Each Ministry has a minister and a number of vice-ministers.

In the Ministry of Education and the Ministry of Higher Education, which are of special interest to us, several changes have been made. In 1949, when the State Council was first organized, there was only one Ministry of Education. In 1951 it was divided into two ministries : the Ministry of Education and

[15] Under the Premier, vice-premiers, and Secretary-General are : 1. Ministry of Foreign Affairs. 2. Ministry of National Defence. 3. Ministry of Public Security. 4. Ministry of Internal Affairs. 5. Ministry of Agriculture. 6. Ministry of State Farms and Land Reclamation. 7. Ministry of Forestry. 8. Ministry of Marine Products. 9. Ministry of Metallurgical Industries. 10. Ministry of Chemical Industries. 11. Ministry of Machine Building No. 1. 12. Ministry of Machine Building No. 2. 13. Ministry of Machine Building No. 3. 14. Ministry of Machine Building No. 4. 15. Ministry of Machine Building No. 5. 16. Ministry of Machine Building No. 6. 17. Ministry of Machine Building No. 7. 18. Ministry of Machine Building No. 8. 19. Ministry of Coal Industry. 20. Ministry of Petroleum Industry. 21. Ministry of Water Conservancy and Electric Power. 22. Ministry of Geology. 23. Ministry of Construction. 24. Ministry of Construction Material. 25. Ministry of Textile Industry. 26. Ministry of Light Industry No. 1. 27. Ministry of Light Industry No. 2. 28. Ministry of Railroads. 29. Ministry of Communications. 30. Ministry of Posts and Telecommunications. 31. Ministry of Control of Material and Property. 32. Ministry of Labour. 33. Ministry of Finance. 34. Ministry of Food. 35. Ministry of Commerce. 36. Ministry of Foreign Trade. 37. Ministry of Culture. 38. Ministry of Higher Education. 39. Ministry of Education. 40. Ministry of Health. (See *People's Handbook*, 1965, published by the Ta Kung Pao, Peking, October 1965.)

the Ministry of Higher Education. In 1954 they were again merged into a single Ministry of Education. In 1964, 10 years afterwards, it was again divided into two ministries, as they stand today. It is difficult to say whether the Government have finally made up their mind. It looks as if the planning and control of higher education for the whole country in relation to economic reconstruction is so gigantic a task that only a separate ministry is capable of handling the matter properly.

In the case of educational and cultural administration, besides a vice-premier who is assigned to supervise the work, there is the Office of Cultural and Educational Affairs with a director and several deputy directors to co-ordinate the work of the Ministry of Culture, Ministry of Education, Ministry of Higher Education, Ministry of Public Health, and other commissions and bureaux in this area of administration.

## The Local People's Congresses and Local People's Councils

Like the People's National Congress on the national scale, there are People's Congresses in the provinces, *hsiens, hsiangs,* and towns, as well as in the municipalities, municipal districts, and national autonomous areas. These are legislative bodies of the respective localities, the representatives of which are elected by the congresses of the next lower level. When it comes to the representatives in the People's Congresses of the lowest level, such as representatives in the People's Congresses of municipal districts, *hsiangs,* and towns, they are directly elected by the electorates. All representatives serve a term of 4 years.

The executive organs of the local people's congresses are the local people's councils which constitute the local people's government of their respective localities. Each local people's council has a number of council members who are elected by their people's congresses. On the provincial level are elected the governors and vice-governors; on the *hsien* level, the magistrates and vice-magistrates; on the *hsiang* level, the *hsiang* heads and vice-*hsiang* heads. In the municipalities they are called mayors and vice-mayors; in the municipal districts they are called district heads and deputy district heads. The functions, authorities, and duties of such bodies and offices are further prescribed by law which we need not go into here.

On the judicial side, under the Supreme People's Court, which belongs to the Central Government, there are the local people's courts and special people's courts. Again, under the Supreme People's Procuratorate, which belongs to the Central Government, the local organs of the people's procuratorate and the special people's procuratorates exercise similar authorities over the local organs of State.[16] Such authorities are so prescribed on paper, but in actuality they are exercised by the party organs of the various levels. Anyway, this branch of government does not particularly concern us in this study.

### The Educational Administrative Structure

What we are interested in specifically is the educational administrative system in the central and in the local governments.

First of all, we must clarify the conception of central government and local government. In democratic states, local governments have a good deal of legislative and executive powers. Although such powers are diminishing in the democracies, there is still considerable local freedom and initiative to make the term local government worthy of its name. The democratic traditions in the Western world are still being guarded jealously. The spirit of local responsibility is still strong. But in the case of China today everyone turns to the Central Government for authority and directions. It would be considered subversion or anti-government, anti-party, and anti-socialism if one were to try to take a departure from central directives or even to be hesitant or slow in carrying them out. This obedience and subservience

[16] According to the Constitution, the procuratorates are supposed to exercise procuratorial authority over the respective departments of the State Council, persons working in organs of the State, and citizens, to ensure the observance of the law.

to the central authority in China dates back to the long history of Chinese monarchical government, but the Chinese Communists have been exploiting this tradition to the very fullest. For this reason it is correct to say that there is no "local government" as such in China in the Western conception of the term. This is similar to the absence of local government in a national army. What is called local government is only the extension of the central government. While the submissive and unified character of the Chinese people accounts for a large part of the success of centralization in China, the Communists certainly deserve special credit, if credit there be, for being able to exercise such a high degree of centralization in a country so vast in area and so huge in population which had been so disorganized and where the means of communication are so inadequate. The fact that Peking is retained as the capital, having been China's capital since the Ming Dynasty with its imperial splendour and prestige, is contributory to this success.

In China, the administrative structure is generally spoken of as being of three levels : the national level, the provincial level, and the *hsien* level, that is to say, the national government, the provincial government, and the *hsien* government. In the matter of educational administration, we have the Ministry of Education in the national government, the Department of Education in the provincial government, and the Bureau of Education in the *hsien* government. (The municipalities also have bureaux of education.) For the first 5 years of the Chinese People's Republic there was an intermediate administration between the national government and the provincial government when there were six great administrative areas, each having an oversight of several provinces. During that period, there were also area ministries of education which stood between the National Ministry of Education and the Provincial Departments of Education. Now the great administrative areas no longer exist. The three levels of administration still hold.

It may be worth while to supplement, in passing, an earlier statement on the co-ordination of the work of the Ministry of

Culture, Ministry of Education, Ministry of Public Health, etc. In 1949, when the People's Central Government was first founded and before the reorganization of the Government in 1954, there was in the State Council the Committee on Culture and Education which was charged with the supervision of the Ministries of Culture, Education, Public Health, the Academy of Science, the Bureau of News, and the Bureau of Publications. There were forty-seven members including the ministers and vice-ministers.[17] Kuo Mo-jo was Chairman of the committee. Lu Ting-yi, Chief of the Propaganda Department of the Chinese Communist Party, was one of the four vice-chairmen. Since 1954 this committee has been replaced by the Office of Cultural and Educational Affairs under the supervision of a vice-premier.

Let us come back to the three levels of educational administration. There are three levels in educational administration as there are in other major branches of administration such as finance, public health, security, etc. On each level of administration, there are the chief executives and associate chief executives, the secretaries, the division chiefs, and division assistant chiefs, etc. The size of the organization and number of personnel for each category decrease as they move down the scale from the ministerial set-up to the *hsien* level. The titles of the offices and officers are not much changed from those used in the pre-Communist period, but there are a few obvious differences which may be observed. (1) In the Nationalist régime, the Ministry of Education was charged with the control of higher education and the Provincial Department of Education was charged with the control of secondary education. In the Communist régime such functions are not so specifically defined. (2) In the Nationalist régime there have never been two ministries of education with a separate one for higher education. (3) While there used to be a division in

---

[17] It is interesting to note that among the members of this committee many have been purged in the last 10 years. Those who were able to hold out but were later purged include: Wu Han, Chou Yang, Li Ta, Tien Han, Chien Pe-tsan, Yang Han-sang, and Lu Ting-yi. Even Kuo Mo-jo had to submit himself publicly to severe self-criticism.

each level of educational administration in charge of social education, this function is now delegated to the ministries, commissions, and bureaux of culture and run on a much bigger scale. (4) The personnel division is almost the key branch of administration in each level today. It looks after all educational personnel under its jurisdiction, looking after their records, activities, thinking, promotions and demotions, appointments, and transfers. (5) Another outstanding difference is that there are no such posts as school inspectors, ministry school inspectors, provincial school inspectors, and *hsien* or municipal school inspectors as there were in the Pre-Communist régime. In the former régime those were out-duty posts and the various levels of administration depended on the inspectors for co-ordination and oversight. But now such functions are performed by many other persons, the chief of which are the party cadres and particularly the party propaganda personnel in each locality. The minor functions of improving the curriculum and methods of teaching are left to the schools in group studies and discussions as well as to the conferences.

## PARTY CONTROL OF GOVERNMENT AND OF EDUCATION

Let us examine how the Chinese Communist Party controls the government in general, and how it controls education in particular. We shall leave the discussion of the structure of the Chinese Communist Party for the following chapter on the Formative Institutions in China.

### How the Party Controls the Government

In outward form the Chinese People's Republic is a democracy. As we have stated above, government bodies in the form of state council, provincial council, and *hsien* council are elected by the corresponding People's Congresses, while the representatives in the People's Congresses are elected by the representatives of the congresses at their respective lower levels. In the case of the *hsiang* or the municipal districts, the representatives are directly elected by the electorate. This is straight representative government, government of the people. It would be too naïve, however, if we were to accept these outward structures at their face value. Those who are inexperienced in the actual operation of the Communist régime are easily misled by its façade.

The most obvious way in which the Communist Party controls the Government is through the control of the congresses. All the representatives in the congresses are Communist party nominees. The candidate list is carefully prepared by the party, and there are only as many candidates for nomination as there are vacancies. No competition or choice is provided. The candidates are usually elected *en bloc*. That is why unanimity is always obtained in the elections. When the tone of party control is pitched so high, there is no chance of a person not in party favour being elected to the legislature or to the Government. Indeed, it would be a great folly to nominate a person outside the party's nomination list, and a greater one to accept the nomination without the party's previous approval.

A more direct method of party control over government is the system of establishing party committees or party fractions within the governmental organs and agencies. This method of party control applies also to the people's organizations. Such party committees are additional to the party committees in the various levels of administrative units, such as the national, provincial, and *hsien* units. This method of guardianship over the Government is openly expressed in the provisions of the Chinese Communist Party Constitution.[18] Each party committee or party

[18] According to the Chinese Communist Party Constitution there are two articles in Chapter 9 which specify the structure of the party fraction in non-party organizations. Article 59 states: "When there are three or more Party members holding responsible posts in the leadership organ of a government agency or people's organization, a Party Fraction shall be formed. The task of such a Party Fraction in the said agency or organization shall be: to assume the responsibility of carrying out Party policy

fraction in these organizations has a secretary; and what he decides is accepted as from authority, no matter whether he is the chief executive of the governmental unit or not. Such party committees or the party fractions, however, are supposed to receive directions from their higher party levels from time to time and are truly representatives of the party and its policies.

So when centralization of government in China is coupled with this party superstructure, where the party is "one and indivisible", the rigidity of control is obvious.

More than the control of governmental administration is the control of the life of the people, both their personal life and their corporate life, and in particular the control of their political thinking. The Communists, Communist youth, and the young pioneers are the watchdogs of the party. They make sure that no organized or unorganized opposition to the party exists. They function more effectively than secret police. They live and work in the midst of the people and penetrate into all corners of life. Such an operation should make the police states, which have to depend on a limited number of paid police, feel inferior.

### How the Party Further Controls Education

The party's further control over educational affairs is through its personnel in charge of propaganda. The term *hsuan chuan* or propaganda carries with it some disfavour in the non-Communist world. But in Communist China the term is used with great respect. The Communists do not feel the need to use a milder term such as "publicity" as in the West.

---

and decisions, to fortify unity with non-Party cadres, to cement the ties with the masses, to consolidate Party and State discipline and to combat bureaucracy." Article 60 states: "The members of a Party Fraction shall be specified by an appropriate Party Committee. A Party Fraction shall have a secretary, and when necessary, may install a duty secretary in addition. A Party Fraction must obey the direction of a Party Committee on all problems."

Since schools are places which handle ideas and where intellectuals assemble and where young intellectuals are trained, and since the function of the propaganda organ is to promulgate ideas and policies from the formulating body of the party, it is only logical that those in charge of propaganda should have charge of the schools. In the Western world, particularly in the United Kingdom and the United States, the use of education for political ends is looked upon with contempt. But in the Communist world it is openly admitted that education is used as the instrument of politics. In fact, Communists claim that education is used everywhere for political ends, though the process is more obvious in certain places and certain times than in others.

Those who have lived in Communist China will know that the head of the propaganda organ of the party is the highest authority for the schools of the area. This was the practice of the Chinese Communists before they took over the whole of China. It was their practice in the "liberated" areas then to have the propaganda chief serving concurrently as the director of schools. Today he is not only the highest authority of the schools but also the highest authority for all cultural affairs, including the press, broadcasting, the theatre, publications, etc. Now that he has so many important duties to perform, he is too busy to be the director of schools, as he cannot afford the time to be involved in daily routines. The director of schools knows that his duty is to execute the orders of his immediate party propaganda chief.

The propaganda chief must be one who is well versed in Communist ideology, Marxism–Leninism, party policies, and now in Maoism. He must be one who is able to interpret the meaning of the party directives; what they do mean and what they do not mean, without forcing his own ideas into the interpretation. Originality is unbecoming. To give more meaning or less meaning to the central authorities directives is considered political dissension. The best qualification for such a person is his ability to understand and interpret party policies and programmes for that moment and in that situation. He does

not need to be an orator. For instance, Lu Ting-yi,[19] the head of
the Propaganda Department of the Central Committee of the
Chinese Communist Party for 17 years, is not an oratorical type
as one might expect him to be for a similar post in the West.
In fact, he stutters occasionally.

[19] Lu Ting-yi was in that post for 17 years since 1949, until his
removal in July 1966 in connection with the purge of the Great Proletarian Cultural Revolution.

# CHAPTER 4

# The Most Formative Institutions

IN EVERY society there are certain institutions which are more formative in nature for the fostering of the social and cultural values which the society upholds and on which its existence depends. Some are more obvious, others are more subtle. If one were to speak of the formative institutions in Chinese society 20 years ago, that is before the coming of the Communist régime, he would have treated this subject very differently from the way he would today. In speaking of them now, one has to acquire a new outlook and to examine the subject in an altogether different light. What has been fostered in a subtle manner is now thrown into the open and attacked, while new institutions have arisen to expound on the ideals and values of the new order.

All reformers feel suspicion for old institutions. But by the Communists whose conception of the new social order is so diametrically opposed to the existing one, every old institution is suspected of being in service to the ideas and ideals of the old régime. The major assumption is, of course, that all social institutions are formative in nature, serving either this master or the other master. They either work for the building of the new order or work against it. If they do not work deliberately against the building of the new order, they at least work as a deterrent to the advancement of the new order. For this reason, nothing is to be taken for granted. Every institution has to be scrutinized with suspicious eyes and its assumptions and implications must be brought to the fore. The Communists feel that all old institutions must be destroyed if possible. But as they cannot do this they have to start cracking the major ones and minimize the influence of the rest. In place of the old, the remnants of feudalism and the bourgeois ideology, new ones have to be installed to serve the cause of the socialistic and proletarian revolution. Their vigilance is brought to such a high degree that no stone is to be left unturned. Not only are the old institutions to be terminated, but also any chance of their revival is to be guarded against. Those who are radically inclined have to be ruthless in the battlefield as well as in the social struggle. They say : to be kind to the enemy is to be cruel to the "people"; without destruction there can be no construction; in order to correct an error one has to go to the other extreme. The social institutions must be torn apart. Figuratively speaking, like an old piece of porcelain, no matter how beautiful it may be in its own design, it must be broken into pieces; and a new mosaic is to be constructed out of the fragments according to the ideas of the new designer. So when the moderates are after reformation, the radicals are after transformation. This is the tenor of the Chinese Communist revolution.

As an introduction to the subject, let us have a look at the Chinese kinship system which has been so well established in Chinese society and so well known to the outside world.

In order to bring out the contrast between China in the past and China under the Communist régime, let us have a look at the Chinese communities outside China today. We may take New York's "China Town" and Hong Kong's Chinese community as examples. We need not consider Taiwan. In the system of kinship, in each of these places, there are many traditional organizations which play a significant role in the personal and social life of the Chinese overseas. In New York's China Town, as one walks in the streets, one finds many large sign boards of associations of many kinds : Surname Associations of the Chens, Lis, Lins, Huangs, Tans, Liangs, Meis, etc.; Native Associations (Fellow-districtmen Associations) of Chung Shan District, Hui Chou District, Tai Shan District, Ch'iung Yai District, Ta P'eng District, P'an Yu District, Nan Hai District, etc. Many a man belongs to one association for his surname and another association for his district at the same time. This kinship tie is strong. A certain amount of social influence and pressure is exerted over association members, and a good deal of common concern is shared by them. This explains in a large measure why in times of economic depression or unemployment, the Chinese are seldom seen in the city's bread lines. They are largely taken care of by their kinship associations. This explains also why there is less delinquency in the Chinese communities though they are also in the slum areas. The formative effect of the kinship system of the Chinese is not to be denied.

In Hong Kong such kinsmanship associations have become more prominent in recent years. In fact, kinsmanship has been greatly emphasized by the British Colonial Government as a method of social stabilization and cultural conservation. There are over 100 such associations[1] registered with the Colonial Government of Hong Kong and blessed by it, many of which were formed in Hong Kong in the last decade or so after the Communist régime was established in the mainland. This acceleration in development of kinsmanship ties in Hong Kong is due partly to the colonial policy of the British and partly to the home-sickness of the Chinese who are refugees in Hong Kong.

The point we want to bring out here, as we discuss the formative institutions in present-day China, is not so much to argue the existence of such kinsmanship institutions in Chinese traditional society, as to point out the sharp turn of events in China's homeland today where none of those surname associations and district associations are permitted to exist in the whole stretch of its vast land. Not only are these associations, but all institutions of a kinship nature abolished : such as the Association of Returned Students from Japan, Association of Returned Students from America and Europe, Association of Returned Students from France and Belgium, Peking University Alumni Association, Lingnan University Alumni Association, etc. This

---

[1] According to the *Hong Kong Yearbook*, 1965, there are fifty-three surname associations and seventy-five native district associations in Hong Kong.

social change is part of a social reform which is known as the "Down with the Five-identity Relationship Campaign" in the early years of the People's Republic.

The term which the Chinese Communists call *wu-tung*, literally meaning "five-sameness", may be translated as "five identities" or "five kinds of identity in social relationship". They are : (1) *Surname identity* (people with the same surnames); (2) *Clan identity* (people of the same clan); (3) *District identity* (people from the same native district); (4) *School identity* (former schoolmates); (5) *Office identity* (former colleagues of any kind). There is a sense of personal attachment for people who belong to or who have belonged to the same group. A certain amount of affection in this "we" feeling is developed through the sharing of a common history, common experience, common acquaintance, common pride, and common likes and dislikes. If some sense of attachment among people of such identities is existent anywhere in the world, this sense is certainly keener among the Chinese, whose culture is known for its special regard for human relations.

It is exactly the warm human feeling and appeal of such identities that the Communists cannot tolerate. Such feelings are social, it is true; but they are not socialistic. It is for this reason that the five-identity relationship must be demolished. In its place, one *tung* or "identity" is to be substituted, and that is *tung chih* or "same purpose" or "identity in purpose" which is often translated as "comrade". It is common in China today to address one another as *tung chih*. It is complimentary to be so addressed,[2] as it is meant to be the way members of the party address each other. As sensitivity to ideological concepts develops in the course of time, the application of the term is more

[2] At the border between Hong Kong and Communist China on the Canton–Kowloon railway station there was once an interesting incident. As an old Chinese woman stepped on the Hong Kong side, she saw a policeman. In showing her travel document to him, without thinking, she addressed him *tung chih* (comrade). The policeman rebuked her and said : "There is no comrade here. If you want comrades, go back to the other side."

restricted. Of course, one would not address the reactionaries and the anti-socialists as "comrades".

The masses of the Chinese people have learned by now to avoid identifying one another with traditional concepts of relationships. It is very unbecoming now to take up as subjects of conversation their common clan, their native district, their former school-mates and school days, or their former business association. When it comes to political purges and screening, however, one has to reveal all his former social relationships of all kinds.

## THE CHINESE COMMUNIST PARTY

Many people have called communism a religion and have pointed out how the Communist Party has tried to model itself upon the Catholic Church in its operation. Like Christianity, communism has a world view and a world programme. It is a faith, as uncompromising as Christianity, where there is only one god and no other god. It has its own doctrines, its sacred literature, its saints and apostles, its theorists, its apologetics, its hierarchy, its religious orders and priesthood. It demands of its followers simple-minded devotion, undivided loyalty, selfless sacrifice, unconditional subordination, and absolute discipline.[3] Like the consecrated clergymen who submit themselves completely and who are willing to go where the Lord wants them to go and do what the Lord wants them to do, the Communists

[3] In Liu Shao-chi's lecture delivered at the Institute of Marxism–Leninism in Yenan, July 1939, entitled "How to be a Good Communist", there is a section entitled "A Party member's personal interests must be unconditionally subordinated to the interests of the Party". To quote from it: "A Communist must be clear about the correct relationship between personal and Party interests. The Communist Party is the political party of the proletariat and has no interests of its own other than those of the emancipation of the proletariat. The final emancipation of the proletariat will also inevitably be the final emancipation of all mankind. . . .

"The test of a Party member's loyalty to the Party, the revolution and the cause of communism, is whether or not he can subordinate his personal interests absolutely and unconditionally to the interests of the Party, whatever the circumstances.

also submit themselves and go where the party wants them to go and do what the party wants them to do. Being much younger than Christianity, the Communist Party seems to be more serious, more offensive, more resolute, more rigorous, and more challenging than we would find the Christian Church today.

When we speak of the Communist Party as a most formative institution, we do not only refer to the formative role it plays in the life of the party members but also to its role in the life of the whole population. The Communist Party members are consecrated to the cause of communism as the members of the Christian religious orders are consecrated to the cause of Christianity. While people in the Western world can now stay away from the church if they so desire and even criticize Christianity freely, the people in Communist China cannot stay away from the Communist Party. Communism is only to be accepted and not to be criticized. The party comes to everybody's door and forces every door open, if necessary, for its propaganda and tutelage. While there are many religious orders and sects within the Christian Church, the Chinese Communist Party is, so far, a solid unity. It has been so for the last 35 years since Mao Tse-tung assumed its leadership. The party's formative influence is, therefore, much more formidable, with no deviation

---

"At all times and on all questions, a Party member should give first consideration to the interests of the Party as a whole, and put them in the forefront and place personal matters and interests second. The supremacy of the Party's interests is the highest principle that must govern the thinking and actions of the members of our Party. In accordance with this principle, every Party member must completely identify his personal interests with those of the Party both in his thinking and in his actions. He must be able to yield to the interests of the Party without any hesitation or reluctance and sacrifice his personal interests whenever the two are at variance. Unhesitating readiness to sacrifice personal interests, and even one's life, for the Party and the proletariat and for the emancipation of the nation and of all mankind—this is one expression of what we usually describe as 'Party spirit', 'Party sense' or 'sense of organization'. It is the highest expression of communist morality, of the principled nature of the party of the proletariat, and of the purest proletarian class consciousness." (See Liu Shao-chi, *How to be a Good Communist*, pp. 45–7, Foreign Language Press, Peking, 1965.)

or dissension permitted. It has been able to live up to the motto : "No party outside the Party, no clique inside the Party". The so-called democratic parties in the CPPCC exist only in name today.[4] They are only echoes of the Chinese Communist Party and have become its shadows. They recruit no more new members.

Some Christian theologians say that when three people pray together in the name of Christ, there is the Church. The Communists, likewise, provide for the formation of a party cell when there are three party members.[5] So throughout the whole nation, people in all walks of life and in all corners of the land have to submit to the supervision and tutelage of the Chinese Communist Party under its nationwide party network.

It is generally said that the effectiveness of the Chinese Communists' campaign can be explained by the ingenious methods they employ, the high quality of their party members and the thoroughness of their organization. But we should also bear in mind some additional factors. In the first place, the veteran Chinese Communists were imbued with a strong hatred of the political and social order that had existed. As revolutionaries they are still more fearless and ruthless. Having to work underground and constantly under persecution during the Nationalist days, many of them had been schooled in hardship, adversity, and vigilance. If they had not been resolute in their purpose, they would have long ago fallen away from the ranks. However unpopular a Communist appears in Western eyes, it is not easy for anyone to become a party member. A lot of screening is required

[4] In August 1966, when the Red Guards organized by the students in Peking posed as the vanguard of the Great Proletarian Cultural Revolution, they demanded the democratic parties to dissolve themselves.

[5] According to the Constitution of the Chinese Communist Party, 1956, Chapter 6, The Primary Organization of the Party, Article 47, has this provision: "Primary Organizations of the Party shall be formed in all factories, mines or other enterprises, in every *hsiang* and nationality *hsiang*, in every *chen*, in every agricultural production cooperative, in every organ, school and street, in every company of the People's Liberation Army and in all other primary units where there are three full Party members or more."

before one is admitted as a provisional member, and a further period of observation is required before he is admitted as a full member. Once he gains full membership, he shares many of the party's secrets. It is because of this that it becomes even more difficult for him to get out if he wants to quit than it was to get in. It is no joke sharing the Communist Party's secrets. The Communist Party is more severe in its persecution of a party member who has quitted than of a person who has always been opposed to communism. Those who are not experienced in Communist Party operation must think twice before they make up their minds to become its members. It is no child's play.

In the second place, the Chinese Communist Party has many ingenious ways of cultivating the members for its use. It goes without saying that they have to study the major works of Marxism–Leninism and Mao Tse-tung's writings. They also have to study party documents and directives from time to time. Before a major campaign is launched or a programme announced, that is, before the public knows anything about what is to take place, the party members are told in advance what is coming and are prepared for it. When the campaign or programme is in progress, they receive party instructions and hold discussions among the members in advance. This makes the party members both very intelligent and resourceful in the eyes of the people for the execution of party policy. The method of criticism and self-criticism is extensively used in the training of party members and leaders in order to break down any trace of individualism and to weld them into the party line. Once in so many years, a rectification campaign is conducted to wash out the undesirable elements and to streamline the political thinking and behaviour of party members. These campaigns often go beyond the party and go down to the masses of the people. As a result, disciplinary actions and purges follow. To be a welcomed party member, one must not only depend on his old glory and meritorious deeds, but must keep up with the party line at its frontiers.

The Chinese Communist Party is a huge organization based on a complete system of philosophy and ideology. It is surprisingly well-run. It is at the same time well consolidated. Iron rule, on such a big scale, finds no parallel in Chinese history except, perhaps, in the reign of Chin Shih Huang. At the moment it does not appear that there is any political power in China, existing or in the making, which can challenge the Communist power. Sporadic opposition cannot overthrow it, just as "a cup of water cannot put out a cartload of wood on fire", as the Chinese saying goes. If the present Communist régime collapses, it will probably be because the Chinese people cannot sustain a rigid way of life which is beyond human nature and human endurance for long. As to whether or not there will emerge a different sector within the Chinese Communist Party itself to take over the reins of government, by which a different policy might be adopted, that is anybody's guess.

We may very well say, at this point, that the whole Chinese nation is now at school, learning to shape and reshape the lives of all to the ideology of communism as interpreted by Marx–Lenin and Mao Tse-tung. The whole nation is a school; the enrolment is approximately 700 million; the study programme is communism; the staff is the Communist Party, and the headmaster is Mao Tse-tung.[6]

It may be appropriate here to give a description of the structure of the Chinese Communist Party. According to the Constitution of the Communist Party of China which was adopted by the Eighth National Congress of the Communist Party of China on 26 September 1956, the organization of the Chinese Communist Party may be summarized as follows:

1. *Membership.* In order to be eligible for party membership, one must be of 18 years old and upwards. An application must be recommended by two full party members. In order to be admitted, one has to be accepted, generally, by the general

---

[6] The editorial of the *Renmin Ribao* (*People's Daily*) on 1 August 1966 in commemoration of the 39th anniversary of the founding of the Chinese People's Liberation Army was entitled: "The Whole Country Should Become a Great School of Mao Tse-tung's Thought."

membership meeting of a party branch and approved by the next higher party committee. Applicants have to serve a probationary period of a year before becoming a full member.

2. *Central organization.* The highest leading body of the party is the National Party Congress which elects the Central Committee. The Central Committee directs the entire work of the party when the National Party Congress is not in session. The Central Committee carries out the decisions of the party, sets up various party organs, directs their activities, and takes charge of and allocates party cadres. It also guides the work of the central state organs and people's organizations of a national character through the leading party members' groups within them.

3. *Local organization.* The highest leading body in each local party organization is the local party congress, which elects its local party committee. The lower party organizations must present periodical reports on their work to the party organizations above them, in addition to carrying out instructions from them.

4. *Geographical and industrial basis.* Local party organizations are formed on a geographical or industrial basis. That is to say, there are provincial party congresses and their respective provincial party committees, municipal party congresses and their respective municipal party committees, *hsien* party congresses and their respective *hsien* party committees, etc. The same pattern applies to the autonomous regions, autonomous *chou*, etc. As for the primary units, such as the factories, mines, and other enterprises, *hsiang*, *chens*, offices, schools, streets, and companies of the People's Liberation Army, and the like, the party organizations are the delegate meetings or the general membership meetings of the particular primary units and their respective primary party committees.

From the above description we not only see the organization of the Communist structure but also see more clearly what we had said before of the superimposition of the party over the Government. In order to guarantee the smooth operation of party control over the Government, there is a party congress and a party committee for every legislative and executive body at every level; each exists in parallel, in which an overlap of membership is bound to exist. What goes deeper than this superimposition is the absolute authority which the party has over all legislative and executive organs of the Government. The fact that Chairman Mao is the final authority of all things in China is the clearest evidence of this position. Mao Tse-tung is known and spoken of as Chairman Mao. But of what is he Chairman? In the first 10 years of the Chinese People's Republic he was chairman of the People's Central Government, which is the Chinese People's Republic. But beginning from the convening of the Second People's National Congress in April 1959, that chairmanship has been transferred to Liu Shao-chi. Then of what is Chairman Mao chairman? He is Chairman of the Central Committee of the Communist Party of China. In other words, the Chairman of the Chinese Communist Party is the Superchairman of the Chinese People's Republic, as the Communist Party National Congress is the Super-Chinese People's National Congress, and so on.

Organically, the Chinese Communist Party also runs two junior organizations for the training of prospective members and for the boosting of its programmes among the masses. One is the Chinese Communist Youth League[7] and the other is the Chinese Communist Young Pioneers Brigade, both of which are also modelled on the pattern of Soviet Russia, and whose organization

---

[7] The Chinese Communist Youth League as it is now called has changed its name several times. In 1922, when it was founded, it was called the Chinese Socialist Youth League; in 1927 it was changed to this name, the Chinese Communist Youth League; in 1949, when the Chinese Communist Party advocated what Mao Tse-tung called the New Democracy, it was named the Chinese New Democratic Youth League; in 1964 it changed back again to the name the Chinese Communist Youth League. Such a development reflects also the winding path which Communism in China has taken. (See *China Monthly*, published by the Union Research Institute, Hong Kong, Vol. 1, No. 2, p. 468.)

and activities are familiar to many Western readers. The Chinese Communist Youth League is for young people between 15 and 25 years of age, and the Young Pioneers Brigade is for children from 9 to 15 years of age; the former covers mostly the age of senior middle school and university students, while the latter covers mostly the age of primary and junior middle school children. The Communist Youth League is considered by the party to be the party's assistant. Regarding its role, the Chinese Communist Party Constitution states :

> In all spheres of socialist construction, the Communist Youth League should play an active role in publicizing and carrying out Party policy and decisions. In the struggle to promote production, improve work, and expose and eliminate shortcomings and mistakes in work, the Communist Youth League organizations should render effective help to the Party, and have the duty to make suggestions to the Party and to the Party organizations concerned.

The Communist Youth are the party's trainees; the party must take a deep interest in their ideological education so that they will be imbued with the Communist spirit, educated in Marxist–Leninist theory, and kept in close contact with the broad masses of young people. According to the Constitution of the Chinese Communist Party, the leaving age of the Communist Youth League is set at 20; but it also makes provision for the Communist Youth members who hold offices in the Youth League to remain in the league beyond this age. In fact, many of them remain there much beyond that age. Some of them have already been admitted into full party membership. This puts the League under the supervision of people over 20 years of age. As the first secretary of the Chinese Communist Youth League reported in January 1964 : "At present, members in the league who are under 20 years of age are relatively small in number." Some Young Pioneers who have reached the age of 15 still remained in the brigade after they had been admitted as Communist Youths. This interlocking membership system provides for the control of the Communist Party over its junior organizations as well as better co-ordination among them.

From the latest figures we have there were over 17 million members in the Chinese Communist Party in 1961 according to Liu Shao-chi's report at the 40th anniversary of the party.[8] The membership in the Chinese Communist Youth League in 1962 was said to be over 20 million.[9] The membership in the Young Pioneers Brigade is set at 100 million in 1966.[10] With this formidable number its strong solidarity and its tight discipline, the strength of the Chinese Communist Party in the transformation of a new order according to the Marxism–Leninism–Maoism ideology should not be underestimated.

## RELIGION

Religion is often spoken of as a formative institution in any society. In China, however, it presents a very peculiar picture.

### *Communism as a Religion and not as a Religion*

As we have said, some people consider communism a great religion. The ecstatic fervour which the Communists have for their faith, even to the call of death, makes one feel that they are among the most devout of religious men. So in a certain sense, communism is a religion. But if it is, it is an atheistic religion,

[8] The membership was 10,734,384 in 1956. According to the analysis presented by Teng Hsiao-ping in his report on the Revision of the Constitution of the Communist Party of China in that year, the party membership comprised 1·74 per cent of the total population. As to the composition of the party membership, 14 per cent were workers, 69·1 per cent were peasants, 11·7 per cent were intellectuals, 5·2 per cent were of some other social status. Women constituted about 10 per cent of the total membership.

[9] According to the statistics given in the *Chung Kuo Ching Nien Pao (China Youth)*, dated 1 February 1962. There has been considerable increase since then. The *Renmin Ribao (People's Daily)* reported on 19 February 1966 that the Chinese Communist Youth League admitted 8½ million new members in 1965.

[10] According to the *Renmin Ribao (People's Daily)* dated 1 June 1966 the membership in the Young Pioneers Brigade had expanded from 50 million to 100 million in one year's time.

provided such a term is not objected to on the ground of its self-contradiction. Communism is out-and-out materialism. According to the Constitution of the Chinese Communist Party, in an opening paragraph in its Preamble which they call General Programme, there is this statement: "The Party adheres to the Marxist–Leninist world outlook of dialectical and historical materialism, and opposes the world outlook of idealism and metaphysics."

If communism is a religion, it is a religion based on hatred. And hatred often has as great a driving force as love.

## The Meaning of Religious Freedom

Religious freedom is a relative term. When one hears the Chinese Communists say that there is freedom of religion in China, he should take heed of what it really means, particularly if he is a Westerner and is brought up in Christendom. One would concede that there is no such a thing as absolute religious freedom anywhere. But between absolutely unrestrained religious freedom and absolute religious compulsion, or absolute religious deprivation, there can exist many shades in a wide scale. We must be aware that religious freedom may differ in degree and extent as well as in kind, and must not take for granted that religious freedom has the same implications in all countries. Differences exist between a country of Christian origin and a country of non-Christian origin, and between a free State and a communistic State.

According to the Constitution of the Chinese People's Republic, under the Chapter on the Fundamental Rights and Obligations of the Citizen, Article 88 reads: "The citizens of the Chinese People's Republic shall have freedom of religious belief." We must take notice of the phrase "freedom of religious belief". "Freedom of religious belief" may mean something different from "freedom of religion" or "religious freedom", in the sense that "freedom of religion" or "religious freedom" may imply the freedom to preach one's religion, while "freedom of religious belief" may not. "Freedom of religious belief" may imply only that a person has the freedom to hold his own personal religious belief. Personal freedom of religious belief, though conceded to the ordinary people, is not permitted to Communist members. And even outside the Communist ranks, one is much handicapped if he adheres to a religious faith of any kind.

It has been advocated by some Chinese Communists that freedom of religion also implies the freedom to oppose religion. It happened in Canton many years ago, under the agitation of such a view, that when the Christians were holding Sunday worship in their Church, a crowd gathered outside the Church where a speaker stood on a soap box to attack religion. It is fortunate that that practice was later disallowed and the Church-goers can now attend their religious services without being molested either in their church premises or on their way to the Church and back from the Church. Church-goers are now confined to the older people and aged people whom the Communists consider to be unredeemable and soon to disappear from the scene.

As the Communists are such ardent adherents of materialism, it is only logical that they show no favour to religion. It should be no surprise to find them opposed to religions of all kinds. What is surprising is rather their admission of religious freedom in their Constitution, and their tolerance of religious worship and religious activities.

To answer the question of "why religious freedom?", we may find hints from the following. In the first place, the Communists justify any means for their end. They will do whatever is to their best advantage. At this juncture of world revolution, it is more advantageous for them to pose as a social order which tolerates religion and the adherents of different religious beliefs. Since most peoples, particularly the backward peoples who are recently emancipated from the yokes of colonialism and imperialism, have strong religious affiliations, it is good strategy that in selling communism to them the Communists do not antagonize them by attacking their religion. The purpose behind this toleration is to further their programme of world expansion. In the case of

China, tolerance is due more to external than internal considerations. If the religious issue had no bearing on the external world, religious people would face a much worse fate than they are facing in Communist China today.

In the second place, anything is capable of being used as an instrument of communism in the various stages of the revolutionary game. So why should they spare religion at this stage of social development? Just as the Communists play on the minorities as a means to entice other national minorities into their orbit, so they play on the various religions in order to dupe believers of other religions into circling round them. The religious groups in China today, including the Christian Protestant Churches and the Catholic Church, have played into Communist hands. The Communists now go so far as to subsidize the Christian Churches, monasteries, and temples, giving them special grants for upkeep and repair. They provide their delegates with travelling expenses to attend regional and national religious conferences. They once sent guards to the religious premises to provide them with better protection. They furnish them with religious robes so that their clergymen can take part in parades. They even set up a Bureau of Religious Affairs to look after their needs and to help them with their political studies. The Chinese Communists have been successful, in this respect, in that foreign visitors to China have often come out to tell the world that there is freedom of worship and that the Christian Church continues to exist, etc. They serve as eye-witnesses, though very superficial eye-witnesses they must be. But one must not forget that though religions and religious believers are given a permissive status, they are often looked upon as the lowest stratum in society. An illustration will make this clear. Some years ago, in a parade in Canton where all organized groups in the city had to take part, the leading groups in the procession were the People's Liberation Army, the industrial workers, the students, etc. At the tail of the procession was the group of Christian, Buddhist, and Moslem organizations and those who were engaged in the business of incense-sticks, candle-sticks, etc. The banner under which they marched had this title :

"Religions and Superstitious Trades". This is their status in the eyes of the masses of the people.

## Religions in China

For our purpose religions in China may be classified under three categories. This classification reflects the attitudes of the Chinese Communist Party toward the religions in China. They are indigenous religions, religions of the oppressed peoples, and religions of the imperialistic powers. Such categories can, of course, be further divided.

1. *Indigenous religions.* By indigenous religions we refer to Confucianism, Taoism, and Buddhism as well as ancestral worship and idol worship of all kinds. We call them indigenous because they have taken roots in the life of the Chinese people. Buddhism was first introduced to China in the Han Dynasty as early as 2 B.C., and flourished in the Tang Dynasty (A.D. 618–907), but it has been so well integrated into Chinese life and belief that it is no longer thought of as foreign. Of course, whether the religion is accepted by the masses of the people or by just a small fraction of the population, is also another criterion.

2. *Religions with imperialistic affiliations.* To these the Catholic Church and the Protestant churches of all denominations belong. They are considered to be associated with imperialism on a double count. For one thing, the United States, England, France, Italy, Germany, Belgium, the Netherlands, etc., are the countries which profess to be Christian countries. They are considered, however, by the Chinese Communists to be imperialistic powers on the ground that they hold or have held colonies in the lands of many coloured peoples. For another, the propagation of Christianity in China was protected by extraterritorial rights under what the Chinese call the "unequal treaties", which were first forced upon China as a consequence of the Opium War and other conflicts with the Christian

countries. Indeed, the activities of the Christian churches, Catholic or Protestant, in their ministry as well as in their schools and universities, have been branded by some Chinese as cultural imperialism. Since Christianity is not native and has become more and more American–European and less and less Asian, in spite of its Asian origin, it is looked upon as something foreign by the Chinese in general, and as imperialistic by the Communists in particular.

3. *Religions of the minorities and oppressed peoples.* To this category both Mohammedanism and Buddhism belong. Mohammedanism or Islam is the religion of a national minority in China known also as Moslems, about 10 million in number[11] who inhabit mostly in China's north-west. They form the greatest national minority in China today. Islam is not considered as imperialistic, according to the Communist conception, in spite of the fact that it has been accused in Christendom as a religion which is symbolized by the Koran in one hand and the sword in the other. It truly represents a religion of China's minority and a religion of the oppressed peoples or formerly colonized peoples, as found in Egypt, Turkey, Arabia, Pakistan, Malaysia, Indonesia, and certain other countries in Africa and Asia. Like Judaism, Islam is as much a religion as it is a national minority. In China one cannot tell outwardly a Moslem from a non-Moslem. The only observable difference between a Moslem and a non-Moslem in China, however, is that the Moslem does not eat pork or use lard in his cooking. So as a gesture of respect for the habits and religion of the minority peoples, food without pork is served to Moslem members in the congresses and conferences which they attend in China.

With the rationale of religious classification in mind according to the Communist point of view, we shall be able to see the different approaches in China to Communist dealings with the

---

[11] According to the 1953 census, the figure given for Moslems in China was 10 million. But the pre-Communist estimate ranged as high as 50 million. (See *Encyclopaedia Britannica*, 1964 edition.)

religious groups. The indigenous religions are treated as a matter of contradiction within the "people" themselves. Superstition is to be removed in a patient way by means of knowledge and science. This will come gradually and eventually. No special effort is required. Taoism, however, needs to be dealt with differently. The I-Kuan Tao, one of the most organized and influential Taoist sects, was persecuted on anti-revolutionary grounds in the early years of the People's Republic because of the rumours they spread among the lowest stratum of society by word of mouth, in the form of interpretation of religious omens unfavourable to the Communist régime. Buddhism in China, very different from that which we see in Vietnam, is essentially pacifistic and non-resistant in nature. Buddhist monasteries spreading out in all the scenic spots in the mountains throughout China have been confiscated together with the land which they used to own for the support and maintenance of monasteries and temples. Most of their monasteries and temples are now used for governmental and garrison purposes. Some are developed as places of recreation and recuperation for the workers and soldiers.

The Communists will have to put up a staunch fight for a long time to come against Confucianism, which is the basis of Chinese culture. Confucian teaching is accused as the source of feudalistic and bourgeoisie ideology. The Great Proletarian Cultural Revolution summoned by the Chinese Communists in 1966 had this Confucian barrier to overcome. The worst part of it is that Confucianism is diffused and is an accepted way of life. It is not an organized religion with a Pope, a priesthood, or a hierarchy which they could destroy. If it has a priesthood, it is the whole body of old Chinese intellectuals. All Chinese philosophy, history, and literature reflect the system of values of Confucianism. It does not seem possible that the Chinese Communists can burn all Chinese books and bury alive all Chinese scholars as did Chin Shih Huang.

Regarding the Christian religion; practically all its churches were started by foreign missionaries under the support of mission boards which were sent from countries of the imperialist powers.

In the case of the Catholic Church, it is looked upon with even greater suspicion, as it is a world order with its hierarchy, its embassies, and its Pope who dictates from Rome. Catholic priests have been often regarded by the Chinese Communists as spies. There have been a number of cases of Catholic priests accused on such counts and sentenced to many years of imprisonment.

The first step which the Chinese Communists took against the Christian churches was a policy that the latter must sever all relations with foreign agencies. The "Three-self Movement" (self-government, self-support, and self-propagation), which some Chinese Christian leaders had advocated in the 1920's to meet the challenge of rising nationalism in those days, was much encouraged after the Communists came into power. They now add the word "patriotic" to the movement and call it the Chinese Christian Three-Self Patriotic Movement, which has had in its National Committee some forty Chinese Christian leaders who were approved by the Communists to serve as members. As for the Catholics, they were coerced to form the Chinese Catholic Patriotic Association of a similar nature.

The Christian Church, including the Catholic Church, used to undertake many social, educational, medical, and philanthropic as well as religious activities. But now it is stripped of all those functions, leaving it with the pure religious function. This has changed the whole picture of Christianity in China. Take the Catholic Church, for example. According to the statistics of the Catholic Church in 1948, the year before the inauguration of the Communist régime, when such statistics were available, there were 3,300,000 Catholics in China. Among the schools they operated, there were 3 universities, 189 secondary schools, 1500 city primary schools, 2243 village primary schools with a total enrolment of 320,000 students. There were 216 hospitals, 781 dispensaries, 5 leper asylums, 254 orphanages with 16,000 orphans, 29 newspapers, 55 periodicals, 1 observatory and 1 big library in Shanghai, and 2 museums. The only school that survived until recently was the one in Peking conducted by the

Catholic sisters[12] for the children of the diplomatic missions. The Protestant Church had an even larger educational programme. While the Catholics had only three universities, there were 13 Christian (Protestant) colleges and universities in China, among which the Yenching University in Peking, St. John's University in Shanghai, and Lingnan University in Canton were the most outstanding. The names of the thirteen universities and colleges do not exist in China today. They have been amalgamated into state universities.

Now the Christian Church in China has no foreign missionaries, accepts no foreign funds, and receives no ecclesiastical communications from abroad. It would be a crime if the foreign tie were maintained. In order to keep alive when the church members have little means to contribute, many of the pastors are engaged in some kind of productive work to earn a livelihood, such as vegetable gardening, chicken raising, goat raising, and shoe-mending.

The Chinese Church has moved into obscurity in Chinese society today. It may as well be so. Any claim to prominence and influence or any word of praise of Christian steadfastness and ingenuity would only invite greater Communist antagonism and more religious persecution.

It is of special satisfaction to Christians to be told here that the name of "Christ" was mentioned, not disrespectfully, in the CPPCC on 27 September 1949 in a session to decide on certain important matters in the establishment of the Chinese People's Republic. In his report on the proposal for the adoption of Christian era as the Chinese era, Chou En-lai said that the Chinese People's Republic was to adopt the universal era, "dating from the year in which Christ was born". Chou En-lai was a student in Nankai College, which was a Chinese private Christian school in Tientsin.

---

[12] This school was finally closed down in August 1966 when the eight nuns of the Franciscan Mission were expelled from China at the demand of the Red Guards, accusing them as foreign spies in consequence of the Great Proletarian Cultural Revolution.

## MARRIAGE AND THE FAMILY

The family is looked upon as the primary social institution in any society and is often regarded as the social institution with the most formative character. In the situation in China today, when the Chinese family, which has been so highly developed as a distinct institution through thousands of years, has to be integrated into a communistic society which has scant regard for kinship relations, the change is revolutionary. The problems involved are enormous.

### *The Traditional Chinese Family*

There is probably no other people in the world which has developed the family system so thoroughly and completely as the Chinese people. Not only has its structure been well developed within the family institution which embraces the extended family and the clan, but the whole structure of society is built on the concept of the family. The family system of values is manifested in and integrated with the political, economic, cultural, and social life of the people.

In order to show how well developed the institution of the Chinese family is, we do not need to refer to the great classics, *Li Chi* or the *Book of Rites*, dated to the time of Confucius, though it has served as the code of ethics for centuries and centuries. We see it in Chinese daily life. For example, the exhaustive terminology of family personal relationships is as appalling as it is unparalleled in the terminology of any other language. Take the word "aunt" which we find in the English language. "Aunt" applies to the elder sister of one's mother, the younger sister of one's mother, the elder sister of one's father, the younger sister of one's father, the wife of one's father's elder brother, the wife of one's father's younger sister, and the wife of one's mother's brother. In China, they each have a different nomenclature. Indeed, we do not have in the Chinese language the word "aunt" as such. The same thing holds true with the term "uncle" and "cousin", simple as they are in Western usage. One of the earliest things a child has to learn in this family relationship is to know how the various persons of his kinship belong to his family tree by learning how to address each one of them in the proper familial appellation. From this training one is conscious of the sense of kinship, knowing how one is related to another, who is who, who is related to whom, and so on through many degrees of kindred.

We do not need to dig deep to search for evidence of the influence of the family on the political, economic, social, and cultural life in China. A scratch on the surface will show. In the political sphere, we have heard of the "Chiang-Kung-Soong family" in contemporary Chinese politics. After Sun Yat-sen, founder of the Chinese Republic, died in 1925, Chiang Kai-shek, Sun Yat-sen's most able lieutenant, married in 1927 Sung Mei-ling, Madame Sun Yat-sen's younger sister. Madame Sun Yat-sen's maiden name is Soong Ching-ling. She had an elder sister, Soong Ai-ling, who had married H. H. Kung. Madame Sun's brother is T. V. Soong. With this "apron-string" relationship, H. H. Kung and T. V. Soong were appointed alternately as Ministers of Finance, Presidents of the Executive Yuans, etc., under Chiang's Government. This family clique in the Nationalist Government with its accompanying corruptions has made it ridiculed as the Sung Dynasty. (The Sung Dynasty in Chinese history dated A.D. 960–1279. "Sung" and "Soong" are the same word in Chinese. It is more commonly romanized as "Sung" than "Soong". The dynasty was called "Sung", not the surname of the royal family, which was "Chao".)

In the economic sphere, take Hong Kong today as an example. Most of the industries and business of the Chinese, particularly the smaller factories and shops, employ many people in their establishments who are their own relatives or relatives of their friends. Economic operation is intermingled with the effort to give one's own family and kinsmen employment, and the prospect of such enterprises depends on their trustworthiness and personal loyalty. As another example, the amount of money which the overseas Chinese remit to their family in China every year is enormous, making it one of the main sources of foreign exchange for the People's Republic. It is not the Communist régime that the overseas Chinese like, but it is family concern that prompts them to do so in spite of their hatred for the Communist government.

In the social sphere there are certain features in Hong Kong which cannot escape even a casual observer's eyes. In the Ching Ming Festival every spring, thousands and thousands of Chinese carry their incense, candles, and sacrifices to visit their ancestors' tombs. On that day one may see the heaviest traffic of the year, when all means of transportation are taxed to the full. Long queues are seen waiting for the trains and buses outside the terminals to take them to the graveyards in the countryside. Again, wedding feasts are elaborate, even for people with small means; family relations from the closest to the distant come, not only to congratulate the bride and bridegroom but also their parents, and to use the occasion as a family social gathering. For funerals of elderly people, one may see in the Chinese newspapers obituaries which reproduce the list of the names of the deceased's mourners, their sons and daughters, grandsons and granddaughters, great-grandsons and great-granddaughters, and the names of the descendants' spouses.

In the cultural sphere, the Chinese take special pride in men of achievement with their own family surname. For instance, when Lin Yu-tang, the noted Chinese writer, was in Hong Kong in 1965, the people in Hong Kong with the surname Lin held a big banquet in his honour which he attended and where he also spoke. There are schools in Hong Kong today called Family Association Schools which are run for the children of the same surname and which are often free in tuition. There are family schools of the Chans, the Lees, and the Wongs. The idea is that they do not want to see their clan's children uneducated. One does not find in the United States or in the United Kingdom, School of the Smiths or School of the Joneses established by the Smiths and Joneses, or special banquets given by the unrelated

Johnsons to a distinguished Johnson. The closest resemblance to this kinship belonging is perhaps observed in the story of the "Red-headed League" as presented in the adventures of Sherlock Holmes.

We have been citing many examples taken from Hong Kong because Hong Kong is closest to China; Westerners can still make their observations there, and one can still see the last vestiges of the social institutions of traditional China.

### The Communist Concept of the Family

What we have said about the Chinese family is not an attempt to explain the structure of the family system but to show how deeply set is the family concept in the minds of the Chinese people and how strong its influence is in Chinese life. Much of what has been said here is an amplification of our earlier discussion of the Anti-five-identity Campaign. Since the family institution has been so strong in its formative function in the past, we have not tried to avoid a certain amount of repetition in order to give the reader a fuller background.

The Chinese Communist régime in general has not yet attacked the family system, particularly the nuclear family and its immediate blood-relationships such as that of the parents and children. So long as the filial considerations do not get in the way of loyalty to the State in the building of a socialistic society, the family is not molested.

Before the Chinese Communists took over China, rumour was spread in the Nationalist territory that the Communists carried the slogan : "I don't want papa, I don't want mama, I only want *Kuo-Chia* [the State]". There was rumour also that the Communists practised promiscuity. As has been said : "The home and the family must go also, for in the family are the springs of all individualism. There must be community of possessions and community of wives. No one must know his offspring, just as no one must know his father or his mother. A generation will beget a generation."

So far the Chinese Communists have not advocated a disregard for parents in any positive way, though a lesser regard for parents is urged when the call of the party and the State is sounded. The family is not abolished altogether, but its importance and its function are minimized. Certainly there is no such a thing as community of wives in Communist China. Irregular sex relations, though common, are unsanctioned. In fact, improper man-and-woman relationships are considered to be socially corrupt; and when one becomes frequently involved and is accused, those are causes of expulsion from the party.

The functions and influence of the family have been in a decline. This is true not only of Chinese Communist society but also of all modern societies. The factors, such as the substitution of the family's function of education by that of the school, the lack of parental supervision because parents are both in employment, the growth of cities and urbanization, the demand of youth for greater freedom, and the like, account for this decline. Such familial deterioration is further aggravated by factors peculiar to Chinese Communist society. In the first place, the occupational function of the family is entirely gone. The family owns no means of production, and the employment and assignment of jobs are in the hands of the Government, which is the sole employer. In the second place, parents hesitate to educate their children in their own way for fear that their old ideologies might ruin their children's future and might also be the cause of persecution in case their unguarded opinions are known to the party and the public through their children's exposures. In the third place, what the parents can provide is little compared with what the State can provide. If family inheritance has been a factor in the inducement of the younger generation to accept parental authority, what the parents have in China today in terms of personal property is considered to be more of a liability than an asset. What is said here does not imply, however, that parental love is gone or that filial affection is absent; nor does it imply that the family has lost all its social and ethical significance in China.

*Marriage*

Marriage is the nucleus of the family institution. Whatever
we may say to criticize the family institution under the Communist régime, much credit has to be paid to the institution of
marriage under the Chinese People's Marriage Law.

Marriage in feudalistic China called for much severe con-
demnation. One can hardly defend the licensing of concubinage,
the prohibition of widows from a second marriage, the inferior
position of the female in the home, the blind marriage (that is,
arrangement of marriage by parents without the children's con-
sent), use of duress to coerce a marriage or to prevent a marriage,
the custom of child betrothal, and the like. While no one should
forget that the feudalistic marriage system has been under attack
all along, and that laws have been made in the Chinese Republican era since 1912, and though much progress has been made
toward the direction of reform, there was nothing so drastic and
thorough as the Marriage Law of the Chinese People's Republic
which was promulgated in 1950 and has been enforced since.

It may be worth while to outline the main provisions in the
Marriage Law.

1. *The new democracy versus feudalism.* The aim is to
abolish the marriage system of feudalism in which are allowed
manipulation, compulsion, male superiority and female inferiority, disregard of children's rights, and to bring into
being the marriage system of the new democracy in which
there is freedom of marriage, with one husband and one wife
(monogamy), equal rights between men and women, and
protection of the legitimate rights of women and children.
(Article 1.)

2. *Prohibitions.* Double marriage, concubinage, child-
betrothal, interference with the freedom of widows to remarry,
extraction of money or goods by anyone in connection with
marriage are all strictly prohibited. (Article 2.)

3. *Mutual willingness.* Marriage must be based on the complete willingness of the man and woman; no one party is permitted to compel the other party nor may a third party come in to interfere. (Article 3.)

4. *Registration of marriage.* Marriage shall be registered at the local people's government by the man and the woman in person. (Article 6.)

5. *Marriage age.*[13] It is only when a man has reached the age of 20 and the woman 18 and neither of them has genital defect, that marriage is allowed. (Article 4.)

6. *Freedom of husband and wife.* Both husband and wife have the freedom of choice of occupation, participation in work, and in social activities. (Article 9.)

7. *Divorce.* If the man and woman both wish to divorce, a divorce will be granted. Registration of divorce shall be made at the local people's government which issues the certificate of divorce. (Article 17.)

One should notice in the Marriage Law that some traditional practices are still preserved, such as the prohibition of marriage between close blood relations, the obligation of parents to children and children to parents, and the privilege of mutual inheritance between parents and children.

1. Marriage is not allowed between persons of direct blood relationship, such as brothers and sisters of the same parents or of the same father and different mothers or same mother and different fathers. As to whether the *side-line* blood relations within the five generations are allowed to marry or not, the decision shall go by customary practice. (Article 5.)

[13] The age has been modified in practice. See the following section on "Birth Control".

2.  Parents have the responsibility to rear and educate their children, and children have the responsibility to give financial support and help to their parents. (Article 13.)
3.  Parents and children have the right of inheritance from each other. (Article 14.)

The Family Law has been well publicized and it has been the legal document which was thoroughly studied throughout the country. Marriage has taken on a new look in China. It is one of the social reforms in China which has been most successful and accepted by the Chinese people. There are, of course, still abuses and violations of the law. Some party leaders do use their positions to impose on women for marriage. But such practices are much less common today than in the pre-Communist days. On a whole, marriage is contracted in the spirit of liberty, equality, and fraternity.

## Birth Control

The issue of birth control has been a controversial one even among the Chinese Communists themselves. Birth control was attacked by the Communists earlier as the product of bourgeois ideology of the capitalistic countries. But in recent years, because of the serious consequences of the population explosion, which made any amount of increase in production ineffective, the Chinese Communists have come forth to advocate birth control. The birth control campaign takes on various methods. (1) It appeals to the class consciousness of the proletariat to put the needs of the State above personal consideration in the building of a great socialist society. (2) The age for marriage is raised to 30 for men and 25 for women. If children are born before their parents reach these ages, the children will have no ration cards of their own for food and clothing. According to certain propaganda literature, it is urged that men before 38 and women before 34 should not be married. (3) Knowledge of birth control is widely disseminated and contraceptive devices are made easily available. (4) Abortion is legalized. Abortion up to 3 months of pregnancy is performed free of charge in any hospital for any woman who asks for it without requiring investigation.

The Chinese Communists, from the standpoint of building socialism, find it congenial to make family interest subordinate to that of the State, and to postpone the formation of the family to a later stage of one's life; it seems appropriate for the parents to have fewer children to look after so that they can have more time for social service. It is interesting to note in a modern contrast, that while the Chinese are encouraging late marriage and late parenthood, people in the West have been encouraging early marriage and early parenthood since World War II.

## OTHER FORMATIVE INSTITUTIONS

There are many institutions of a formative nature in the new régime in China, and every institution is used by the Communists as a formative instrument of human behaviour. There are the workers' unions, the communes, the Liberation Army, the press, the radio, the festivals and national days, the transport system, recreational centres, the theatres, and a host of others, all of which are institutions with distinct formative functions. Whether one is at work or at play, there is no escape from exposure to the formative designs of the Communist framework.

Since it will take too long to describe how each of these institutions functions in the formation of a new outlook and a new pattern of behaviour, it may suffice to take the theatre as an example of the role it plays and the problems involved.

However interesting the subject of the Chinese theatre is, particularly the Chinese opera, from the standpoint of its formative values, space does not permit a full discussion nor does the study justify a disproportionately long treatment on the subject. Brief as the account is, the significance of the theatre or the opera is not difficult to see. Indeed, it was precisely the anti-party and anti-socialist nature of the opera *Hai Jui Dismissed from Office*, written by Wu Han in 1961, for which he was accused, that caused the dismissal of the playwright from the office of vice-mayor in Peking in 1966. Among other writings, the play was the cause of the campaign which broke into the open in spring 1966, and which is known as the Great Proletarian Cultural Revolution.

Let us go back to the theatre as a great formative institution in traditional Chinese society. In the past there were regular theatre houses in the cities. In the countryside, where such luxuries were not afforded, temporary theatres, usually bamboo structures, were put up to accommodate the roving operatic teams which came to perform. Usually they came in the leisure seasons of the year when there were local festivals. The performances lasted 3–5 days at a time with one performance in the day time and one at night. Men and women, young and old, rich and poor, went to watch the shows. Such shows were the greatest community affairs of the year. The plays were taken from Chinese history and from popular stories. The ideologies were, of course, chiefly Confucian. The themes usually exemplify the five cardinal human relationships, of loyalty to the king, filial piety to parents, fidelity of wives to their husbands, fraternal love between brothers, and faithfulness among friends. The right always triumphed over the wrong and the virtuous over the wicked. In a country which was largely illiterate, in the absence of such modern mass media such as the movie, radio and television, the influence of the operas in the formation of the common mind in the traditional ideology cannot be overestimated. The voluntary nature of attendance and the aesthetic presentation of the artists make the plays as much social entertainment as cultural assimilation.

The policy of the Chinese Communists toward the Chinese stage has made several swerves in the last 17 years since the establishment of the People's Republic. The earliest policy was to give to the people what the people enjoyed. The people had always enjoyed the traditional Chinese opera, proletariat and non proletariat alike. What was needed then was to make the opera accessible to the masses, making the masses of the people the real beneficiaries of their rich cultural heritage. The actors and actresses in traditional China, in as much as they had always come from the poorer classes, had often been exploited and abused by the ruling classes in spite of their artistic talents. Now they were raised to a status of public esteem. The great operatic performers, such as Mei Lan-fang, Chou Hsin-fang, and Ching Hsien-chou, by nature of their popularity among the masses, were made delegates in the first Chinese People's Political Consultative Conference in 1949. Of course, the proletariat in the stories as well as in the casts must not be allowed to be portrayed as a clown, a villain, or a laughing-stock in the minds and eyes of the spectators.

The second stage was the further upsurge in dramatic art after the success of the First National Operatic Exhibition in Peking in October 1952. Mao Tse-tung wrote "Let the Hundred Flowers Bloom" in tribute to the excellence of the performances. This became the slogan to develop all types of drama, all kinds of stage craft and dramatic technique, and all varieties of native and local drama. As far as dramatic art goes, this stage of development lasted for 10 years without any set-back. In the meanwhile many old dramas were rewritten and modified while new historical themes were developed; on the whole, however, the traditional pattern of operatic art persisted. During this period many operatic groups with casts of famous artistes were sent abroad to give performances to boast Chinese artistic attainment and to win international good will. As late as summer 1963, the operatic groups came to play on the Hong Kong stage. The performances were excellent. The theatres were fully packed for weeks and weeks during their stay. It did puzzle those who were conscious of ideological differences to know why the traditional operas were still so flourishing under the Communist régime. The only explanation one could think of was that their counterparts, the old Russian operas and the ballet, were also undisturbed in Soviet Russia and that perhaps art should enjoy special concessions.

Now we are witnessing a third stage of theatrical development. As far as the opera is concerned, Communist open criticism of

s and the playwrights began to be heard in the autumn
n the spring of 1966 it burst into the Great Proletarian
_ Revolution, when the first shot was fired in the editorial
of the *Jiefangjun Bao* (*Liberation Army Daily*) of 18 April 1966.
Its title was: "Hold High the Great Red Banner of Mao
Tse-tung's Thought and Actively Participate in the Great
Socialist Cultural Revolution."

Besides Wu Han's play, we may also mention another play,
*Hsieh Yiao-Huan*, written by Tien Han in 1961. Tien Han is one
of China's greatest dramatists and is author of the Chinese
national anthem. He was attacked for using historical events for
the purpose of criticizing the present régime. In the words of the
Communists: "Now the campaign is vigorously to promote
modern plays whose themes must be on the struggles of the
socialistic revolution, of workers and peasants and the Liberation
Army and their heroes." Regarding the period of time to be
covered in the plays, it was suggested by Tao Chu, a vice-premier
and the former governor of Kwangtung Province, who in July
1966 was appointed Head of the Propaganda Department of
the Chinese Communist Party to replace Lu Ting-yi, that it
should cover the period starting from the Chinese Communist
Party's assumption of leadership. He said:

> The sphere of subject-matter of modern revolutionary plays should
> include the two stages under Communist leadership. Subject-matter
> in the democratic revolutionary stage can be and should be used for
> writing, and should be written with organized effort and with good
> planning. But more should be written on events of the socialistic
> revolutionary stage, and the major effort should be laid on the
> fostering of the image of the heroic figures in the Socialistic
> revolutionary stage.

In his capacity as the first secretary of the Central-southern
Regional Bureau of the Chinese Communist Party, Tao Chu spoke
to the delegates of Dramatic Art at a conference in his region
on 20 February 1965 in which he said that Peking Opera should
be the chief fortress to attack. His words are of tremendous
importance, and we quote them here:

> Why must we insist on boosting the performance of modern
> revolutionary drama at the present time? We all know that the

contradiction between Socialism and capitalism is the major contradiction confronting China today. To stand steadfast in Socialism in opposition to capitalism constitutes the fundamental principle and practice of our Party in the past decades. Therefore, everywhere in the country, in the cities and in the country side, we must launch the Socialist Education Campaign and loudly proclaim the socialistic revolution and socialistic construction, and loudly proclaim the class struggle (under the banner) of 'up with the proletariat and down with the bourgeoisie', and loudly proclaim the dictatorship of the proletariat. But on the stage, what is the situation? . . . On the stage what is shown are the emperors and kings, (the imperial) generals and premiers, and the talented élites and virtuous maids. Such things have nothing in common with our revolutionary purposes and needs. . . .

In the past, things of feudalism and capitalism have monopolized the stage, some of them for thousands of years, and some for hundreds of years. Now the feudalistic landlord class and the bourgeoisie class are overthrown, but they (the things of feudalism and capitalism) still cling on the stage and will not go. What is to be done? Ask them to get down and let our themes of the proletariat and socialism come up to the stage to perform.

The stage, then, has become the arena. The kings and princes have been forced to abdicate, and the peasants, workers, and soldiers have come into the limelight. But the issue of what is allowed and not allowed on the stage is not settled and the battle is still on, not between the kings and the workers but between the playwrights and the Communist ideologists. The traditional opera may some day come back, and the people will still welcome it, though it is difficult to say when. Even Tao Chu had to admit that in the traditional operas there are good ones which can be retained. The suspension of their performance, according to him, is only for the time being.

We see, then, that the theatre as a formative institution and as a weapon has not been overlooked in the class struggle.

# CHAPTER 5

# Prevalent Assumptions

LET us examine some of the prevalent assumptions in the recasting of a new social order in China. We shall refer to those which have special implications for the development of the educational system. Students of comparative education are familiar with the concept that every educational system has its underlying assumptions and implications. It is our purpose here to analyse the basic assumptions in order to prepare ourselves for a better understanding of the educational system which we shall discuss in the following chapter.

There are two important documents which reveal the underlying principles and policies of the Chinese Communist régime with regard to education. One is the chapter on Cultural and Educational Policies[1] in the Common Programme adopted in CPPCC

[1] Cultural and Educational Policies (Chapter 5 of the Common Programme):

*Article 41.* The culture and education of the Chinese People's Republic are those of the new democracy. That is, its culture and education are nationalistic, scientific, and popular (in character). The cultural and educational work of the People's Government shall have as its major function the elevation of the people's cultural level, the cultivation of personnel for national reconstruction, the liquidation of feudalistic, compradoristic and fascistic ideas, and the advancement of the idea of serving the people.

*Article 42.* To promote love of the fatherland, love of the people, love of labour, love of science, and love with respect of public property as the common virtues of all citizens of the People's Republic of China.

*Article 43.* To develop rigorously the natural sciences to serve construction in industry, agriculture and national defence. To encourage by rewards scientific discoveries and inventions, and to popularize scientific knowledge.

in 1949. The other is in the Constitution of the Chinese People's Republic adopted in 1955, which contains certain articles of relevance in the chapter on General Principles and the chapter on the Fundamental Rights and Obligations of the Citizen.[2] Although we do not depend on these sources alone for our analysis, it would be a mistake if we underestimated the importance of these statutory documents merely because there is some other more recent documentation under the imprint of the Chinese People's Liberation Army Organs of the Chinese Communist Party which place a strong accent on the proletariat revolution. One must remember that the Constitution was a development from the Common Programme both of which were drawn up principally by the Chinese Communist Party. They still constitute

---

*Article 44.* To promote the application of the scientific historical point of view in the study and interpretation of history, economy, politics, culture and international affairs. To encourage by rewards outstanding works of social science.

*Article 45.* To promote the use of literature and the fine arts in the service of the people, to awaken the people's political consciousness, and to encourage the people's enthusiasm for labour. To encourage by rewards fine works of literature and art. To develop the people's dramatics and motion pictures.

*Article 46.* The educational method of the People's Republic of China is the unity of theory and practice. The People's Government shall make plans and adopt appropriate procedures to reform the old educational systems, educational contents and teaching methods.

*Article 47.* To carry out universal education with planning and appropriate procedures, and to reinforce secondary and higher education; to put emphasis on technical education, and to strengthen spare-time education for working people as well as education for cadres in service; and to provide young intellectuals as well as old intellectuals with revolutionary political education in order to meet the extensive needs of revolutionary work and national reconstruction.

*Article 48.* To promote national physical education. To extend public health and medical services, and to pay attention to the protection of the health of mothers, infants, and children.

*Article 49.* To protect the freedom of reporting truthful news. To prohibit the manipulation of news for libelling, damaging the benefits of the country and its people, and agitating for world war. To develop the people's broadcasting. To develop the people's publication and to put emphasis on the publication of popular literature and magazines which are of benefit to the people.

the basic statutes of the state and until the 1955 Constitution is repealed or amended, it is still the most important document to be referred to. We quote from the Constitution, because the statements there are more recent. We quote from the Common Programme, because the chapter on the Cultural and Educational Policies is the most comprehensive and also the most concise form in which we find the policies presented. (See Chapter 7, section on the Sixteen Points and the Red Guards' activities.)

We shall enumerate the basic assumptions in a sequence which is intended to show, more or less, the rationale of the Communist

---

[2] Constitution of the Chinese People's Republic:

*Article 3.* . . . All the nationalities are equal. Discrimination against, or oppression of, any nationality, and acts which undermine the unity of the nationalities are prohibited. All the nationalities have freedom to use and foster the growth of their spoken and written languages, and to preserve or reform their own customs or ways. . . .

*Article 4.* The People's Republic of China, by relying on the organs of state and the social forces, and by means of socialist industrialization and socialist transformation, ensures the gradual abolition of systems of exploitation and the building of a socialist society.

*Article 86.* Citizens of the People's Republic of China who have reached the age of eighteen have the right to vote and stand for election whatever their nationality, race, sex, occupation, social origin, religious belief, education, property status, or length of residence, except insane persons and persons deprived by law of the right to vote and stand for election. Women have equal rights with men to vote and stand for election.

*Article 87.* Citizens of the People's Republic of China enjoy freedom of speech, freedom of the press, freedom of assembly, freedom of association, freedom of procession and freedom of demonstration. The state guarantees to citizens enjoyment of these freedoms by providing the necessary material facilities.

*Article 88.* Citizens of the People's Republic of China enjoy freedom of religious belief.

*Article 94.* Citizens of the People's Republic of China have the right to education. To guarantee enjoyment of this right, the State establishes and gradually extends the various types of schools and other cultural and educational institutions. The State pays special attention to the physical and mental development of young people.

*Article 95.* The People's Republic of China safeguards the freedom of citizens to engage in scientific research, literary and artistic creation and other cultural pursuits. The state encourages and assists creative work in science, education, literature, art, and other cultural pursuits.

approach to the subject of social and educational transformation. They are interrelated and interlocking. In some minor aspects there may exist a certain amount of self-contradiction.

## EDUCATION AND POLITICS

The first assumption is : the most basic factor in life is politics, and education is the instrument of politics.

Many people would agree with Aristotle in defining man as a political animal. Many more politicians would agree that politics is the most essential factor in life, but few would so readily agree that education is the instrument of politics or should be the instrument of politics. The Communists, however, openly admit that they use education as the instrument of their politics. As Lenin had said : "We do not think of education as outside politics, but very frankly subordinate it to our political aims."

His followers have developed his idea further and claim that education has always been used as the instrument of politics at all times by all peoples. What is different, they say, is that it is not so deliberate and obvious at certain times as at others. They claim that it cannot be otherwise. There is no power structure willing to give up its use. The Communists not only offer no apology but go so far as to accuse those in the Western world who deny that they use education as an instrument of their politics as either liars or hypocrites.

What is said here, however, does not mean that the Communists have not accused other governments of using education for political ends. The Chinese Communists had always instigated the old intellectuals to attack the Nationalist Government for using education as the instrument of politics, such as the requirement to teach the Kuomintang doctrines in all schools, or for the appointment of heads of schools and universities on political grounds, and the like. However, that was when the Nationalists were in power and they, the Communists, were struggling for power. Once they were in power, the story was different. It is pathetic to find the same intellectuals who had been so loud in their protest against the Kuomintang's use of education for political ends so silent when the Communists are many times more ruthless than the Nationalists in this respect. If they speak loud at all, they are loud in their eulogy of Communist practice.

To the Communists what matters most is one's political ideology, one's political consciousness, and one's political stand. If one's ideology is correct, all is well; if it is incorrect, all is questionable. This view is not without support in traditional society. We often hear that if a man has good knowledge but bad morals, he is more harmful than if he has had no good knowledge at all. It follows the same logic when the Communists say that if a man has good knowledge, or a good education, or whatever one may call it, but a wrong ideology, he will be more of an obstacle than a help to the advancement of communism. The State is not interested in giving such a man an education. In fact, the State must change him, indoctrinate him, force him if necessary to accept Communist ideology and serve the Communist cause. Everyone must have his thinking in line with the Communist view of life, of society, and of the world. Everything must be subordinated to these politics. Their slogan is : politics reign supreme. In the exact terminology in Communist China, which has a strong proletarian flavour, the slogan is : *"cheng chih kua shuai"* which means "the political is the banner of the marshal".

The function of political education in the eyes of the Communists may be likened to the function of liberal education in the eyes of educators in the West, as conceived since Greco–Roman times. To the Communists, it is education in "how to think"; "how" not in the sense of methods of thinking or the psychological process of thinking, but referring to the basic viewpoints of life in which one's thinking is to be engaged. Call it liberalizing or encroaching as one pleases, in essence it is the same thing. The Communists are concerned with the advancement of their class while the liberalists are concerned with the advancement of the individual.

Political education, of course, means much more than the teaching of "civics" in the schools, just as religious education

means much more than the teaching of the Bible. Political education must permeate every phase of education, including its
purposes, contents, methods, administration, student selection,
and teacher qualification, etc. The political ends and the educational ends are to be identical. Just as political education is more
than "civics" teaching, so is education more than the school,
though the school is a highly organized and systematized institution to which are delegated the chief functions of education, more
so than to any other institution.

## EDUCATION AND THE WORKING CLASS

The next assumption, as a corollary of the first, is : education
is for the working class.

The working class is a general term. Sometimes the term is
amplified to denote the workers, the peasants, and the soldiers.
At times, more so recently, the term propertyless class (proletariat) has been used. Education is therefore to be used for the
service of the workers, peasants, and soldiers, the proletariat.
This means that educational opportunities must be first given
to the working class and children of the working class in preference to the bourgeoisie and the children of the bourgeoisie; the
aims of education must be in the interest and for the welfare of
the working class, and the control of education must be in the
hands of the working class.

The Communists argue that in the past, going as far back as
the beginning of the history of the school, education has always
been the monopoly of the privileged bourgeoisie class. The
peasants and workers and their children were in practice denied
the opportunity of education. Even in the modern era when
education has been extended to the poor, the latter are limited
to the lower schools, leaving higher education almost exclusively
to the privileged class who can afford to pay, who have the
leisure, and who are considered to be properly bred. From the
standpoint of class ideology, the children of the poor, after being
admitted to the schools, come out imbued with the bourgeois

ideology and serve the cause of the bourgeoisie against their own class.

So the balance has to be tilted. Whether it is to make up for lost opportunity or to seek revenge, the children of the peasants and workers must be given priority in the allocation of educational opportunities. In being sent off to the higher levels of the school system, they are reminded of their obligation to their class. If it were not because of expediency in the face of the immediate needs for trained personnel in the construction programme, where the bourgeoisie and their children are needed because of their superior cultural backgrounds and their better aptitude for school work, the bourgeoisie would have been forced out of the educational field in China today.

But to keep them there does not mean to let them carry on in their own way. They have to be re-educated. The teachers in the universities as well as in the schools are required to denounce themselves in addition to being denounced by others. This is the way to convert them and to break down their prestige in the eyes of the students and the public. The old intellectuals have constantly to admit that the heavy bourgeois burden on their backs is a handicap to their ideological advancement. They pledge to take heed of the revival of their old habits of thinking. They have to show their willingness to learn humbly from those who come from what the Communists call "better family background", that is, people from formerly poverty-stricken families, from the poorest of peasants and workmen. The Chinese old intellectuals used to look down upon the peasants as people "with their feet clogged with cattle manure". Now they have to go to live in homes of poor peasants to learn to work bare-footed and to love the fragrance of cattle manure.

One often hears this slogan in China today : *hsing wu mieh tzu* which is the abbreviation of the slogan "raise the proletariat; liquidate the bourgeoisie". The Communists explain that it is not their policy to destroy the physical bodies of the bourgeoisie. But the bourgeoisie as a class must be destroyed, together with its ideology, mentality, modes of thinking, and ways of life. In the educational realm, they ask : Who to receive education? And education for whom? The reply is : Not only is education to serve the workers, the peasants, and the soldiers, but education is to be obtained by learning from the workers, peasants, and soldiers. It is only after the old intellectuals have successfully learned from the working class that they are fit to be teachers of the working class. As Lenin said : "Those who educate, must first be educated." The burdens of the bourgeoisie are indeed heavy. Recent events in China reveal that even the highest personages in the Communist hierarchy, such as those who have been in charge of propaganda and cultural affairs for years and years are, in fact, according to the accusations of the Chinese Communist papers, hidden agents of the bourgeoisie class. In China, if such is the case, the redemption of the old intellectuals is probably a forlorn hope.

## THE REVOLUTIONARY STRUGGLE AND THE MASS LINE

Another assumption is : The class struggle is the order of the day in the World Revolution. The revolutionaries' political capital lies in the masses who would surely rally to their support.

What society needs is a great revolution which is to be carried on in the interests of those who labour to keep society going and who, though forming the largest majority of mankind, have been downtrodden by the exploiting class, the propertied class. The bourgeoisie class must be pointed out as the deadly enemy whose supports are feudalism, imperialism, and capitalism. In order to win the battle, class consciousness must be stirred up. The struggle will be long and fierce. Without the combatant spirit like that required in the battlefield, the war will never be won. To the Communists, whatever is advantageous to their class war is right and good conduct. The end justifies the means. The key to the success of the socialist revolution lies in the policy of the mass line. The masses always constitute the largest majority of the population, who, when they are organized and mobilized, become a formidable force in any society to crush any minority. The Communists know best how to take advantage of mob psychology and social pressure. Their tactics are to appease the masses and release their grudges. The less educated the masses are, the more easily they can be stirred up, even though they are bound to commit more errors. As a Chinese Communist propaganda chief once said :

> When the masses rise up, there is bound to be inversion; when there is inversion, you can be sure that the masses have arisen. It does not matter, from the standpoint of class struggle, if the bourgeoisie class suffers from maltreatment. It would not be revolution, if one were guided by the bourgeois morality of tenderheartedness and bourgeois standards of fairness. When one is committed to killing, his hands must not quiver in the execution. Tenderheartedness must not enter into his mind. Communist logic is that one must be resolute in the class struggle, for to be kind to the enemy is to be cruel to one's own class. The class war is no game.

The combatant spirit must be constantly kept alive. The creation of tension is helpful to an outburst of the spirit. Military terms are employed a great deal in daily usage, such as "to *combat* with ignorance", "in the cultural and productive *front*", "in our own *ranks*", "the scientific *army*", "to *conquer* the floods", "to *arm with* Marxism–Leninism", "to mount an overall *offensive*", "a mission of *surprise attack*", "the school is a *fierce battle-field* between the proletariat and the bourgeoisie for the *capture* of the young generation", "not to *withdraw* until final *victory* is attained". Social movements and campaigns are designed one after another in order to keep up the fighting spirit as well as to train the sinews of the revolutionary. A function of education is to produce activists for the class struggle.

The abolition in 1965 of military titles with differentiated uniform insignia according to rank (which had been introduced in 1955) is an illustration of the triumph of the principle of combatant spirit and the mass line. The military establishment which was adopted from the Soviet Union and other countries was meant to regularize the national defence organization and to raise the social dignity of the officers. It was a departure from the traditional practice of the Chinese People's Liberation Army in the guerrilla days, when the officers and the privates were considered comrades-in-arms without any mark of distinction among them. As a result of the new military hierarchy, it was said, the officers and the soldiers were alienated and the combatant spirit declined. Now, the officers' insignia on the uniform collars, etc., have been abandoned in order to boost army morale, with a return to the principle of the mass line.

## THE IMPORTANCE OF LABOUR

The assumption is : Labour has an inherent reformative power.

In the materialistic interpretation of history, labour itself possesses creative power. It forms and transforms the human mind. It has the cleansing power to reform a man. The theory is that man developed from the ape, and when he began to stand erect on his feet and use his hands, his brain developed. This is the story of the human brain. According to this view, labour creates mankind and creates the world.

We have heard the slogan "Those who do not work, neither shall they eat". Work may mean manual labour and it may mean mental labour. But what the Chinese Communists emphasize today is principally manual labour. Teachers and students as well as the cadres in governmental offices are mobilized to the rural areas to undertake manual work in the farm. Some of them are sent to the factories and mines. Manual labour is thought to have an educational value as it brings the intellectuals closer to the working people and develops in them the outlook of the manual worker. The half-work half-study school is operated on the same assumption, although the motive of speeding production is not to be ruled out. The Communists would not regard such manual labour as a waste of the students' and teachers' time. One might say that boring manual routine has no educative value to speak of in the development of the mind, but the Communists do not admit it. While intellectuals are sent to the farms and factories to work with their hands and feet, the landlords and anti-revolutionaries are sent to the labour camps for

hard labour. The theme is the same : they are given the opportunity to educate themselves through direct participation in
labour.

Some commentators have paid tribute to the Communist
scheme of enforcing manual labour upon the Chinese intellectuals. They consider it a good reform because working with the
hand and working with the mind had been widely divorced from
each other since the time of Confucius. The Confucian view of
labour is not without criticism. Even Confucius was criticized
for this by one of his contemporaries who, in rebuking his
disciple, was criticizing Confucius. The man said, as recorded in
the Confucian Analects : "Your four limbs are unaccustomed
to toil; you cannot distinguish the five kinds of grain; who is
your master?" Anyway, the disdain for manual labour in traditional Chinese society is excessive. Any casual observation of the
life of the Americans, among whom even university professors
do a lot of manual work at home, would present a sharp contrast
with the life of the Chinese scholar.

But the Communist correction of the Chinese intellectuals in
this respect is not undertaken in a light vein. It is far from being
contented with having manual training and industrial arts included in the school subjects for the sake of diversifying interest
or for the sake of the exploration of personal aptitudes. It means
much more than encouraging students to take physical exercise
as extra-curricular activities after school. It means much more
than writing essays on the sanctity of labour on Labour Day.
Labour in education is a much more serious matter in China
and has much wider implications. Labour is the dividing line
between the ruling class and the ruled. It is a weapon of ideological warfare.

## PRODUCTION AND PRODUCTIVITY

Another assumption is : Productivity is the key to socialistic
success, and education must be linked with production.

Education is not for the leisurely enjoyment of life. It must serve the needs of agriculture and industry. The five-year plans are economic in nature, and education must be mobilized and geared to the requirements of those plans. We have mentioned before the idea of the "three red flags"—the People's Commune, the Great Leap Forward, and the Socialist Main Line—which are all calls to expedite production. The long list of ministries in charge of productive affairs in the Central Government[3] is evidence of this emphasis. The people are challenged to exceed the capitalistic countries in production. As a result of these efforts, the whole nation is made production-conscious.

For a time schools operated farms and factories to boost agriculture and industry, while farms and factories operated schools to train technicians right on the spot. Even where educational institutions do not run productive establishments and productive enterprises do not run educational institutions, education and production are not so disconnected as they are in the Western world. Students look forward to going into the industries and farms, while the industries and farms look forward to absorbing the graduates in large numbers. Producers have to do their jobs well and improve upon their products constantly. Just as there are political study groups for all workers, there are also occupational study groups for them. They have to learn the new techniques, ways and means of increasing efficiency, and improving the quality of production. A glance at the large variety of commodities on sale at the Chinese Native Product Departmental Stores in Hong Kong will convince the outsiders that remarkable improvements have been made in the quality of Chinese products in the last decade. We see this in the preserved fruits, canned goods, embroidery, carving, leather shoes, garments, furniture, machines, bicycles, electric appliances, etc. These represent the light industries which now compete well with other advanced industrial countries in the world market and win for the Chinese their national pride. Other items include marine diesel engines, generators, heavy duty air-conditioning equipment, printing machines, high-speed paper-cutting machines,

[3] See Chapter 3.

micro-jewel bearings for precision machinery, high vacuum coating equipment and high-frequency ceramics, etc., which were on display in Hong Kong in August 1966. These are items which China had always imported and never exported before the Communist régime.

Education for production and productivity means more than learning the know-how and the required skills in production. It means also that the individuals have to learn, through the study groups, how their jobs and their production units fit into the economic scheme of the whole country and the five-year plan. The producers in China today, in that sense, are better-grounded and more intelligent than the producers in old China or his counterpart in the capitalistic countries. They see the meaning of their labour in the great national undertaking and see the relationship of their jobs to the whole process of production, from the source of their raw material to the consumption of the finished products. It is on this basis that attendance at study groups to discuss political and occupational reports, in addition to long hours of work, can find some justification.

## SOCIALIZATION AND CORPORATE LIFE

The assumption is: Corporate life is the foundation of socialism just as individualistic life is the foundation of capitalism. Individualization must be destroyed to give way to socialization.

Individualism is being attacked as the enemy of socialism. Individualism, individual liberalism, individual heroism, individual orientation, are all terms of disrepute in Chinese Communist society. The terminology used a great deal in the educational world in the West (such as individuality, individual development, individual difference, individual consideration, individual interests and aptitudes, individual ability, individual experience, individual freedom, etc.) is not found in the Chinese educational literature today. When it is found, it is in terms of ridicule and subject to attack.

In the schools in Hong Kong, for example, children learn to compete with each other during the whole school career. Because of keen competition for school places, the students are encouraged to outdo the other fellow. The teachers teach their own subjects independently. Mutual comparison of notes is rare. Joint preparation of lessons is rarer still. Selfish motives prevail. But a hundred miles away, in the city of Canton, for instance, co-operation is prominent in the schools. The faster students help the slower students. They help each other. They take pride in having the whole class mastering the lesson they are taught. Each class is divided into small groups. They sit together to prepare, to discuss, and to review their lessons. Teachers of the same subject or of the same class share their knowledge and experience with one another. Good examples of illustration are shared by all. One is considered a bad teacher if one tries to surpass others in his teaching, and a good one if he is helpful to other teachers. The relationship between students and teachers is one of comradeship. We may say that students and teachers have learned to co-operate with each other and among themselves. But it is more correct to say that their school behaviour as students and as teachers have been socialized. They have acquired the habits of team work. Knowledge is a common wealth. Individual heroism or championship has a low status in the schools in China today. To stand aloof from the masses makes other people suspicious.

Everyone is exposed to public scrutiny. Social pressure is brought to bear on the individual, and the individual is overwhelmed by his group. Corporate living starts with the nurseries and the kindergartens. Birthday parties which are popular in the kindergartens in Hong Kong do not exist in the kindergartens in China because they are looked upon as occasions for the cultivation of individualism. Instead, people in China, young and old, come to celebrate the birthdays of great social institutions, the anniversaries of the Chinese People's Republic, the Chinese Communist Party, the Chinese Liberation Army, etc. Awards of prizes for school achievements are dropped from the schools. Children are led to feel that a successful harvest in the commune is their success and that conquest of the flood is happy news to them. Constant participation in group life, as in the parades and campaigns, which the Chinese Communists are so expert in handling, with their banners and music and the tides of people in formation, makes the individual feel himself personally insignificant and socially helpless, and yet so great and magnificent in the collective. This is another technique in socializing the individual. He comes to feel that it is useless to protest, and yet so useful to conform. People learn thus to accept the mass line.

## THEORY AND PRACTICE

The assumption is : Theory must be integrated with practice. The Chinese Communists assume that they have a great revolutionary theory, and that in putting the theory into practice they are the most realistic. Success lies in the unification of theory and practice.

The phrase *li lun yu shih chi i chih* (the unification of theory and practice) has become the shibboleth of the Communists on the subject of methods and educational methods, particularly in their criticism of methods and educational methods. Such a principle is not at all new in the philosophical world. It usually implies that theory must be tested in practice. And in case practice does not agree with theory, theory must be modified to agree with practice. But the Communist interpretation takes on a different slant. Their emphasis is on practice, on right practice, yet essentially on applying the same theory in accordance with the practical circumstances. They do not question their theory.

Let us quote from Mao Tse-tung, in his report at a cadres' meeting in Yenan on the subject "Reform Our Study", in which he attributed the success of the Communist revolution to the unity of right theory and right practice. He said.

> But it was only after World War I and the Russian October Revolution that we found the truth of truths, Marxism–Leninism, as the best weapon to liberate our nation; and the Chinese Communist Party has become the advocate, propagator, and organizer of

the use of this weapon. Once integrated with the concrete practice of the Chinese revolution, the outstanding truth of Marxism–Leninism has made the Chinese revolution assume a new aspect.

The interpretation of the principle of the unity of theory and practice is directed to the need for paying attention to actual problems and local circumstances, assuming that the theory is absolute. Mao further said :

> But we still have defects, and very big ones too. In my opinion, unless these defects are corrected, we shall not be able to push our work forward or make further advance in our great undertaking to integrate the unprecedented truth of Marxism–Leninism with the concrete practice of the Chinese revolution. . . . What we study is Marxism, but the method used by many people in our midst in this study runs directly counter to Marxism. That is to say, they have violated the basic principle repeatedly enjoined by Marx, Engels, Lenin, and Stalin : The unity of theory and practice. Having violated their principle, they have invented an opposite one : the separation of theory from practice. In schools and in the spare time education of cadres, teachers of philosophy do not guide the students to study the logic of the Chinese revolution; teachers of economics do not guide them to study the characteristic features of Chinese economy; teachers of political science do not guide them to study the tactics of the Chinese revolution; teachers of military science do not guide them to study the strategy and tactics suited to China's special conditions, and so on and so forth. The result is that errors are disseminated to the great harm of the people.

In 1941 Mao said : "Marx, Lenin and Stalin teach us to proceed from actualities and to derive from them laws which will guide our action." The principle of the integration of theory and practice should imply that new laws can also be derived from actualities. But "laws", as used by the Communists today, refer only to some minor rules of social action within the framework of Communist theory and not beyond it. Dogmatism has taken such a grip at this stage of Communist development in China that Mao Tse-tung's thinking is held to be fixed and supreme.

It must be a great mental challenge to the Chinese intellectuals, and to the Communist intellectuals as well, to decide what is good practice and what is bad practice, and what is the right practice under certain actual circumstances and what is wrong practice under those circumstances. There is no objective criterion for judgement. It seems that the unity of theory and practice is possible only when there is freedom in theory and in practice, and free interplay of theory and practice.

## CRITICISM AND SELF-CRITICISM

The assumption is: For the advancement of socialism the proletariat have to be self-reliant by resorting to the method of criticism and self-criticism.

This implies that the proletariat cannot expect to have the benefit of advice from other sources. Even if advice is available, it would be too soft for the revolutionary. Criticism is dynamic and dialectic in nature. Progress depends not on mutual encouragement but on mutual criticism. It is only then that the combatant spirit is awakened and the contradiction is maintained. In the Communistic society, when a person is criticized, it is bad taste for him to defend himself; it would be better for him to follow criticism from others by self-criticism which, in a way, is confession. This would indicate that he has come to accept himself not as a unique individual who clings to his old self, but has attained partyhood by becoming a member of the group, whose concern is the party's concern. The self-criticism of Kuo Mo-jo in submission to the attack on the intellectuals for failing to serve the proletarian cultural revolution is the most recent example.[4] Criticism is mild, as a method to be used among the

[4] On 14 April 1966 Kuo Mo-jo, China's most prominent intellectual, spoke at the Standing Committee of the Chinese People's National Congress on the subject "Learn from the workers, peasants, soldiers, and masses; serve the workers, peasants, soldiers, and masses", in which he said: "Among my friends and comrades, I am generally looked upon as a man of culture, and some people even call me a writer, and further, a poet, and a so-called historian. In the past decades, I have taken up my pen to do certain writing and translating. If we count the words, the number must be several million. But, to take the standards of today, what I have written in the past should be completely burned. My works are without an iota of value.

"What is the main reason? It is because of my failure to learn well Chairman Mao's thoughts, failure to use Chairman Mao's thoughts to arm myself; thus, the class standpoint at times became very blurred. . . ." (See *Kuang-Ming Ribao*, Peking, 18 April 1966.)

"people" or within one's own ranks. When used against the enemy, the weapon is persecution. Criticism should be kept within bounds, however. Criticism of a serious nature, or as directed at the party on its higher levels, particularly if it comes from non-Communist fractions, is considered anti-revolutionary and is not tolerated.

The institution of criticism and self-criticism has another effect besides the solicitation of opinion for social improvement. It has the additional effect of socializing the individual. The dignity of the individual is thus impaired and the authority of the public is installed. A person, in order to hold himself together mentally, must learn to submit to the wishes of his social group completely; that is, he must learn to be selfless, or else learn to be a hypocrite by hiding his real self and saying what he is expected to say. It looks as if the latter is often the choice the people make in China today.

When there is constant criticism and self-criticism, there is little danger of social stalemate or sterility. In that sense, a condition of progress is provided. But the danger lies in the absence of the sense of security both for the individual and for society.

## EQUALITY OF THE SEXES

Another assumption is : All men and women are created equal and that the inequality of women is the product of feudalism.

It would not be socialism or any modern doctrine to stand against the principle of the equality of women. Whether or not women are really equal to men, no politician today dares to say the contrary if he wants to obtain women's votes in any place.

In traditional China, the inferior status of women in the home and in society was too deplorable to be defended. Infanticide of baby girls, the practice of concubinage, and the prohibition of widows to remarry are examples of inhumanity and savagery. To declare equal rights for women is to emancipate half of the population. The struggle for this equality began in China with the impact of the West, long before the Chinese Communist Party came into existence. It is of no special credit to the Communists, though tribute has to be paid for the legislation of the Marriage Law of the Chinese People's Republic in 1950 and to its enforcement. In giving women equal treatment in employment, China has released the energy of practically half of its population for production. The effect on the nation's economy is great.

There are a few interesting features in China today regarding the status of women. (1) There is no feminist movement as such in Communist China. The feminist movement was played up by the Communists in the pre-Communist days in China. It was used as an instrument for attacking the existing order and the government then in power. It is also so utilized by the Communists today as a way of social agitation outside the Communist countries. The former leaders in the feminist movements in China are now silent before the Communists who claim that the party looks after the rights of women so well that no feminist movement is called for. (2) Differences between men and women are reduced to the minimum. The sex factor is not allowed to be exaggerated. Sex appeal is reduced to nil. The female figure is not revealed. Men and women are dressed so similarly that Western visitors say that sometimes they cannot tell a woman from a man. One may look upon this as another interpretation of sex equality, though definitely not in the Western sense of the term. (3) Now that women are fully employed and equally paid, the burden on women is much heavier than before. As women, they have the additional burden of bearing children, nursing them, and nurturing them. Until men learn to put on their aprons, the work in the kitchen and other duties of the housewife will make the women more tired out than before. With political meetings in which women also have to take part after working hours, women in China are much overloaded. When comparing them with the women of leisure in feudalistic times, it is difficult to say that the present system is in every respect a blessing for women. It seems that no sooner are Chinese women emancipated from the yoke of feudalism than they are enslaved by socialism in the name of equality.

Now that women are not formally discriminated against because of sex, we find many women doing the work which was once exclusively for men. In the industrial field we find women in metallurgy, in steel furnaces, in locomotive and tractor driving, in ship building, etc. In the educational field, large numbers of women study and teach medicine, engineering, forestry, agriculture, mining, surveying, mineralogy, and any subject which had been almost exclusively monopolized by men. The surprise is that, while there are women in leadership in many fields of activity, there are so few women in leadership in the political field. We find no women in the Political Bureau of the Chinese Communist Party Central Committee, just as we do not find them in the controlling level of the Communist Party in the Soviet Union. There seems to be some underlying elements remaining unresolved in acknowledging the equality of the sexes.

THE CHINESE CULTURAL HERITAGE

What is the attitude regarding China's cultural heritage which is considered to be the product of feudalism? The Communist assumption is : the Chinese cultural heritage should be examined with discrimination. There are desirable and undesirable elements in Chinese culture. The desirable elements should be preserved and developed while the undesirable elements should be eliminated.

Some Communists claim that the works of science and the works of art which constitute China's cultural heritage today are the fruits of labour and imagination of the Chinese working class in the past. They are not to be attributed to the bourgeoisie. What was wrong in the past was the monopoly of science and art—beautiful architectural works, paintings, objects of art of all kinds—by the small minority, the exploiting class. What is to be done now is to use science and art to serve the people. Communists claim that it is only by making art accessible to everybody and not keeping it in the hands of a few that art is truly liberated. When art is so liberated, they believe, the working people will have greater zeal for the advancement of art than ever before.

As to the popular art of the masses, it must be greatly encouraged and elevated to a respectable status. In old China as well as in China before the Communist régime, it was a common sight to see talented proletarian artistes—singers, dancers, minstrels, and acrobats—clothed in rags like beggars. They made their living by singing and performing on the street corners, taking collections from their sympathetic audience to whom they held out their hats and bowls. Now we do not find such artistes ragged or in such humiliation. We find them dressed in beautiful attire, well shaven and combed, using polished instruments, behaving in a refined manner. They are respected for their talents as well as for their persons. From this the Communists claim that they have turned devils into men and have given Chinese art a new life.

Another great change in Chinese art, as we have intimated before, is that the Communists are not contented with the change of the audience from that of the bourgeoisie to that of the proletariat. They insist also on the change in the ideology and motif of art for the cause of the proletarian revolution.

It may be appropriate here to point out a contradiction in the preservation of Chinese culture during the process of the Great Proletarian Cultural Revolution. In as much as the old culture is the product of the old ideologies of feudalism, landlordism, and the bourgeoisie class, the best way to build up a new culture in the new ideology should be to begin with a clean slate. If an individual has been brought up in the old culture, the longer he has been exposed to that culture the more difficult it is for him to forsake it. Similarly, for a State such as China, which has such an ancient and rich culture, the richer the culture and the longer its standing, the more difficult it becomes to forsake it. Take the Chinese written language as an example—if it were not so highly developed and if there were not so much in its literary treasures, the introduction of the system of romanization or phoneticization, as is done in the primitive tribes which have no writing and no written accounts, would have made the liquidation of illiteracy much easier than by having to learn the difficult Chinese characters the Chinese have today. In fact, Mao Tse-tung's versatility in Chinese culture—his high accomplishment in Chinese poetry in the form of *tsu* (lyric) and in Chinese calligraphy—is in itself a conservative factor in favour of retaining the old culture and a deterrent in the advancement of a new culture. It is most interesting that Mao's Red Guards in the Great Proletarian Cultural Revolution have come forth "to destroy the 'four olds', and to foster the 'four news' ". The "four olds" are : old thinking, old culture, old customs, and old habits. The "four news" are : new thinking, new culture, new customs, and new habits.

## LOVE OF THE ANCESTRAL LAND

Another assumption is : The greatest appeal, to the Chinese people, as yet, is nationalism. In mobilizing the people for the socialist cause, the appeal to their love of the ancestral land is now being fully used. The term "fatherland" is used in the West. In China the term is "ancestral land", not "fatherland". But in order to conform to Western usage, we shall use fatherland instead.

Nationalism is based on the group feeling of belonging together with a common concern. This feeling can be dominant or dormant, strong or weak, according to the circumstances with which the group, as a nation, is confronted. The growth of national consciousness and national sentiment in modern China was the result of entanglements with the foreign powers in the last hundred years. The introductory chapter of the book was meant to present this background. In as much as the Chinese Communist Party was formed together with the Student Movement of 1919, and the Communist Party gained its prestige in the 8 years of war against Japanese invasion, the role which patriotism plays in the Chinese Communist Movement is apparent. So behind every social, political, economic, and cultural campaign we see a lining of nationalism—to make the country strong, to destroy the nation's enemies and to surpass other countries. In a way, the Sino–Soviet split is not without the support of the Chinese masses through this anti-foreign feeling. The original slogan of international Communism was : "The worker has no fatherland." But in China the fatherland of the worker is brought into great prominence in the Chinese working class. The Chinese Communist Party has perhaps gone so far in pursuing its national interest as to have been accused of departing from international communism and of now practising "dominant-nation" chauvinism.

In the schools, love of the fatherland is listed as the first of the "five loves"[5] to be cultivated among the students. Indeed, without this appeal of the fatherland, the building of socialism in China would make no stir in the people's hearts. Thus the patriotic element is utilized to the full in all educational appeals.

It is pathetic that many Chinese youths have returned from overseas to China to study because of an unbounded love for the fatherland. They have been disappointed to find that Communist China is not built on the kind of patriotism which people normally understand it to be. Patriotism in Communist China is used as an instrument of the class struggle. A Chinese patriot must be first converted into a proletarian in ideology before he is fit to love his country. To remain a patriot and a bourgeois in ideology as any overseas Chinese from colonial territories and capitalistic countries is apt to do, is considered to hinder the progress of the fatherland and even to endanger its existence. In other words, such patriotic youths will have to find out sooner or later, and often too late, that they must change all over and denounce their own past if they do not want to be branded as

[5] The "five loves" are : love of the fatherland, love of the people, love of labour, love of science, and love with respect of public property. (See Common Programme, Cultural and Educational Policies, Article 42.)

anti-State. Love of the fatherland is not unconditional. It must be harmonious with the interest of the working class as interpreted by its guardian, the Chinese Communist Party. One's naïve patriotism may lead to endless trouble. This applies to overseas Chinese youth as well as to all patriotic Chinese overseas.

## INTERNATIONALISM AND INTERNATIONALITY

As the antithesis of the spirit of patriotism, the Chinese Communists advocate at the same time the spirit of internationalism. The assumption is : Communism, being a world movement, must be engaged in world revolution and world expansion.

Outside the country the policy is to advocate internationalism; inside the country the policy is to win national minority confidence or good will between nations. It is only in so doing that fear and suspicion will not be aroused among the people at home or abroad in matters of race and nationality.

In the educational field, based upon such an assumption, we find that new schools have been established in the minority communities where there had been no schools; new written languages have been created through the romanization of the native spoken word where no written language had existed; new books have been published for them; and new teachers have been trained to teach in these schools. Besides solving the problems of illiteracy, favourable arrangements are made for admitting students of the national minorities to the higher and technical schools. Minority costumes, minority folk dances, and minority art are on prominent display, perhaps more prominently than the infinitely small population of the minorities would call for. Of course, the humiliation which the *Hans* (Chinese) had inflicted on the minorities for centuries and centuries past, by giving those tribes nomenclatures with an animal "radical" is now rectified. The social and political position of the minorities in China today is perhaps higher than any time since the domination of the *Hans* over the Chinese land.

The teaching of foreign languages in the schools and the establishment of special language schools are among the manifestations of awareness of the need to maintain, as well as to broaden, China's international contacts. The sending of missions abroad headed by the top leaders of the State and party and the warm reception of missions from abroad, further strengthen this communication. The rapid expansion of international activities in China in recent years is astonishing. It was reported that in the celebration of the 15th anniversary of the establishment of the Chinese People's Republic in October 1964, delegations from eighty foreign countries were represented in Peking at the reviewing stand of the parade. Even while China's international prestige has declined in the last two or three years since its open split with the Soviet Union and the border conflict with India, foreign delegates and missions from abroad still arrive in large numbers. For instance in 1966, in the Afro–Asian Writers' Emergency Meeting held in Peking from 27 June to 9 July 1966, 161 writer delegates from 53 countries and regions of Asia and Africa attended. And in the Summer Physics Colloquium of the Symposium held in Peking from 23 to 31 July 1966, 144 scientists from 33 countries attended.

It must be pointed out with all seriousness that one must not be as simple to infer that increased international contacts and communications will bring about better international understanding and international goodwill. Indeed, from the standpoint of the free world, of which the United States is the chief exponent, such international activities of the Chinese will only increase international tension, international misunderstanding, and international hatred, and greater antagonism towards the United States and things American.

There is one decided gain in China's international life, and that is the broadening of the horizon of the Chinese people in world affairs with finer discernment of affairs outside their country. Limited and prejudiced as they may be, the Chinese have learned to look at their own problems in the light of the world background and in clearer international perspective. The

Chinese used to think of Westerners as all alike whether they were American or Europeans, but now they know the difference between the Frenchman and the American, between the Russian and the Albanian, between the East German and the West German, and even between a British Communist who is considered to be their friend and a Chinese landlord who is considered to be their enemy.

## REPETITION AS A SOCIAL METHOD

It is assumed that: In political education, particularly for the masses, the method of repetition is to be constantly employed.

In order to create a common mind in a new ideology, the masses of the people must be familiar with the slogans and plans of the socialistic society at all its stages. Slogans are devised which come easily to one's lips and are easy to remember. The slogans must be repeated, posted everywhere, shouted in rallies, printed in the newspapers, and talked about everywhere until they trip off the tongue, are familiar to one's ears, and readily recognized on sight, so much so that one is able to say them in his sleep. China now is a country of slogans.

Documents and directives from the State and the party are studied as soon as they are released. Throughout the whole country, in every corner, one may hear the top party authorities reporting on their contents, meaning, and purpose. After the higher authorities have made the reports, the cadres of the lower levels relay them to their respective constituencies. Then everybody takes part in small group discussions. To discuss in China today means to support what has been reported. The national and local newspapers print the reports on their front page. Then the editorials and articles come out to endorse the reports day after day. One of the most outstanding characteristics of the editorials, articles, speeches, and comments is that they are all alike with no new ideas for implementation. The idea of Communist propaganda is that the documents and directives from the top places are complete and final, "far beyond one's power to add or detract". Any new interpretation is looked upon in Communist eyes as deviation from the party line.

The application of the law of frequency is not without parallel. The commercial advertisements in the Western world offer many examples of this law in application. It has been said that even the most popular cigarettes have to remind the public of their brands all the time. On cutting down their advertisement, their sales drop. The difference between the Communist and capitalistic societies is that the law of frequency is used by the capitalistic countries in commerce, while the Communists use it in politics. The catch phrase is : "Lest they forget."

It might be supposed that repetition after repetition in the shouting of slogans could produce boredom which might even lead to reaction and repugnance. This may be true in a free society, where over-repetition produces resentment which defeats its own end. But it is less true in a socialistic society where freedom of expression is not permitted; in which case, repugnance is reduced to the minimum. From the standpoint of materialistic philosophy, outward behaviour can change a man's inside. After one has heard them so many times, even apparent falsehoods begin to appear as truth. After he has said them so many times, the words gradually come to be his own. The frequency method is particularly useful in a socialistic society where the masses are illiterate and are used to subjugation.

## PERSISTENT VIGILANCE

The assumption is : Enemies are all around, inside and outside, open and hidden, whose aim is to destroy communism. So unless the Communists resort to persistent and untiring vigilance, the enemies will catch them napping. In order to attain victory, vigilance is imperative; after attaining it, and in order to solidify the fruits of victory, vigilance is equally imperative; and in order to push victory forward, vigilance is again imperative.

It is not difficult to understand the precautions they take, as the success they have so far attained was not without a heavy price. One remembers that in the early days of establishing the Soviet Union, the Soviets also sounded the alarm that the anti-revolutionary forces were attacking them within the country and international imperialism was encircling them from the outside. As for the Chinese Communist Party, between its establishment in 1921 and its victory over the Kuomintang in 1949, in spite of constant vigilance, many comrades were captured and executed and others' existence was constantly in peril. The fact that the top Chinese Communist leaders now often have their meetings at night is a reflection of the habits they had acquired during their long struggle when they had to work underground under the veil of night. One might allege that the enemies they say exist are more imaginary than real. However, considering the existence of the Nationalist Government at Taiwan and the Korean and Vietnam wars where United States forces came close to their door, their fear is perhaps not entirely without grounds.

In consequence, people are taught to be constantly watchful of what is going on and what might happen, on the assumption that enemies who work for the interests of feudalism, landlordism, imperialism, capitalism, and the bourgeoisie might be disguised as supporters and friends in their midst. Recently the Communists have even accused some of their high-ranking leaders of "waving the red flag to oppose the red flag" and "putting on the outer cloak of Marxism–Leninism and Mao Tse-tung's thinking to oppose Marxism–Leninism and Mao Tse-tung's thinking". In one sense, the Communists are more suspicious of their own comrades than they are of outsiders. In the words of Liu Shao-chi, "the fortress is more easily attacked from the inside".

There are two mottoes which are specially popular. One is, *Ti kao ching ti* (Raise high your vigilance) and the other, *Ta tan huai i* (Be suspicious without reserve). As a result, everybody is suspicious of everybody else. Mutual trust and personal confidence find practically no chance of cultivation. The father is suspicious of his son and the son of his father. The teachers and students are suspicious of each other and among themselves. As long as such vigilance is maintained, any organized attempt to overthrow the Communist régime from the inside by non-Communists is probably impossible.

Some time ago a group of young athletes from China came to Hong Kong to play in a table tennis tournament. An enthusiast in Hong Kong requested the Chinese players to sign his autograph album. At first they signed their names and put on their addresses. At a second thought, they decided not to expose their addresses. So that page was torn, and on the new page only their signatures appeared. This is an example of the result of education for vigilance.

Now with the basic assumptions and implications in view, let us proceed to a discussion of the school system in the new régime. The school system itself could have no significance apart from the conceptual bases which give it its life and soul. On the contrary, a different set of assumptions might give the same outward structure of a school system totally different implications and interpretations.

# CHAPTER 6

# The School System

Now we come to the formal educational system—the schools. What has been said about education in its broad sense applies also to the schools. In China today, when society is undergoing a revolutionary change of unprecedented character, the school cannot be an isolated institution, but is part and parcel of the whole scheme of things. For such a society and at such a time, the outward structure of the school can have no meaning apart from the total setting. In many respects, the school reflects on the nature of the society and its problems and demands.

To follow general practice, we shall first present the picture of the school ladder in People's China today. But before we do so, we should give a brief account of the developments of the modern school system in China up to the establishment of the Chinese People's Republic as well as since its establishment. There are certain topics of a general nature which apply to all levels of schools. In order to simplify matters we shall take up those topics when we come to the level of school to which they are more related. We shall take up the topics of the liquidation of illiteracy, Chinese language reform, and the unification of speech in the section on elementary education; the topics of half-study half-work schools, physical and health education in the section on secondary education; and the topics of the teaching of foreign languages, the private schools, the place of the intellectuals, in the section on higher education.

## MODERN SCHOOL SYSTEM IN CHINA BEFORE THE CHINESE PEOPLE'S REPUBLIC

China's adoption of the school system of the modern world is usually dated to 1903, when the Imperial School Regulations drafted by Chang Chi-tung and others were promulgated by the Manchu Government. It was a year preceding the abolition of the Civil Examination, a system which had existed in China for over a thousand years. The school system as promulgated was modelled after the Japanese which had more resemblance to the French than to that of any other Western country. The system consisted of 5 years of primary school, 4 years of higher primary school, 5 years of middle school, 3 years of higher school, 3–4 years of undergraduate college, and 5 years of graduate school. After the overthrow of the Ching Dynasty, a new system was established in 1912, the first year of the Chinese Republic. There were 4 years for the lower primary, 3 years for the higher primary, 4 years for the middle school, 6–7 years for the undergraduate college, with graduate school for an unspecified number of years. In 1922, 10 years after the establishment of the Chinese Republic (not the Chinese People's Republic), when American educational influence was specially strong in China, the Ministry of Education introduced a new school system adopted from the United States which had become popular in the western states and in some cities in America. It is commonly known as the 6–3–3 system, with the general pattern of 6 years of primary school, 3 years of junior middle (high) school, and 3 years of senior middle (high) school. On top is the 4-year undergraduate college, which is followed by the graduate school. This system has been the system in China for the past 40 years. It is the system we find in Taiwan today. It is also the system we find largely in operation in Communist China today.

It is not our special duty here to outline the development of the modern school system in China since its installation in 1903 up to the establishment of the People's Republic, however interesting and important such a subject may be to the student of education. Nevertheless, it will be worth while to point out here a few salient features in Chinese education of the period from 1903 to 1949 as a background for understanding and evaluating education in China today.

(1)  In order to see the educational picture in People's China

in a proper light, we must bear in mind that there had been great educational achievements for almost half a century preceding it. The first battle to overcome tremendous antipathy to the introduction of the modern school system as against the old traditions had been won by the Mandarins of the Ching Dynasty.

(2) The Manchus not only overcame the inertia but also made the first 10 years of modern education a laudable decade. In spite of their inexperience in modern schools and the danger of revolutionary ideas which would inevitably come as a concomitant of the new learning, and which they had not failed to envisage, the Ching Dynasty did encourage the development of new schools without reservation, once the regulations were promulgated. Thus new schools of all levels and kinds, public as well as private, developed everywhere in the country, growing like mushrooms. Enthusiasm for the new learning has been almost unmatched ever since. Take students going abroad to study as an example. At one time there were as many as 15,000 students going to Japan in one year, most of whom came back to teach and to open new schools. The eight higher normal schools in different centres in China at that time for the training of secondary school and normal school teachers laid such a good foundation for modern learning that they have since developed into famous universities.

(3) The period from the establishment of the Chinese Republic in 1912 to the establishment of the Chinese People's Republic in 1949 was a period of about four decades. In spite of the constant disruption of civil wars and 8 years of resistance to Japan, there was still considerable educational progress. According to the latest statistics released by the Ministry of Education of the Chinese Nationalist Government before its collapse on the mainland,[1] there were 207 universities and institutions of higher education with 20,133 on the teaching staff, 155,306 students enrolled, and 25,098 graduates (1947); there were 5892 secondary schools, with 143,502 members on the staff, 1,878,528 students,

[1] See Chinese Ministry of Education, *The Second Chinese Education Yearbook*, published December 1948.

and 389,465 graduates (1946); there were 290,617 primary schools, 785,224 primary teachers, 23,813,705 school children, and 4,688,606 graduates (1945). So one can see from these statistics that the Communists did not start from scratch. However, the university students, secondary school graduates, and teachers of all levels have constituted a large army of old intellectuals which give the Communists constant headaches in their cultural and educational revolution. The Communists inherit the old intellectuals who are as much a liability as an asset.

(4)    There was a good deal of liberalism in education in the first two decades of the modern schools, which covered roughly 10 years in the Ching Dynasty and 10 years in the Chinese Republic. It was only after the rise of nationalism since 1920 and particularly after the establishment of the Nationalist Government, first in Canton in 1925, that the rigid control of education came to the foreground. The Kuomintang, in its 25 years of party dictatorship, did a great deal to unify and standardize the school system, and to take into their hands the control of administration, curriculum, methods, textbooks, teacher registration, graduation examinations in the lower schools, and entrance examinations to the universities, and the like. The Kuomintang also had party branches and cells in the schools and in the universities. In a real sense, the Kuomintang paved the way for the Communists to exercise party control over the school in China.

(5)    It should be borne in mind that practically all the great Communist leaders in China were brought up in this period of liberalism in Chinese education. Practically all the Chinese Communist leaders now in the age bracket of 60–70 were in the new schools in the period from 1905 to 1925. Mao Tse-tung's autobiography as recorded by Edgar Snow reveals much of the liberal spirit in the schools in his student days. Seeing the small number of outstanding leaders in China since the tightening of control in education makes one feel that liberalism has been able to produce more leaders of thought than a régime of rigidity. One can perhaps say that the Communist movement in China

benefited by the modern schools in China in its early days of liberalism, which blessed Communism with its present leaders.


THE SCHOOL SYSTEM IN CHINA
AFTER THE ESTABLISHMENT OF THE
CHINESE PEOPLE'S REPUBLIC

There has been no radical change in the school system since the establishment of the Chinese People's Republic in 1949. As we have said before, the school system is still largely the 6–3–3 system. When we say the school system is "largely" the 6–3–3 system, we should supplement the statement with a few words of explanation. In the first place, the educational authorities in the People's Republic have not been too particular about the marking off of divisional lines in the school ladder. While they have had certain decrees to modify the structure of certain schools at certain levels, they have not established a complete school system as such, nor have they announced the abolition of the 6–3–3 system.[2] In the second place, after one has accepted the single track, there is no great significance one way or another whether there is one year more or one year less in the primary school, or whether the primary school ends at the age of 12 or 13, particularly as education is not yet compulsory and there is no specified age for compulsory education. In the third place, when flexibility is desirable and the 6–3–3 system in actual practice in China provides for a great deal of flexibility, there is no urgent need to change it just for the sake of change. In the fourth place, one must remember, the 6–3–3 system was used not only in the

[2] According to the Editorial of *Renmin Ribao* (*People's Daily*), dated 18 June 1966, in supporting the decision of the State Council on 13 June to suspend the admission of new students to the colleges and universities for half a year in order that the work of the Great Proletarian Cultural Revolution shall not be interrupted and sufficient time is available to plan for the new scheme of college and university admission, it further said that the reform must not be confined to the system of college and university admission and senior middle school admission, but must be extended to the reform of the whole school system, the examination system, the class promotion system, and the like.

Nationalist territory prior to 1949 but also in the Communist "liberated" territories during all those years when they were able to have regular schooling. So it was as much a perpetuation of the Communist system as it was the perpetuation of the Nationalist system. For this reason one cannot say that the Communists adopted the 6–3–3 school system from the Nationalists after they took over the country as if they had given up their own. It may be mentioned here also that the Communists had developed some kind of educational theory and practice for the primary and secondary schools in their occupied territories before 1948, which they posted as guides for the reorientation of education for all schools after they took over the whole country. In the matter of school system, unlike the Nationalist Government which was concerned with the outward form, as all bureaucracy is, the Communist Government is concerned with the spirit of the school system, its control, its contents, and its methods.

After these preliminary explanations, let us now present the structure of the school system in People's China today (see diagram). Our purpose is to make the diagram as simple as we can. We must, however, substantiate it in order to give a correct picture of what it really means. The following explanations may be necessary as well as helpful.

1. In appearance, the school system today is very similar to the school system one finds in Taiwan or in China in the pre-Communist period. But, as we have said, what differs is essentially the spirit, the exercise of control, the contents, and the methods which we shall note in the later sections.

2. It is evident that there is a marked change at the beginning of primary school, which starts at the age of 7 instead of 6 as before. The primary school is not the first educational institution for many children. A large number of them have attended kindergartens, and before the kindergartens, the nurseries.

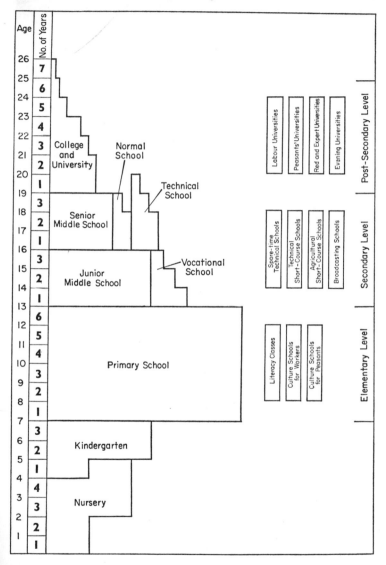

Left, the school system of the Chinese People's Republic. On the right, *Part-time and Spare-time Schools* (age and years in wide range).

3. There was once, in the early years of the People's Republic, an agitation to adopt the Soviet Union's 10-year school, but it was only tried out in certain schools in certain cities and later given up. Experimental 5-year primary schools are also seen in certain cities to save 1 year's time; but they are in negligible numbers and do not make headway. Starting school at the age of 7 instead of 6 was definitely adopted from the Soviet system, and has remained unchanged.

4. In the primary school, for convenience of administration, some like to mark off the first 4 years as lower primary, and the next 2 years as higher primary, while others like to group the first 2 years as lower classes, the next 2 years as middle (intermediate) classes, and the last 2 years as upper classes. In the kindergarten, when it runs for 3 years, the first year is called lower section; the second year, middle section; and the third year, upper section. When it runs for only 2 years, there is no middle section. Nurseries are not exactly schools. Most of them accept children from the age of 2–4, and some up to 5. Some nurseries also accept infants of 1 and 2 years old.

5. There are many more schools on a part-time and spare-time basis than before. They enrol large numbers of young people and adults and play an important role in the cultural life and technical life of the country. They may generally be classified according to their functions in the three levels of education—the elementary, the secondary and the post-secondary. The numbers of years for the part-time and spare-time schools are usually limited to 1, 2, or 3 years, while the range in age is very wide. They chiefly serve the adults and youth.

6. There are many half-cultivation half-study schools and half-work half-study schools. But since the school years remain the same and are not doubled or even prolonged in spite of the fact that the study time is reduced, we classify them as the regular school type in the school system.

7. In the regular school system the vocational schools and technical schools are of a great variety. Unlike the vocational and technical schools in pre-Communist China, where such schools were only symbolic, the enrolments in these schools today are in huge numbers.

8. In the schools of a vocational, technical and professional nature, the length of training for each school is determined, not by its academic level i.e. whether it is on the junior middle school level or on the senior middle school level, but by the requirements of the course and the needs at that time.

9. While an upper school is usually an extension of its lower school, articulation between one and the other is not stressed, nor is admission to the upper schools limited to the graduates of the lower school. There is a great deal of cross-transfer within the school system.

10. There are very few graduate departments in the colleges and universities. Graduate work is mostly done in connection with the research institutes. Some university courses such as medicine take 7 years, though there are medical courses which take only 3 or 4 years. The age index in the diagram for the upper level of the university and for research is only arbitrary.

11. The width of each type of school in the diagram indicates roughly the proportion of students attending it as compared with other schools of its level or with schools immediately below or above.

12. Each school year is divided into two terms throughout the whole school system, starting in autumn, ending in summer. There is a long summer vacation. A great deal of flexibility is allowed for vacations. Some city schools even suspend classes for many weeks for the teachers and students to work in the rural areas during sowing and harvesting seasons.

13. Military schools, party schools, political training schools, and cadre schools are not included in the diagram.

After this explanation, we may give a brief account of the structure of the school system in China today.

In the pre-school stage there is the nursery for children from infancy to the age of 4–5, which is followed by 2–3 years of kindergarten. Formal schooling starts at the age of 7 in the primary school, finishing normally at the age of 13. As a main stream, students proceed to the regular or general secondary schools (which in China have been called middle schools), where there are two divisions—the junior middle school and the senior middle school, each with 3 years normally. Many schools have the junior middle school and the senior middle school on the same campus under the same administration. Parallel with the regular type of middle schools, which more or less keep to the academic pattern, are the vocational middle schools of junior middle school level and the technical and normal schools of senior middle school level. Their years of training vary according to the nature of the course and the needs at that time. It often happens that they graduate their students earlier or keep them in the courses longer in accordance with topical needs and not with the formal pattern. On the top of the middle schools are the colleges and the universities, and professional and techno- logical schools. The crowning academic institutions are the graduate departments, some of which are affiliated with the universities, while others are attached to independent research institutes.

The school system has been criticized for being too long in its courses. It is urged that studies be shortened, especially in the upper schools.[3] How this is to be worked out remains to be seen. It is doubtful whether, with so much manual labour required and so many political meetings to attend, a further reduction of study time would enable schools to produce trained personnel who are really competent.

[3] It was urged in the editorial of *Renmin Ribao* (*People's Daily*) in connection with the Great Proletarian Cultural Revolution in the summer of 1966 that the arts course (non-science) in colleges and universities should be shortened to 1–2 years, with 3 years at the maximum.

Parallel with the regular school system is the wide range of schools of a vocational, technical, literacy, and cultural nature corresponding to the regular schools, except that length of study, age of students, and standards of admission are much more flexible. Most of them are part-time and spare-time schools.

We shall concentrate on the regular schools.

## THE NURSERIES

The Chinese term for "nursery" is *t'oh-erh-suo* (child trust institute) which means the centre where one entrusts his child to be looked after. The term as well as the idea, though not of Chinese origin, has been familiar to the Chinese workers in the cities in the last 30 years. The need for such institutions became obvious when parents who both worked outside the home had to leave their young children to someone's care. There was a small number of nurseries in the cities in China before the People's Republic. It was only after the establishment of the People's Republic that nurseries flourished on a big scale and spread from the urban areas to the rural areas.

Now we find nurseries a common feature in China. Practically all the communes, factories, mines, economic enterprises, and governmental organizations have nurseries in their community. In the cities there are also nurseries established by the neighbourhood groups. They are usually free of charge and maintained by government or public funds. The children's meals have to be paid for by their parents. In the day nurseries, parents leave their children and take them home when their work is over. In the comprehensive nurseries,[4] the children go home only on weekends and holidays.

Life in the nursery is, by and large, a happy one. One hears little of the crying of children or the scolding and whipping that we commonly find in Chinese homes in Hong Kong, particularly the homes of the Chinese workers who have no time to look after

[4] According to 1959 statistics, there were 3,690,000 nurseries in the Chinese rural areas which took care of 67,700,000 children (*People's Daily*, Peking, 1 June 1960).

them. There is a genuine atmosphere of respect for the personal dignity and rights of the child in People's China which is a joy for any educator and humanitarian to see. Although there are old folk and unemployed people who we think might be useful to look after children, one will be surprised that for the up-bringing of the young in a socialistic society they rely more often on people trained as nursery teachers with the Communistic ideology who to start with are usually teenagers. The young children call the nursery teachers *ku-ku* (aunt), which still carries with it the familial intimacy in which perhaps the children feel more at home. The nursery children have a great deal of activity in play as well as in work such as keeping themselves and the place clean. Group life is predominant. One often finds the nursery children in cities going out to the park in groups, holding each other's hands, and guided by a nursery teacher. Right from infancy, they are brought up to the feeling that they are part of the great society and have their share in its assets and its well being. They feel that their parents are also part of the same society and have the same share as themselves. The children feel that they belong to the public, the society, and the State more than they belong to their parents. Of course, when the parents have no opportunity in terms of possessions or in terms of authority to exercise domination over their children, the parents and children are both conscious that the only concern and authority is the State's, which is indisputable.

Childhood is probably definitely happier in the People's Republic than before. In the buses, people offer their seats to the children and help them alight or board. In the trains, special coaches are marked off for young children and their mothers. The nurseries are so impressive that a social worker from Canada after her visit to China remarked that Canada should learn from the Chinese nurseries. We find few nurseries in the United States. The nurseries which catch one's attention on the sign-boards by the roadside in the United States are for the nurture of young plants.

## KINDERGARTENS

The kindergarten which had existed in China before the People's Republic was of 2 years for children from 4 to 6. Now it is extended to 3 years, including children up to 7 years of age, when children are admitted to the primary school. The kindergarten, in non-Communist China, as well as in the Western world today, is looked upon as a sort of educational luxury for the children of the well-to-do, before they enter school. It may be pointed out, here, while we are still alert to class consciousness, that the kindergarten and the nursery had different origins. The kindergarten movement, as we see it in the Western world, was inspired by educational ideals for the development of the child as an individual, while the nursery was necessitated by the needs of the working class in modern industrial society. The kindergarten may be regarded also as the lower extension of the primary school, while the nursery may be regarded as the upper extension of the function of the home. The difference of these two institutions in idea and in function is becoming less and less, noticeably so in a socialistic state, especially as kindergartens and the nurseries grow and multiply in huge numbers and the line between the rich and the poor is blurred.

In the past the kindergarten in China was called *yu-chih-yuan* as it is still so called in Taiwan and Hong Kong. In the People's Republic, it is called *yu-erh-yuan*. There is no special significance in the change of the middle word except that the new term conforms more to the colloquial usage in reference to children of that age. A big difference between the kindergartens in the Nationalist régime and in Hong Kong, and those in the People's China today, is that reading and writing are taught in the former and not in the latter. In the former, textbooks are used and daily home assignments are given, making the pre-school child literacy-conscious, book-conscious, and academic-standard conscious. In the kindergartens in the People's China, life is comprised chiefly of group games, hand-work, singing, story-telling, sight-seeing, and group activities. Formal subjects as conceived in the schools are not found in the kindergartens. Although no literacy is taught in the kindergartens, language ability in speech is much more developed. For this reason, the children in the primary schools now are more capable of expressing themselves in speech and in writing than in the past. Their knowledge of what is going on around them is wide.

Unlike the children in the nurseries, those in the kindergartens usually go home for their lunch. When motor traffic in the cities is not much of a problem and the kindergartens are generally in their own neighbourhood, the children do not mind the walk and the change in the daily routine.

## PRIMARY EDUCATION

Schooling starts at the age of 7. Most children go to school. Education is not compulsory but we may say that it is quite universal. There is no law for compulsory education. The absence of legal compulsion may be explained by the fact that, in China, people consider going to school a privilege. It is never looked upon as an obligation to be avoided if possible. It may be explained also by the fact that legislating such a law compels the Government to establish enough schools to accommodate the children of school age more than it compels the parents to send their children to school. The Chinese Communist Government does not want to tie itself to such a commitment. Until the passing of a compulsory education law in China, one may be contented with this speculation.

At present, some schools charge tuition fees of a few dollars per school term, that is, per half year. Parents who cannot afford to pay may ask for a reduction or exemption.

### The Curriculum

The curriculum in the primary school is simple. There are very few subjects. That is one of the reasons why they are taught well. The principle throughout the whole school system is the simplification of the curriculum, teaching fewer subjects but teaching them more thoroughly. In the first 4 years, up to the age of 10 or 11, the child learns the same six subjects each year : language or *yu wen* (which means speech and writing) takes up 12 out of the 24 periods a week, that is, half of the total time; arithmetic[5] occupies 6 periods; handwork and activity each occupy 2 periods; drawing and singing each occupy 1 period. (A period is usually of 45 minutes in the primary school.) The early part of the primary curriculum is thus almost reduced to the 3 R's. In the last 2 years of the primary school, nature study, history, geography, and physical education are added to the curriculum, with the number of periods per week increased to 28. This is the general pattern of the primary school curriculum. One is struck by its simplicity, which forms a sharp contrast to the primary schools in Hong Kong, where they generally teach fourteen or fifteen subjects. Overloading the child is not found in the schools in China.

As we observe, language study is the main subject in the lower classes of the primary school. It includes a wide range of subject-matter but does not create a sense of segregation or departmentalization of knowledge. The political tone is very strong in the selection of the material as well as in its presentation. In order to give a picture of what the language subject is like, let us have a brief analysis of a textbook in the language, *Yu Wen*, used in the autumn term of the fourth year class in the primary school. For want of a more recent textbook, we use the one published by the People's Educational Press, Peking, in 1957, which happens to be available. Russian influence is prominent, as it was published before the Sino–Soviet split.

> The book contains 72 pages with the last lesson running into the inside of the back cover to save the space of one page, sold at 12 cents. The size is 5 × 7 inches. Simplified Chinese characters are used. Words are arranged in horizontal lines reading from left to right. There are 40 lessons. Eight of them are poems, none of which are Chinese classical poems. There are 18 illustrations. The length of the lessons is uneven. The shortest has 229 words, while the longest one has 1478 words.

---

[5] Beginning from the 4th grade, arithmetic includes teaching the use of the abacus.

These are some observations: (1) Mao Tse-tung is the hero to worship. One lesson is on his childhood; one lesson is a poem, entitled "Sing Praise to Mao Tse-tung". There are other lessons, poems, and prose, which either have as their main theme the glorification of Mao or pay tribute to him in one way or another. (2) Patriotism and tribute to the People's Liberation Army are prominent. The opening lesson is a poem entitled "Sing to the Fatherland". One lesson is a narrative of "Gaiety at the Capital on the National Day's Eve". Five lessons are on the Liberation Army's heroic deeds, with one, a poem, on the enthusiasm in service of a Liberation Army cook. (3) The desire to learn from the Russians is strong. The story of Lenin's childhood precedes the one of Mao's. Its title is "Lenin at School". In addition, there are many lessons translated from Russian primers. Five are distinctly Russian stories, because they have Russian children's names and a Russian setting. (4) Science and production are brought to the attention of the children. Five lessons are grouped on the main theme "water", ending in the lesson on the big Reservoir at Kuan Ku. Six lessons are on industry and agriculture, with one on the iron works at An Shan and another on an experimental farm. Four lessons are on forestry, beginning with a lesson on the growth of the pine and ending with one on where the desk comes from. Four lessons are on animals, with one on the camel, one on the ostrich, one on feeding the calf, and ending with a lesson on a Visit to a Russian State Farm. The lessons in the textbook often take the forms of stories and descriptions as well as poems. Not only is there no classical Chinese poem in the book, but Chinese stories are scarce. There is only one on "Weighing the Elephant" which can be truly called a Chinese story. Only three stories which had been popular in Chinese primary school primers are now retained. One of them is about the conspiracy of mice against the cat; another, the story of a man and his horse, on the folly of procrastination; and another on the father and his son and their ass.

It would be interesting to contrast the primers of 1957 with those of 1968; and it would be even more so to study how Mao Tse-tung's youth, who were trained through the rights and wrongs of 1957, react today to the rights and wrongs of today.

## Life of the Primary School Children

Life in the school is a happy experience for the child in China today. The curriculum is light and assignments reasonable. Teachers respect the children, and children can voice their opinion on things which concern them. Pupils are helpful to each other. The spirit of co-operation and comradeship is seen in every aspect of school life. The Chinese Communist Young Pioneers'

Brigade is found in every school. Though according to past regulations the pioneers accept children from the age of 9–15, the brigade now takes in children as early as 7 and groups them from 7 to 12 in the *Erh T'ung Tui* (Children's Team), and then from 12 to 15 in the *Shao Nien Tui* (Early Adolescent Team). Joining the Young Pioneers' Brigade is voluntary, but practically all primary school children join. All of them put a red scarf around their neck as a symbol of membership and they are normally called the "red scarves". A class of about 45 to 50 children usually form a platoon, which is composed of 5 or 6 squads of about 8 to 10 children in each. For schools of a certain size, the platoons combine to form a company. There is a leader in each of the squads, platoons and companies, who is elected by the children from among themselves. Teachers who have good political records are appointed to be their supervisors; they also put on the red scarf while they direct the activities of the pioneers. The children take pride in wearing the scarf in spite of the fact that it is not a mark of personal distinction. On the other hand, a child would feel frustrated if denied admission to the Pioneers' Brigade or as a penalty deprived of the privilege of wearing the scarf. The pioneers form the most enthusiastic throng in parades and in welcoming foreign visitors and national heroes. All the Red Guards of the Great Proletarian Cultural Revolution in 1966 have either been young pioneers or are young pioneers now.

Education aims at the all-round development of the child, in the sense that it aims to develop a child's body, mind, and morals. The motto of the young pioneer is to be a "five-good" student, that is, good in study, good in work, good in body, good in thinking, and good in labour. The leaders in each squad are children who are accepted as excelling in these virtues, take the lead in helping the slower children to learn their lessons; in mastering these skills they often prove more effective than their teachers. Each squad has two to three afternoons a week for group study. This explains why the average standard of the primary schools in People's China can be regarded as reasonably high in spite of their many drawbacks. The schools adopt, principally from the Soviet Union, the five-point grading system, with 5 as the highest grade and 1 as the lowest, instead of the per cent marking system used in pre-Communist China and elsewhere. What is significant is that most students receive 5 or 4 for their grades. This reflects the fact that the principle of encouragement is employed on the part of the teachers, and the desire to reach the expected goal on the part of the children is strong. Grades are used to indicate the progress of the individual, and how well he has come up to the general expectation, rather than to indicate who is better than who.

One hears a great deal about school children participating in labour in China and often wonders what they do. There are in general two regions for labour, one in the urban areas and the other in the rural areas. We shall discuss here only the type of labour which children do in the cities. The following are some of the things they do.

(1)   The children clean the parks, roads, governmental compounds, their neighbourhood, and their own school. For example, a group of primary school children had a contract with a movie theatre to help clean the staircase, seats, floors, etc., at certain times every week. They went at the appointed times with their cleaning apparatus, and worked in a systematic and organized manner. The theatre management admitted that they did a better job than adults, because with their small bodies they could even crawl under the seats to clean. As a reward the children were often permitted to see a show without charge.

(2)   Alternatively, children go to the factories two or three afternoons a week to do their voluntary labour. Some go to the toy shops to help to assemble toy wagons, putting the parts together, stuffing dolls, or packing them in boxes. Some go to preserved fruit factories and help to take the seeds and stones from the fruits, to fold bags, or to wrap candies and fruits.

(3)   Some children go to the bus stops and tram stops in hot weather to offer drinking water to the drivers and conductors. They bring water and cups. They also bring manganese dioxide solution and towels to make sure that the cups are sterilized and

wiped clean. The drivers and conductors often write letters thanking the children and praising their fine spirit.

(4) When there is any social campaign, these young pioneers use their own initiative to plan a working programme. For example, when the campaign for public hygiene was on, the pioneer squads went to the stations, bus stops, and street corners, holding their pioneer flags. There they made speeches and sang songs, repeating slogans asking people not to spit in the streets. They even provided paper for the offenders to wipe up the sputum from the pavement and put it in an antiseptic tank which they carried with them. These are but some examples.

Each child is provided with a handbook in which to keep records of his studies and his labour. For example, after the child finishes work in the factory for that week, the supervising workman writes in his handbook his comments of the performance. This record is examined by his group as well as by his teachers and parents.

The children seem to enjoy the participation in such socially useful activities. They are alert to what is going on in the real world around them and they are positive in their attitude toward study and labour. Their counterparts in Hong Kong, for instance, by contrast, seem to be unaware of what is going on around them and are negative in their attitude toward study and work. With a real taste of factory life and farm life, the barrier between the school and industry and agriculture is broken down. Children also learn by doing and learn in real life how to negotiate with agencies for practical work and how to manage their own affairs.

## Primary School Teachers and Teaching

Teachers are still held in high esteem among the students.[6] The relationship is generally a friendly one. There are exceptions,

[6] In the United Kingdom the term "student" applies to those who study in the universities, whereas the term "pupil" applies to those who study in the primary and secondary schools. In China, the term "student" applies uniformly to those who study in the universities as well as to those who study in the kindergarten. This book generally follows the Chinese usage.

of course, when there are social movements in which the teachers are involved. But as soon as these are over, cordial relationships are resumed. All students address their teachers as *lao shih* (old master) such as *Chen Lao Shih* (Old Master Chen) whether the teacher *Chen* is old or young, and indeed whether the teacher *Chen* is a man or a woman. The teacher is not addressed as "Mr., Miss, or Mrs. So-and-So" nor is the teacher addressed as "Comrade So-and-So". Students rise when the teacher enters the classroom. The usual greeting is for the teacher to say : *"Tung hsueh men, hao!"* which means "Fellow students, how are you?", with the reply by the students : *"Lao Shih, hao!"* (Old Master, how are you?). Then the teacher would say, *"Tung hsuen men, ching tso"* (fellow students, please sit down). This maintains the respectful role of the teacher and creates a friendly atmosphere in the classroom.

All teachers have to plan their lessons and write them down before they conduct the classes. They are considered unsatisfactory teachers if they cannot produce their lesson plans when the principal asks for them. Such lesson plans are carefully made, often in consultation with teachers of the same class or teachers of that subject in other classes. Discussion groups for the interchange of teaching experience are held regularly and classroom visits to observe each other's teaching take place frequently. The teacher whose lesson is to be observed is usually notified ahead of time and after each visit a discussion follows among the teachers themselves. A teacher's good points are always first pointed out, followed by constructive suggestions for improvement. The spirit of mutual assistance and of everyone working for a common enterprise is prevalent. When students fail or get a low grade, it is the teacher who is more worried than the students. He has to find out the causes for the failures, and devise ways and means of helping the students get over the barrier. This applies to the primary schools as well as to secondary schools and universities.

Teachers are carefully selected so that those who are non-socialistic and non-proletarian in ideology are gradually weeded out of the schools. New teachers are first trained in the normal schools. New teachers as well as old ones are constantly being trained and retrained while in service. Training involves the political and the professional, with the emphasis always on the political. Training takes many forms: listening to party reports, attending lectures, seminars, conferences, and institutes of various duration, visitations, and interchange of teaching experience within the schools and in school systems of wider areas. The Communists claim that they help the teachers to improve themselves all the time so that they can be of better service to the people.

The young students, because of the political education which they receive in the Young Pioneers' Brigade, can distinguish a progressive teacher from a non-progressive teacher. Assuming the role of "pioneers" of the party, they often try to push their teachers forward. Let me cite an example. When the movement first started to use Mandarin, or the Peking pronunciation, as the spoken medium of instruction in all the schools, some teachers, because of their unfamiliarity with the national tongue, still dragged on with the local dialect in teaching, while the youngsters, being fast learners, picked up Mandarin in a short time. When the teachers spoke to them in the local dialect, the children replied in Mandarin. This made the teachers blush. Many teachers were impelled to drill themselves in the Mandarin speech so that they could teach in that medium and catch up with the students.

Some primary school teachers are graduates of normal schools and some are not, but training in service goes on all the time, keeping the teachers, whether normal school graduates or not, in pace with the times both politically and professionally.

According to recent information, the teacher is paid a monthly salary of JMP ¥38.50 to ¥99.50.[7] Salary differences between

7 JMP is the abbreviation for *jin-min-pi* (people's currency). JMP ¥1.00 (¥ is the symbol for the JMP dollar) is equivalent to HK $2.34 or US $0.40 at the official rate of exchange, which has been kept very steady. According to the latest information, the monthly salary of a primary school teacher is JMP ¥38.50 to ¥99.50; for a middle school

teachers of different school levels in China are not as great as in Hong Kong.

## Liquidation of Illiteracy

Closely related to the subject of primary education are the movements for the liquidation of illiteracy, the phoneticization of the Chinese writing, the simplification of Chinese characters, and the unification of Chinese speech. One could include the movement for literary reform in which the spoken style is used in place of the classical style in writing. But that reform which started at the Chinese Renaissance had been successfully brought about long before the People's régime, so it does not belong to our discussion here.

It is of universal agreement that illiteracy is a mark of backwardness. The Communists further say that illiteracy is a stumbling-block to the building of socialism. Now after 19 years of Communist rule, what one can say is that illiteracy in China has been much reduced. But to say that everyone knows how to read and write is far from being true. Even as late as 1965 there were many young people in China who had never been to school.[8] Figures for literacy or illiteracy cannot be taken too

---

*Footnote 7 (continued)*

teacher it is from ¥47.50 to ¥165.50. An ordinary worker in the factory gets on an average about ¥40 to ¥50 a month. The stability of the Chinese People's Currency in the last 15 years is remarkable and can be compared favourably with any currency in the world. The purchasing power of the JMP is high. Though wages seem low in terms of dollars, a single person can live on ¥25.00 a month. A family of four persons in Canton, for instance, can live on ¥60.00 a month in a simple way (¥8.00 for clothing, ¥36.00 for food, ¥8.00 for housing including water and electricity, ¥4.00 for transportation, ¥4.00 for toilet and miscellaneous articles). From information for Canton in 1966, rice is about 12 cents a catty (13 ounces), peanut oil 96 cents a catty, coal ¥1.25 per 50 catties, sugar 80 cents a catty, pork ¥1.00 for catty, tomatoes 15–20 cents a catty, biscuits 70 cents a catty, rubber shoes ¥5.00 a pair, cigarettes (20 cigarettes) 15 cents per package, bus fare 5 cents per division, railway fare from Canton to Shanghai ¥65.00, air ticket from Canton to Kweilin, Kwangsi, Y75.00.

seriously, anyway, before one is clear what the criterion of literacy is or how they are obtained. So we shall not quote literacy figures here.[9]

Since the Communist Revolution in Russia, literacy has taken on a wider connotation. It adds to the new concept of political literacy. The Chinese Communists give a greater emphasis to political literacy than linguistic literacy. Even the promotion of linguistic literacy is chiefly concerned with learning political terminology and phraseology, making it a rather dull affair for the majority of the adult illiterates. Literacy classes are found in the rural and urban areas for those who have missed the opportunity of schooling. In the cities, where the educational and cultural level has always been higher, literacy has never been a problem. With the well-known special respect for education of the Chinese there is no reason to believe that China cannot attain, in years to come, as high a percentage of literacy as any other country in the world.

## *The Phoneticization of Chinese Writing*

The movement for Chinese language reform is chiefly concerned with these two aspects : the phoneticization of Chinese writing and the simplification of Chinese characters. Let us first take up phoneticization.

Chinese (*Han*) writing is ideographic, symbols representing ideas, not sounds. There is no alphabet and writing is not phonetic. According to the standard Chinese dictionary prepared

[8] According to the New China News Agency of 14 August 1965 : "The students in the graduating class of the Peking Normal University who participated in the Socialist Educational Movement in certain villages in the mountains in remote areas noticed that there are innumerable young people in the rural areas, particularly sons and daughters of the poor peasants and lower middle peasants, who have never been to school. This makes political study and scientific and technical study difficult." (*Renmin Ribao (People's Daily)*, 15 August 1965.)

[9] According to the Communists' admission, among the workers, about 20 per cent are illiterates or semi-illiterates. (*Renmin Ribao (People's Daily)*, 26 January 1964.)

under the reign of K'ang-hsi (A.D. 1662–1723) of the Ching Dynasty, there are 42,174 characters, each with its own symbol. One cannot tell its pronunciation merely by its structure. Of these about 14,000 characters are of really practical use. For common usage, it is further reduced to about 5000. Some modern educators at the close of World War I picked out through statistical investigation 1000 words (later modified to about 1200) of most frequent use as a basic vocabulary for literacy education. Even then, 1000 words mean 1000 symbols, and it is a very laborious job to remember both their structures and their sounds and to be able to reproduce them in writing with proper strokes. There are simple words with one or two strokes only, while some run to as many as thirty-seven strokes. To some people it looked a hopeless task to have all people in China able to read and write.

Lu Hsin, one of China's greatest modern writers, advocated the abolition of Chinese writing. He said : "If the Chinese (*Han*) characters are not abolished, China will certainly perish."

The quickest and easiest way to reform is to adopt an alphabet and spell out every word by its sound. This is what is called "romanization",[10] once very commonly called by the Chinese Communists, "latinization". After one has learned the alphabet and the standardized rules of spelling and pronunciation, he can read the newspapers and write letters in Roman letters in one or two weeks' time. The advocates claim that culture and education would thus be much accelerated through the use of the typewriter and linotype machine. Those who cherish the aspirations of Esperanto claim that the adoption of phonetics in Chinese writing would help to make Chinese into a world language. Proper names for persons such as Stalin, Khrushchev, Churchill, Wilson, Lincoln, Johnson; places such as Moscow, London, Washington; and scientific terms such as oxygen, radium, Fahrenheit, vitamin $B_2$, etc., need not then be translated.

---

[10] The Christian missionaries in China have long used romanization in the promotion of literacy among the Chinese converts. There are many romanized versions of the Bible in China in various dialects.

In the name of liquidating illiteracy and in the name of the proletariat, the romanization of Chinese writing should have made much greater headway in China. In spite of some very ardent advocates of this movement in the Communist Party, the chief exponent among whom is Wu Yu-chang, little progress has been made. The movement is still confined to the research and experimental stage and its supplementary functions. The rich cultural heritage of Chinese literature explains this retardation in part, while the conservatism of Mao Tse-tung in this respect may also explain much of it.

After many years of research and deliberation, and benefiting by the various schemes proposed in the last 60 years, a draft scheme for a Chinese phonetic alphabet was promulgated by the State Council of the People's Republic in 1957. The scheme is not to create a new alphabet or to introduce new letters to the alphabet. It is, in form, the twenty-six letters of the Latin or English alphabet.[11]

Romanization is now used in China not as a substitute for the written language, but rather as its supplement, just as the *chu yin tse mu* (phonetic transcript)[12] has been, to aid the pronunciation of the Chinese character according to the accepted national sound.

## Simplification of Chinese Characters

Between two extreme views, one to abolish the Chinese characters altogether, and the other to keep them unchanged, there is a middle course which is to simplify the Chinese characters. The way to do this is to keep the Chinese characters but reduce the strokes whenever possible. Many Chinese characters

---

[11] See *Reform of the Chinese Written Language,* published by the Foreign Language Press, Peking, 1958.

[12] Wu Chih-hui was one of the earliest advocates of this scheme. The letters are like the "radicals" in Chinese script. They resemble the Japanese *katakana* syllabary, which has nothing in common with the English alphabet.

had been simplified or reduced in strokes and had been in common use all along. What the People's Government has done is to standardize them and invent new ones to increase the list. The Government also makes these simplified characters official. By official, is meant their use not only in hand writing but also in print and their recognition as the right form to use in place of the old characters.

After some years of careful study by the joint efforts of philologists, etymologists, phonologists, semasiologists, writers, teachers, educationists, journalists, cultural workers, labour union representatives, and army representatives, two lists of simplified characters containing 515 words in all, were promulgated by the State Council in January 1956. Since then, all books, newspapers, documents and writings of all kinds, with the exception of the old classics, have been printed in the simplified characters. Indeed, all Chinese characters have since then been in simplified form and in simplified form only. It is only in that way that simplification could have any meaning; otherwise it would add to confusion, and furthermore people would have to learn two forms for every word instead of one.

Since 1956 other supplementary lists have been produced. In 1964 a cumulative list, consisting of 2328 words, was published. We notice on the simplified list there are five words with two strokes which were originally eight to seventeen strokes. We may also use Mao Tse-tung's name to illustrate. The word "Mao" is not simplified, because it has only four strokes; the word "Tse", originally of sixteen strokes, is now simplified to eight strokes; the word "tung", originally of eight strokes, is now simplified to five strokes. Although the list of 2338 simplified characters seems long, the change is not really so great as to render the new words unintelligible to an educated Chinese. For instance, he can read the *Renmin Ribao* (*People's Daily*) quite intelligently by inferences and guesses without having to turn constantly to the conversion table to find what the simplified word is.

Those who are familiar with Chinese culture will know that unlike European writing which runs in horizontal lines from left to right with lines succeeding each other from the top to the bottom of the page, Chinese writing for thousands of years has run in vertical lines from top to bottom, with the lines following each other from the right to the left. For the last 40 years, some Chinese publishers have been printing Chinese books according to the Western style. The Western style has many advantages when it comes to books with foreign names or when there are mathematical and scientific formulae; but this practice has been the exception rather than the rule in Chinese publications. The newspapers were particularly conservative in this matter. But beginning from January 1955 new books and newspapers in China have adopted the Western style. The *Renmin Ribao (People's Daily)* and the *Hsin Hua Yueh Pao* (later called *Hsin Hua Pan Yueh Kan*) took the lead in January 1955 and were followed by all others.

This brings us to a very interesting point in connection with Mao Tse-tung's thinking. Mao is very fond of Chinese calligraphy and is proud of his handwriting. He inscribes in big Chinese characters for almost all the newspapers in China starting from the *Renmin Ribao* which was first published in June 1948. As recently as the Red Guards' revolt in Peking in August 1966, he inscribed for two magazines, the *Xien Bei Da (New Peking University)* and the *Zhong Guo Fu Nu (Women of China)*. The format adopted in the publication of his works is not without significance. The *Selected Works of Mao Tse-tung* has been translated into many languages. In the Chinese edition the books are printed in the traditional Chinese style, that is, in vertical lines from top to bottom following each other from right to left. More than that, all the words appear in the old characters and no simplified character is used. If that was his preference, his position in the Chinese language reform is certainly not on the frontier.[13]

[13] In September 1966 under the pressure of the Great Proletarian Cultural Revolution, it was announced that hereafter simplified characters would be used in the publication of the Selected Works of Mao Tse-tung and reading would be on horizontal lines from left to right.

*Unification of Chinese Speech*

The Chinese people have a unified written language, but they have many dialects. Some dialects are so widely different from each other that interpreters are needed. This has been a disgrace to the Chinese people. The movement for the promotion of a unified spoken language has been going on but has proceeded in a half-hearted way. There were arguments on choice of the standard dialect of pronunciation and whether the need for it was more idealistic than realistic. However, as years went by, with regionalism being broken down gradually and particularly with the great mobility and migration of the Chinese people during their flight from the Japanese-occupied areas in the 8 years of anti-Japanese war, Mandarin or *kuo yu* (national language) or *pu-tung-hua* (a general term for the common pattern of northern dialects), became more and more popular, not only among the intellectuals and students but also among soldiers, merchants, and the working people. Radio broadcasting, of course, has been an effective instrument for its advance.

The People's Government has all to gain in pushing forward the movement. The school is certainly the best place to start. Beginning from 1956, teaching in the primary schools has been carried on in the medium of *kuo yu* (national language), with the Peking pronunciation which had always been regarded as of excellent phonetic quality, as the standard. To make the movement successful, primary school teachers were first trained in the National Pronunciation Training Centre—again the principle, "those who educate must first be educated", applied. They had to master also the rules in the phonetic spelling of Chinese words. Now primary school children from the start have to learn the letters of the Roman (English) alphabet and how they are used. In the primary school language textbooks, the phonetic spelling in Roman letters is placed above every Chinese word. With this aid, children in every locality can read out the lessons in correct Peking pronunciation, including the words new to them. This is a tremendous help in the teaching of Chinese language and Chinese literature. Now Mandarin is spoken in the classroom and all children after the third year in the primary school can understand and speak Mandarin. The value to the individual of knowing the national language is immense; the significance to the Chinese nation is immeasurable. To provide a population of 700 million people with a common written language is a formidable enough task; to break down the dialect barriers of centuries and centuries and speak in the same tongue achieving a unification of spoken language, could be a threat to the rest of mankind if this unity is misused.

From the above, we see that while the movements for the liquidation of illiteracy, the phoneticization of Chinese writing, the simplification of Chinese characters, and the unification of national speech have implications beyond the primary school, the primary school is very heavily involved in all these movements.

## SECONDARY EDUCATION

Secondary schools in China are mainly of three types : (1) the *pu tung chung hsueh*, the general middle school; (2) the normal school; and (3) the vocational and technical school. The general middle school is the main type of secondary education. It was almost the exclusive type in pre-Communist China. The normal school, in a way, is a type of vocational and technical school, but since it is quite distinct in itself and has always existed in large numbers, it is usually named separately. For teacher training on the higher education level, it is called *shih fan hsueh yuan* (normal college), the biggest one of which is in Peking which has a long history and has retained its old name, *Peking Shih Fan Ta Hsueh* (Peking Normal University). In recent years the vocational and technical secondary schools have developed rapidly and are beginning to catch up with the general middle schools in number.

### General Middle Schools

The general middle school is the academic type of secondary school which has always been "college preparatory" in its curriculum. That is to say, the subjects examined in the college or university entrance examination are based on the general middle school syllabus. It is difficult for students who come from other types of middle schools to get into the colleges and universities, unless certain subjects are waived or unless students enter technical and professional institutions of higher education with other standards of admission. The general middle school in China, different from the *Mittelschule* in Germany, has the highest status in the Chinese secondary school system. Since its curriculum is quite uniform throughout China, Table 1, taken from the schools in Canton gives a representative picture of the framework of the general middle school curriculum.

We do not want to go into a detailed study of the general middle school curriculum. But a casual observation reveals its academic nature, with three distinct emphases : the linguistic emphasis, the scientific and mathematics emphasis, and the social and political emphasis. Such a heavy programme also shows how difficult it is for graduates of other types of secondary schools, technical schools for instance, to attain this standard, and how much more difficult it would be for the half-work half-study secondary schools to maintain the standard without increasing their years of study. It will help us understand why those who do not come from the general middle schools have asked for the abolition of the entrance examination to the colleges and universities which is based on the general middle school curriculum.

Middle schools usually charge some fee, a few more dollars a term than the primary school. There was once a slogan : "He who studies, pays." There are exceptions. For instance, some middle schools specially established for returned overseas Chinese students are free of charge. Room and board are also provided free.

Teaching efficiency is quite high, as teachers are constantly under the pressure of criticism from their colleagues and from the students, particularly from members of the Communist Youth League. The teachers have always to be at their best.

TABLE 1.  THE GENERAL MIDDLE SCHOOL CURRICULUM

| Level of school: | Junior middle school | | | Senior middle school | | |
|---|---|---|---|---|---|---|
| Year: | 1 | 2 | 3 | 1 | 2 | 3 |
| Language and Literature | 6 | 6 | 6 | 6 | 6 | 6 |
| Foreign language | 4 | 4 | 4 | 4 | 4 | 4 |
| Political science | 3 | 3 | 3 | 3 | 3 | 3 |
| Chinese history | 3 | 3 | | | | |
| World history | | | 3 | | | |
| Chinese modern history | | | | 3 | | |
| World modern history | | | | | 3 | |
| Chinese geography | 3 | 3 | | | | |
| World geography | | | 3 | | | |
| Chinese economic geography | | | | 3 | | |
| World economic geography | | | | | 3 | |
| Biology | 3 | | | | | |
| Physics | | 3 | | 3 | 3 | 3 |
| Chemistry | | | 3 | 3 | 3 | 3 |
| Essentials of agriculture | | | 2 | | | 2 |
| Essentials of hygiene | | | 2 | | | |
| Algebra | 5 | 2 | 3 | 3 | 3 | 3 |
| Plane geometry | | 3 | 2 | | | |
| Solid geometry | | | | 3 | | |
| Analytic geometry | | | | | | 3 |
| Plane trigonometry | | | | | 3 | |
| Drawing | 1 | 1 | | | | |
| Music | 1 | 1 | | | | |
| Physical education | 2 | 2 | 2 | 2 | 2 | 2 |
| Total No. of periods per week* | 31 | 31 | 33 | 33 | 33 | 29 |

\* Each period is of 50 minutes.

Therefore, overloading the students with assignments, cramming for examinations, lack of clarity in explanation, attending classes without sufficient preparation, laziness in correcting students' papers, rudeness towards students, prejudice against students, and lack of enthusiasm in conducting classes are simply stamped out of school life. The practice of the principle of criticism and self-criticism in the schools really helps to raise the academic standard of the schools in spite of their many short-comings.

The textbooks are generally very well prepared. They are the product of joint efforts by outstanding teachers in the subject after a long process of trial and criticism. There are not many textbooks for any one subject, with the exception of books for distinct localities on a trial basis. Those which are formally published are really very fine. One finds middle school science textbooks, for instance, very interesting and practical with many excellent illustrations. The presentation of scientific facts seems fair. Even at the time when Russian influence was strong and much was credited to Russian science, the history of science was not as distorted as one might think. For instance, the senior middle school first year physics textbook, published by the People's Education Press in 1955, introduces Newton's three laws of motion in the chapter on Combination and Resolution of Forces. Isaac Newton's portrait is printed there. It begins with this statement: "The founder of dynamics was the English genius Newton." Then it goes on with half a page on his life, his discovery, and his contribution. It also gives Newton's dates (1643–1727) and the day of his birth (5 January 1643).

## *The Vocational and Technical Schools*

Only about one-third of the primary school graduates are admitted to the junior middle school and a still smaller number to the senior middle school. Those who fail to gain admission to either go to the vocational and technical schools or into employment. Some go to normal schools to be trained as primary school teachers, but the number is comparatively small.

The development of vocational and technical schools has made great strides in the last 19 years, as seen in the variety of schools opened, the number of students enrolled, and the improvement of their curricula. In pre-Communist days, during a period of over 40 years after the adoption of modern education, technical schools existed only in name. Even in the technical schools which existed, such as the agricultural schools on the secondary school level, the curriculum was academic, and the method of teaching was bookish. By contrast, agricultural education in China today is of a practical nature. The syllabus of an agricultural middle school illustrates the point. Besides physics and chemistry, there are these subjects : the general use of agricultural machinery and appliances, rural hydraulics, sericulture, rice planting in wet land, sugar-cane planting, peanut planting, domestic animals and their feeding, essentials of farm management, common animal diseases and their cure, the programming of agricultural production according to the twenty-four agricultural seasons (solar terms) of the year, protection of plants, essentials of climatology, scientific use of fertilizers, protection against frost.

*Half-work Half-study Schools*

The development of the half-work and half-study schools in China might be attributed to several factors. (1) Theoretically it was based on the Communist principle of education : "The intellectualization of the working people and the cultivation of labour habits and attitudes in the intellectuals." (2) Historically it was based on a movement, the *Chin Kung Chien Hsueh* movement (the campaign for being diligent in work while thrifty in study), initiated by Tsai Yuen-pei in 1915, the year in which the *Hsin Ching Nien (New Youth Magazine)* was published. Tsai was then chancellor of Peking University, and had been to France. Many ambitious students in China at that time who had not the financial means to go to the United States, went to Europe, particularly to France. Among them were some Chinese Communist leaders today, such as Chou En-lai, Teng Hsiao-ping, and Chen Yi, who organized themselves into the Chinese Communist group in Europe almost simultaneously as the Communist Party in China. The motto *Chin kung chien hsueh* has been popular in modern Chinese educational history; it is still repeated in its exact words in the Communist campaign of today in the promotion of half-work half-study programmes. (3) In practical terms, it aimed to increase school places for those who ask for them by spreading the butter thinner, as it were, and to supply a larger intellectual force to meet the needs of agriculture and industry. It helped to satisfy a large number of young people who had quit schooling early and were anxious to study again. This movement started as early as 1958, at the time of the Great Leap Forward. It grew fast in 1963. In 1965 many cities and provinces even created new bureaux for the promotion and administration of the half-work half-study schools and the spare-time schools, which are also closely related.

Such schools are sometimes named as half-work half-study schools, half-agriculture half-study schools, and are sometimes simply called work-study schools, cultivation-study schools. Some study half a day and work half a day, some study one day and work another day, while some study and work in alternative weeks. These schools are not confined to the secondary school level, but there are more of them on the secondary than on the college level. Half-work half-study schools are chiefly in the cities, but are not very numerous. The half-cultivation half-study schools are in the rural areas, and since they are on the primary school level mostly, they form the largest proportion of the half-study schools. The half-study schools are often converted from full-time schools or are added to them as extra units. In the last 4 years, as a result of this campaign, there has been a great increase in number of half-work half-study secondary schools, but the number of full-time general middle schools has not substantially increased. According to a report, there were 386 half-work half-study secondary schools in Shanghai in 1965 with an enrolment of 49,000 students. Some of these schools are operated by the factories in the cities and by the communes on the farms. Whether they are schools of a general, technical, or agricultural nature and whether they are at the primary, secondary, or college level, one has reason to doubt the quality of their performance. Because of their rapid expansion and the shortage of teachers, some experienced farmers and skilled workers are recruited to the teaching staff. In spite of the publicity and propaganda surrounding the rise of these schools, it seems that they are only a transient phase of education in China and doomed to failure.

## *Participation in Rural Construction*

Closely related to the half-work half-study scheme is the programme of participation in rural life and in agricultural production. This applies to the students and teachers in the cities particularly, not only affecting large numbers but also crucial in their political influence on society. The programme involves two aspects. The first is to mobilize the students and teachers to the rural areas to help in agricultural production. There are two major seasons in the year when they are sent to the villages, in summer and in autumn. In the city of Shanghai it was reported that in the autumn of 1965 there were over 160,000 secondary school students who went to the villages to help the peasants. It is not farming alone that the students and their teachers have to do; the political part is really the most trying. They advocate the principle of *san tung* (literally, threefold sameness), that is, to live together with the peasants in the same place, to eat the same food together with the peasants, and to labour together with them at the same work. They have to learn from the poor peasants the stories of their past hardships and write their village class histories. They have to help the peasants to clean the place and help them cook and draw water wherever they are old and weak. In leisure hours they have to stage recreational performances for the peasants and help them to organize village schools. Students now often carry with them a little sewing compendium and know how to mend shoes and do haircutting.

The second aspect is that when the students pass school-leaving examinations but fail to be admitted to the higher schools, they are mobilized to the far away areas to farm and work. In Shanghai, during the last few years, over 70,000 students were sent off to Sinkiang, China's furthest western province. It is reported that in June 1966 the first dispatch to Sinkiang was 900 students, followed by new dispatches every two or three days. This explains why there is no unemployment in the cities and no sign of the existence of discontented youth there. It is reported that in Canton, as early as April 1966, 3000 young people were sent to Hainan Island to settle down there. The Communists have their way of manipulation, so that the young people who go appear to be volunteers migrating at their own request. In order to make the young people more at home in the new environment, their teachers are sometimes asked to accompany them and stay with them for the early period of their settlement.

## The Communist Youth League

As far as the age of secondary school students is concerned, it falls largely in the age-range of "Communist Youth" and their subsidiary young pioneers. For this reason alone, life in the secondary schools is constantly under the supervision of the Communist Youth League. According to the Chinese Communists : "The school is the fiercest battle ground between the proletariat and the bourgeoisie for capturing the generation of youth." It is in the schools that the Communists look for their successors. It is natural that the secondary schools are not overlooked by the Communists for their ideological training and in their pattern of life. As the students move up from the primary school to the junior middle school, from the junior middle school to the senior middle school, and from the senior middle school to the university, the selection of students for admission grows tighter and tighter. The criteria of selection are : first, the family background of the student; second, the progressiveness of the student's thinking; and third, the student's political reliability. Whosoever survives the screening must be either a Communist youth activist or one who is not objected to by the League. Teachers, too, go through the same screening and can hardly carry on if they are constantly objected to by the League. While primary education is supposed to be for everybody and class distinctions cannot very well be drawn in admission to it, secondary education is the stage where the demarcation has to begin. It is only in this context that one can understand the meaning of secondary education in China today.

The Communist Youth League has its headquarters in every secondary school and university, with its secretary, officers and the rest. It is of no special significance to describe how the League's headquarters are organized and how they work. What is significant is the general fibre of the Communist youth. This should not escape our attention. They are usually good at studies, good at work, good in health, good in thinking, and good in labour. These are qualities socially acceptable and respectable, similar to those things the Western world would expect of Boy Scouts. From what one hears and reads of the recent events in China, the Red Guards seem to differ from the Communist youth and are selected on the basis of other qualities. It looks as if the radicals in the Chinese Communist Party do not agree with the Communist Youth League and with its past leaders for "soft-pedalling" the control of youth; and that is why they have to count on a different selection of teenagers to help them launch the Great Proletarian Cultural Revolution. The fact that publication of the magazine, *Xhongguo Qingnian (Chinese Youth)*, national organ of the Chinese Communist Youth League, was suspended in September 1966, is an evidence of this distrust. It is only when the cloud over the Chinese scene which arose in mid-1966 is dispersed that one will understand more intelligently why the Communist Youth League has been kept in the background and the Red Guards have been installed in their place.

## Physical Education

Mao Tse-tung has often spoken of developing education in its three aspects—the moral, the intellectual, and the physical. It is possible that the symbol of the YMCA triangle left him with the idea of the three aspects of education. A good physical body is needed from the standpoints of productivity, of military defence, and of social well-being. Physical education is emphasized inside as well as outside the school system. Since it is closely related to the secondary schools, we shall take it up here.

We may say there are two parts to the physical education programme. One is what is called the "Broadcast physical exercises". Several sets of physical exercises are broadcast in sequence over the radio early every day, sometimes with musical accompaniment, for the public to participate in for about 5 minutes. In the schools, at recesses between classes, such exercises and music are broadcast over the microphone every day. Students and teachers know how to exercise in formation in the athletic grounds or in the corridors, and how to participate to best effect. These broadcast exercises are also followed daily in offices and factories at specified hours. They are popular because of their recreational value. Collective action and socialistic discipline are seen as the concomitants of such physical training. It is a blessing that the people's physique in China is not being neglected. Providing them with sufficient diet and nutrition is an indirect result of this emphasis.

The other part of the physical education programme is what is called the "labour-defence scheme", in which certain standards in physical or athletic achievements are set for certain age groups, with a slight variation for the female sex. The slogan is to train the body for the defence of the fatherland. The performances include running, jumping, throwing, and shooting. The military tenor is high. Throwing includes throwing the grenade, running includes charging, and jumping includes jumping over barricades. Those who have an aptitude for sport become national athletes, taking up sport as a profession or becoming physical education teachers after proper training. For the rest, it is also a good preparation for those who intend to enter military service.

Youths between the ages from 18 and 25 are recruited for military service. Not everyone is conscripted. In fact, it is only those who are physically fit and politically trustworthy that are accepted. It is considered an honour to be drafted. If recruits are found to be unsuitable after enlistment, they are sent back to the schools to study or to places of employment with favourable terms of placement, similar to those accorded to Liberation Army personnel who retire or who are rehabilitated. In the secondary schools there are military camps in the summer to which some students go for several weeks of pre-military training.

## HIGHER EDUCATION

### *Types of Colleges and Universities*

In this section on higher education we shall present the general features of the universities, colleges, post-secondary technical schools, and research institutes in China. In certain countries, such as the United States, the universities constitute the main body of higher education. But in Communist China it is not quite the case. As far as numerical strength is concerned, according to the latest estimate,[14] there are only forty-three universities[15] in

[14] Based on the article "Institutes of Higher Education in Communist China", *China Monthly*, November and December Numbers, 1965, published by the Union Research Institute, Hong Kong. It gives as detailed an account of the names and structure of the institutions of higher education in China today as one can find anywhere. While the information and statistics there cannot be taken as accurate on every minor point, as its author did not claim them to be, it gives us a good picture of the present situation of higher education in China.

[15] Our criterion here of a university is that the institution is purely called *ta hsueh* (university) without any qualifications, such as the University of Peking, University of Nanking, University of Foochow, Sun Yat-sen University, Nankai University, etc. They offer a variety of disciplines in the arts and sciences, as distinct from other institutions which are specialized or specific to one branch or one general field of higher studies, such as the University of Communication of Shanghai, the Industrial University of Harbin, the Medical University of Chekiang, or the Agricultural University of Shantung. This figure forty-three includes, however, three universities—Tsing Hua University, Tung Chi University, and the University of Tientsin—which are actually *technical* universities without having *technological* added to their names.

China as compared with a total of 664 institutions of higher learning. These universities are sometimes called *tsung ho ta hsueh* (composite universities), which are interdisciplinary in nature—interdisciplinary in the sense that they embrace both the arts and the sciences. Take the Sun Yat-sen University in Canton as an example, a university with which Lingnan University was amalgamated : there are at present these departments : mathematics, physics, chemistry, biology, geology, geography, history, Chinese, foreign languages, philosophy, economics, and oceanography. The departments are not grouped in faculties as in pre-Communist China or in Taiwan, where the regulation is that no higher institution is permitted to be called a "university" unless it has three faculties or more. The Nationalist pattern of formalism is not found in the school system of People's China today.

The function of the composite universities is to strengthen the theoretical foundation of higher learning and perhaps the academic foundation as well, so that men of high calibre will be produced to do pure research and to teach in other institutions, such as the technological and professional schools, the normal schools, and the secondary schools. For the supply of normal school and secondary school teachers there are also the normal universities, normal colleges, and colleges of education on the higher educational level, of which there are 113. Out of this number, eight are called normal universities and the rest are variously called normal colleges, colleges of education, technical normal colleges, industrial normal colleges, special subject higher normal schools, etc. For the supply of a great variety of teachers for the schools of secondary level, there are also the colleges of physical education, music, foreign languages, and a host of technological and professional colleges.

The key concept in the institution of schools of higher education is the "mono-technic" concept as distinct from the polytechnic concept. The idea of the comprehensive and all-inclusive university is rejected. While such a pattern of higher education is not generally found in the United Kingdom and in the United

States, it is not strange to the German system or to the Soviet system of education.*

* We may observe that among the 237 schools of higher education which serve the industries listed in the *China Monthly,* there are still many types. For instance, besides 52 which are industrial colleges and universities with a broader curriculum, there are 27 which are specific, as their names indicate, including colleges of petroleum, mineral ores, mining, oil refining, coal-mining, etc.; 8 are specified as colleges of geology, geological surveying, and planning; 18 are specified as colleges of electrical dynamics, electrical-hydraulics, hydraulics, and water conservancy, etc.; 10 are specified as colleges of iron and steel, ferrous and non-ferrous metals, metallurgy, metallurgical construction, etc.; 13 are specified as colleges of machinery, electrical machinery, optical precision machinery, electrical engineering, etc.; 3 are specified as colleges of surveying, meteorology, etc.; 13 are specified as colleges of light industry, textile industry, silk weaving industry, paper industry, chemical fibric industry, food industry, etc.; 16 are specified as colleges of chemical engineering; 11 are specified as colleges of construction industry, construction material industry, construction engineering, cement industry, etc.; 13 are specified as colleges of postal communications and telegraphy, broadcasting, telegraphic engineering, radio equipment, etc.; 30 are specified as colleges of communication, railway, ocean transportation, highways, shipping, bridge engineering, river transportation, water transportation engineering, etc.; 13 are specified as colleges of forestry engineering, agricultural machinery, agricultural mechanization, etc.; 13 are specified as colleges of aviation, oceanography, city construction (planning), ceramics, etc. Of the 75 schools of higher education which serve agriculture, many are simply called colleges of agriculture, of forestry, of agriculture and forestry, but some are specified as colleges of tropical plants, sericulture, horticulture, animal husbandry, veterinary science, marine products, soil science, etc. Of the 87 medical colleges, 9 are colleges of Chinese (traditional) medicine. The 33 schools of higher education in the field of political science and law, economics and business administration are variously specified as colleges of political science and law, commerce, diplomacy, finance and trade, foreign trade, international relations, economics, industrial accountancy and statistics, social science, law and security, etc. Of the 14 schools of higher education for foreign languages, some are colleges of foreign languages in general, while 2 are specified as colleges of English, and 1 is specified as a higher preparatory school for students who are to study abroad. There are 37 schools of higher education in the field of art. They are variously called colleges of art, literary art, movie, drama, operatic art, music, fine art, etc. There are also 15 colleges of physical education.

In illustrating the mono-technic concept in the establishment of schools on the university level in detail, we hope we have, at the same time, presented a panoramic view of the structure of the colleges and universities in China.

We have not included in the above analysis other types of universities and higher schools which do not belong to the regular type such as the labour universities, of which it is reported that in 1965 there were eighty-seven in Kwangtung Province alone in the various *Hsiens*. Besides, there are the spare-time universities, evening universities, "red and expert" universities, broadcasting universities, television universities, correspondence universities, peasants' universities, short-course high schools, etc. They exist as universities in name only and are far below any appropriate standard. In speaking of their low standard, no implication is made that the 664 schools of higher education mentioned above are all of an acceptable collegiate standard.

According to the figures given by the Chinese Government official organ,[16] there were 170,000 graduates in 1965 from all schools of higher education, with the largest number from technical colleges, second largest from the normal colleges, then from medical colleges, next from agriculture colleges, and finally from the colleges of natural science.

## Administration of Higher Education

*Ministry of Higher Education.* The Ministry of Higher Education in the Central Government administers higher education over the whole country. As we said in an earlier chapter, there have been several changes in the administration of higher education. There have been times when higher education was under the administration of the Ministry of Education without having a separate ministry of its own, as it again has now. What is more significant is that many schools of higher education are partially administered by the various ministries of the State Council. An examination of the names of the technological

[16] *Renmin Ribao (People's Daily)*, 11 August 1965.

colleges and the names of the ministries[17] will reveal the close parallel between the colleges and the ministries. Those colleges or schools of higher education are usually initiated and supervised by the ministries concerned according to their specific needs. While those ministries often have special departments to control their colleges, the Ministry of Higher Education is the co-ordinator and overseer. Some colleges and universities are more directly the responsibility of the Ministry of Higher Education, such as the composite universities and the normal universities and colleges, but even then this does not exclude other bodies from exercising their control. For instance, the Sun Yat-sen University, a composite university in Canton, is not only controlled by the Ministry of Higher Education in Peking, but also by the Provincial Government in Kwangtung which has its own bureau of higher education, and by the local party. What is said here, however, does not mean that the administration of the technological colleges is in a state of confusion. Rather, it indicates that they are well co-ordinated in so far as the Chinese Communist Party is an integrated unity and everything within its jurisdiction must work in harmony with the directives of the party, without any tolerance of deviation from the party line either because of regionalism or independent-kingdom thinking. The over-all policy is in the five-year plans.

*Private colleges and universities.* It is obvious that for a régime based on the assumptions that education is the instrument of politics and education is in the service of the proletariat, as under the Chinese régime today, there is no leeway for private education. Private schools and private universities, including missionary universities, existed for a short time after the establishment of the People's Republic. But in 1952 there was a campaign for the "Readjustment of Colleges and Departments" in which the breaking up and merging of various colleges and departments took place. New ones were also set up at that time, but they were in very small numbers. It was, in appearance, a

[17] See Chapter 3, footnote 15.

scheme to consolidate the colleges and departments operated on the principle of rationalization, eliminating duplications, concentrating the nation's resources, and providing for better distribution. But, in essence, it was to abolish all private colleges and universities and break down the institutional identities which had existed. As a result of that campaign, the thirteen Christian colleges and universities in China,[18] which had been established and subsidized by mission boards, mostly American, were merged with other government colleges and universities. Their names were all wiped out. Catholic universities met the same fate. On the secondary and primary school level, the private schools, particularly those connected with the Christian churches, were at the same time reorganized with their names also changed. Some private schools, realizing the futility of opposition, offered their schools with their property and assets to the Government unconditionally. The Government at that stage of its developing power, was willing to take them over so long as they had not been established by Kuomintang reactionaries. This is something of the past, and yet it gives one some idea of how the transitional period was bridged from the former system to the new system.

*University administration: In whose hands?* After the campaign for the readjustment of colleges and departments was successfully carried out and the earlier movements for thought reform had run their course, the professors in the universities began to feel their way in the university community. The issue raised then was of who should run the university. The questions were : Should the university be under the administration of a university council or should it be run by a chief executive such as the president of the university? How should the university

[18] The thirteen Christian colleges and universities were: Fukien Christian University, Ginling College (for women), Hangchow Christian College, Hua Chung University, Lingnan University, University of Nanking, University of Shanghai, Cheeloo University, Soochow University, South China Women's College (Fukien), St. John's University, West China Union University, Yenching University.

council be set up? Since the university is concerned with higher learning and scholastic pursuit, why is it not administered by those distinguished in scholarship? To boil it down, it was a registration of complaint over the domination of non-academic party cadres in the affairs of the university. The argument was : those who do not know should not lead those who know, as those who are not in the trade are not qualified to lead those who are. The outcry of the university academics, not without the support of the party's intellectual, was : *chiao shou chih Hsiao*, which means "the universities to be administered by professors". This would look like following the practice of some British universities where the professors form the senate, which has the final say in academic matters concerning the university. The professors in the universities in Peking were more vocal in their opinion during the period of liberalism in 1956 and 1957 when the "Let the Hundred Schools Contend" campaign was having its day. The naïvety of the academics only led the Communists to step up their tactics into a higher gear for the struggle. The Communists advanced the slogan "both red and expert", as a result of which the university teachers were sent to the rural areas to participate in manual labour in the farms in order to help them to become "red". This slogan of "both red and expert" was designed more to forge the "experts" to be "red" than to require the "reds" to be "expert". Now, no matter whether the administration is in the hands of a president or in a university council, or whether the university council is composed of more party cadres or more academic people, it is the party that takes the initiative and has the final word. Even when a pure academic or a group of academics is placed in the highest position in the administration of the university for tactical reasons or expediency, it is not true that the position is accompanied by authority.

*Student admission.* The admission of students to the schools of higher education in People's China is based throughout on several factors : the need for that type of technical and professional personnel and the number to be admitted, the preference of the applicant, the qualifications of the applicant and his results in the entrance examination, the social status of the applicant's family, the political status and record of the applicant, and his age.

The needs of each field of enterprise and the number to be trained are, in general, decided by the Ministry of Higher Education and the ministries concerned in consultation with the various technological and higher schools as well as with the various agencies of production and services, in accordance with the five-year plans. The number to be trained is under control, and varies from year to year. It has been the practice for many years that applicants with proper qualifications are further required to take the National Joint Entrance Examination for colleges and universities.[19] Examinations are in three major divisions of which the applicant chooses one. They are : (1) Engineering and Natural Science; (2) Medicine and Agriculture; and (3) Arts and History. A foreign language is a required examination subject for all the three divisions; it may be English or Russian. An exception is made for applicants who belong to the national minorities. Applicants who apply for the arts and history division who have been workers, peasants or soldiers for 2 or more years, are also exempted from the examination in foreign language.

Each applicant is asked to name his preferences, to as many as five or six, indicating the field or fields of study he wants to take up and the colleges and universities he wants to attend in his order of preference. The Ministry of Higher Education, basing its decisions on the results of the joint entrance examination, then quotes for each college and university the preferences of the students and other salient factors, and finally publishes the list of successful candidates and the subjects and schools to which

[19] As a drastic measure in response to the Great Proletarian Cultural Revolution, the annual National Joint Entrance Examination for colleges and universities for 1966 was abruptly suspended. According to the *Renmin Ribao* (*People's Daily*) of 18 June 1966, the entrance examination is to be abolished and hereafter admission to the colleges and universities shall be made by the selection and nomination of the Communist Party.

they are assigned before the academic year begins in the autumn. This is what is called "unified distribution".

By "other salient factors" we refer first to the social status of the applicant's family. A young student should have no social status barrier of his own. For instance, he could not have been a landlord. He has had no chance to be a bourgeois. What troubles him, however, is probably the status of his family or of his father. Now the Communists trace one's status even to the status of one's grandfather and his ancestry. We see, then, that grievances and revenge are still in the hearts of Chinese Communists. Regarding the political status of the applicant, preference is given to membership in the party or in the Communist Youth League or to one who has been a political activist as shown in his past records. It is reported that about one-sixth of the secondary school graduates get admission into the college and universities. With such a high selectivity, the chance of studying the subject of one's first preference or entering the college of one's choice is very small. Again, with such political screening, the chance of admission is slim for a student from a family of disadvantageous social status.

It has been the regulation that the upper limit of age for application to colleges and universities is set at 25. For peasants, workers, and soldiers there is an extension to the age of 27.

The problem of college and university admission is again a problem of the class struggle. It is another aspect of the answer to the question : "Education in whose hands?" The leftist extreme wing in the Chinese Communist Party would rather give access to higher education to mediocrities whom they consider politically trustworthy than have the talented whom they do not trust. When such a drastic measure was taken in summer 1966, as the abolition of college and university entrance examinations, especially at this stage of Chinese educational development, it makes one suspect one of two things : either the Communists' political education and re-education of the young intellectuals who come from non-proletarian families has been unsuccessful or else the discontent of the proletarians and the pressure to get their sons and daughters into the colleges and universities are so great that the Communists have to bar the children of the formerly privileged classes from entrance. In 1963 the Communists reported with certain satisfaction an increase in the proletarian and party ratio, declaring that among the graduates of the colleges and universities of that year, 54 per cent were of worker and peasant family origin and 62 per cent were members of the party or the Young Communist League.[20] It looks as if the extremists do not share this feeling of satisfaction.

One can predict that such a measure as the abolition of entrance examination, which implies a disregard for academic standards, will not last long. It is strange that such a measure was not taken earlier but actually after the Communists had held the reins of government for 17 years. Those who are familiar with the history of education in the Soviet Union will recall that such a measure, adopted in the earlier years of the Soviet Revolution, was soon given up as the process of regularizing their educational system came into effect. But the Communist extremists in China seem to want to start the revolution all over again. This revolution is directed against what they themselves have taken years to build up. If this is what is meant by the application of the principle that the revolution is a continuous process, it seems to be a very rude application of it.

This is not what the Chinese Communist extremists would like to hear. There was an old Chinese saying that "It takes ten years to nourish trees, and a hundred years to nourish men". The cultivation of the mind is a long process. It takes more than one generation to rear a generation. If "by laying down the butcher's knife one can become a Buddha right on the spot", then it may be easy for the children of the peasants and workers, in the absence of intellectual background, to become intellectuals by enrolling in the universities.

[20] In 1965 the percentage of party and Communist Youth League membership came up to 70 per cent according to the *Renmin Ribao* (*People's Daily*), 11 August 1966.

## University Teachers and Teaching

University teachers have a high status in China. They enjoy the esteem handed down from thousands of years of Chinese tradition which was accorded to teachers and scholars both by students and by society. An exception occurred, of course, during the social movements in Communist China in which teachers were the objects of struggle. The absence of monetary motives in the Chinese scholar calls for respect even from some Communists. The need is real for their scholarship and technological knowledge in the training of new personnel as well as in carrying out the various projects of construction. The Communists do not fail to value this cultural asset which is now put to their use. University teachers are very well paid compared with other occupations. Generally the junior lecturer starts with a monthly salary of about ¥100, the assistant professor with ¥165, and the professor with ¥240 up to the maximum of ¥400. Most of the university teachers are provided with quarters on the campus for a nominal rent. Such salaries are equal to those of the high-ranking officers in the Liberation Army.

Teachers in the colleges and universities are organized into "teaching and research groups" according to the nature of the subjects they teach. Such groups are found in the secondary schools as well. Each teacher presents for discussion in his group, the syllabus, lecture contents, teaching methods for his own course, the research work he and his students take up, and the problems that arise. Most teachers teach only one course and not infrequently teach it jointly with other teachers. As years go by, the content has become well organized and the methods are improved to a high degree of efficiency. The main emphasis of higher education is specialization. For the student, it means studying fewer courses but more thoroughly. For the teacher, it means teaching only one subject, but digging deep into it and teaching it well. College and university teachers are kept in touch with new knowledge, new techniques, and new methods. They are sensitive to developments in other parts of the world.

In the examinations, "open book" examinations are brought into use; that is, students are allowed to open their books during the examinations. This helps to reduce the mental labour of rote memory which is specially advantageous to older students. Thinking is more developed in this method than in examinations based on the reproduction of lecture notes. Oral examination is also occasionally used. One of its methods is that the student is asked to select a question slip at random from a box containing many such slips. Given a little time interval, he has to go to another room to elaborate his answers before a group of teachers. The student is often given hints for his answer by his teachers, so that any slip of memory or emotional tension will not deprive him of a fair performance. It indicates, in a way, the atmosphere of socialization in teaching in the schools.

Students, before they graduate, are usually required to write a thesis on a piece of research, sometimes doing it alone and sometimes doing it jointly with others. Quite often the theses are projects which have direct use in agriculture, industry, science, and the professions. The practical nature of higher learning and its service to production is predominant in the content and methods of higher education in China.

## *Foreign Languages in Higher Education*

Knowledge of a foreign language, particularly English or Russian, is considered necessary in the pursuit of higher learning. The ability to read foreign textbooks and journals is the goal to be attained. As China is backward in science one might expect that foreign textbooks would be used extensively for the scientific and technical subjects in the colleges and universities, just as they are said to be necessary in the universities in Hong Kong, but that is not the case. Many standard textbooks have been translated or are being translated into Chinese. According to the 1965 list of scientific books published by the Chinese Scientific Press, out of 192 books 101 were translated works of various subjects in mathematics, physics, chemistry, biology, astronomy, electronics, seismology, geology, etc. Besides this, thirteen dictionaries and encyclopedias of scientific and technological terms were published in that year, most of which were translated from English and Russian.

In the early years of the People's Republic, Russian was very popular. Many schools switched from English to Russian. As the demand for teachers of Russian was so great, even the White Russians who had fled from Russia in the October Revolution (1917) and settled down in China's big cities, found good jobs teaching Russian. Many former teachers of English, because of their linguistic aptitude, went to study Russian and became teachers of Russian in the schools. Russian experts and university professors came to lecture in the Chinese colleges and universities. They taught through Chinese interpreters and their lecture notes were translated into Chinese to serve as textbooks until new textbooks were ready.

Russian influence in Chinese education died out gradually as the rupture between the Chinese Communist Party and the Russian Communist Party developed. The glamorous picture of Russia which was painted for the Chinese people when China was pursuing the policy of "falling on one side", as advocated by Mao Tse-tung in his article in 1949 "On the People's Democratic Dictatorship", faded away. The Russian language, together with Russian theory, Russian science, and Russian education became less popular, particularly as the Russian experts and technicians (1390 in number) formally withdrew from China in July 1960 *en bloc*. As a result of the Sino–Soviet split, English has come back to the schools.

Although foreign language teaching is not confined to Russian and English, yet these two are the main ones. Japanese is not popular. Speaking of popularity, even English is not popular in the sense that it is a subject which students are very fond of. Since language and culture are not easily separable, it is difficult to study English without studying English culture, or to be interested in English without being interested in the Anglo–Saxon culture. The social movements and thought reform movements have scared the people to such an extent that, as far as possible, they keep away from any association with imperialism. It was reported that the sons and daughters of the professors of English in the universities were unwilling to take up the study of English. It was explained that they did not want to face the same misfortune of their fathers in the social movements and thought reforms when they had to pay the penalty for having been English scholars. At one time, in elementary English in the lower schools, "Jack" and "John" were superseded by such Chinese names as "Li Fong" or "So Ming", and "sir" was replaced by "comrade". Progress in foreign language learning is handicapped by this emotional strain.

## Graduates and Foreign Students

In the last few years, close to 200,000 students graduated from the colleges and universities annually. Graduates are awarded graduation certificates. No academic degree is conferred.[21] A few go into research. It was reported that in 1965, in about 180 colleges, universities, and research institutes which admitted graduate students for research, only 1200 were admitted out of a total of 12,000 applicants. This means that only 10 per cent of those who applied, or less than 1 per cent of the total number of graduates, were admitted. Those who were admitted were mostly members of the Communist Party and the Youth League.

As a rule, 99 per cent of the graduates who do not go on to study are given jobs. Again, as they did at the time of the undergraduate admission, they are also asked to name their preferences for the type of work they want to do. Through the process of

[21] In 1956, the programme for the degree of "associate doctorate" was inaugurated in the Chinese Academy of Science, following the Soviet pattern. After being admitted by the Academy of Science, students work in the Academy's research institutes or in other universities and institutes to do research. Upon the completion of all requirements, including a thesis on a research project, they are awarded the degree. It was once announced that in the future no one would be promoted to the professorial rank unless he is a holder of the degree of "associate doctorate". But so far this ruling has not been enforced.

"unified assignment", they are notified by their own colleges and universities where they are to go and what they have been assigned to do. Unlike their counterparts in many countries in Asia who are confronted with unemployment upon graduation, none of the college and university graduates in China are out of a job, provided they accept whatever is assigned to them. It would be very bad to refuse the offer, for disobedience to "organizational assignment" would deny anyone a future appointment. It is almost impossible to get a job anywhere, since the Government is the sole employer in the country. Normally, a college graduate starts with a monthly salary of ¥48.50, certain adjustments depending on living conditions in one's locality.

Some graduates are sent abroad to study. In the early years of the People's Republic, large numbers were sent to the Soviet Union and some to the countries of eastern Europe. Now the number to the Soviet Union is much reduced. Many were recalled before they completed their studies. Students are beginning to be sent to Western countries. In 1964, 102 students were sent to France. In that year, through an arrangement with the British Council, twenty-five students went to England to study. Among the graduates from the colleges and universities in Peking city in 1964, 100 were sent to sixteen countries to study.

In return, foreign students come to China to study. It was reported that from 1950 to 1964, China received some 1300 foreign students from forty-six countries. In 1964 there were 150 foreign students studying in China. How successful such a programme is for the foreign students who come or for the Communist régime, it is difficult to tell.[22, 23] But at least the fact that

[22] The account of the African student, E. J. Hevi, who was expelled from Communist China in 1962, seems to indicate that the programme is far from being satisfactory to the students from abroad or favourable to the course of international Communism.

[23] The People's Government in Peking announced in September 1966 that all foreign students in China had to leave the country within a month. All classes in the universities and in secondary schools, including the special classes for foreign students, had been suspended because of the activities of the Great Proletarian Cultural Revolution since June 1966.

foreign students came from forty-six countries to study, a fact unprecedented in Chinese history, is a good talking point in Chinese Communist propaganda.

There is another category of students from abroad which we may include in this discussion, and that is the overseas Chinese students returning from abroad. On the secondary level, there are many schools which admit overseas Chinese students. A few in the coastal cities are established for overseas students. On the higher educational level there are two universities established exclusively for overseas students : one is the Chi-nan University in Canton and the other is the Overseas University in Chuan Chou. Since most of the overseas Chinese are natives of Kwang-tung and Fukien provinces, it is natural that the universities are established in these two provinces, with one in each. The Chi-nan University, originally established for overseas Chinese students in the Ching Dynasty in 1906, was in Shanghai before the Communist régime. In 1958 it was moved to Canton. The Overseas University at Chuan Chou was established in 1960. Chuan Chou is in Fukien, near Amoy. Its president is the chairman of the Commission on Overseas Affairs of the People's Republic. The departments which these two universities offer are similar to those in the composite universities.

*Research*

We have selected some topics of general interest in higher education for discussion. There are many more, but one cannot prolong this discussion indefinitely, particularly if we do not want to have any one section disproportionate to the whole theme. We should like, therefore, to conclude this section on higher education by presenting a general picture of research work in People's China.

All colleges and universities are supposed to have research hand in hand with teaching. We have seen that in every college and university there are many "teaching and research groups" but by "research" is meant more or less the search for better ways of teaching rather than pure academic or technological research. Real research is usually done by the specialist departments whose function it is to undertake research and to train research personnel. Besides the research departments in the colleges and universities, there are independent research institutes.

There are two major bodies which assume the responsibility for research on a national scale. One is the Chinese Academy of Science or the Academia Sinica, the other is the Commission on Science and Technology which was established in 1958 under the chairmanship of Nieh Yung-chen, a vice-premier, who for many years was chief-of-staff of the Chinese People's Liberation Army.

The Chinese Academy of Science was established as an organ within the State Council when the People's Republic was established in 1949. Kuo Mo-jo has been its president ever since. It is now separated from the State Council with a higher organizational status, parallel to that of the State Council. It has many institutes of research which are grouped into five major divisions : (1) the Division of Mathematics, Physics, and Chemistry; (2) the Division of Life Science; (3) the Division of Earth Science; (4) the Division of Scientific Technology; (5) the Division of Philosophy and Social Sciences. There is a director for each division and under each division are many institutes. Most of the institutes have their own publications including learned journals. Some of the institutes are the Institutes of Heredity, Botany, Micro-biology, Geology, Geography, Chemistry and Physics, Chemistry of Silicates, Marine Biology, Electronics, Physiology, Mining, and Meteorology.

The establishment of the Commission on Science and Technology in 1958 under the chairmanship of a military man is not without significance. One may recall that 1957 was the year when the intellectuals were under serious attack in the rectification campaign as a counter measure to the "Hundred Schools Contend" campaign. The Chinese scientists and technological experts would have been badly involved and their research work would have been interrupted if they had not been so protected. Evidently Kuo Mo-jo was too weak politically to be able to shield them. It needed a military man, representing the Liberation Army, to gather the scientists and technologists under his wings. We must bear in mind also that science and technology in China do not exist for their own sake, but for the sake of national defence, which, in its broader sense, includes national construction. Nieh is also a vice-premier. His commission is within the State Council but it enjoys a status higher than the ministries. The function of this commission is to co-ordinate all scientific and technological work and research throughout the country. It also oversees the Academy of Science and other projects of scientific and technological nature under the auspices of the People's Liberation Army which are "classified" or secret, and unknown to the civilians. By "classified" establishments we refer to such projects as nuclear weapon development and to such organs as the "hush-hush" agencies which have no address or signboard.

There are two named universities of science and technology, both established in 1958, which seem to resemble the pair in the United States: the Massachusetts Institute of Technology (MIT) and the California Institute of Technology (Cal. Tech.). The one in Peking is called the University of Science and Technology of Peking; it is under the presidency of Kuo Mo-jo, assisted by a group of vice-presidents of great scientific fame. They are Yen Chi-tzu, Lo Hua-keng, Wu Ju-yang, Wu Yu-hsun, Chien Hsueh-sen, Chien Chih-tao, and Chin Tseng-I. The University covers a group of departments from nuclear physics and nuclear engineering to bio-chemistry and departments for the rare elements. The programme of study is 6 years. In Shanghai, a city more advanced in the development of science and technology than Peking, there is the University of Science and Technology of Shanghai, which is under the presidency of Chou Jen. It has similar departments and its programme of study is from 5 to 6 years.

The efforts in developing science and technology may also

be seen in the publication of books on these subjects, the exchange of contacts with the outside world in what they call "international scientific and technological co-operation", the organization of learned societies, and the convening of scientific and technological conferences. It was reported that between 1949 and 1961 China published 51,900 titles on science and technology, including popular reading. The popularization of science and technology runs parallel to academic research. Between 1959 and 1963, 927 foreign scientific publications were translated and republished in Chinese. There were fifty-seven learned journals according to the 1963 figures. Efforts have been made in recent years to obtain scientific and technical assistance and co-operation from other countries to replace former reliance on the Soviet Union. One can cite many instances of China's success in this attempt, but the political tone is so strong in any of China's manœuvres, that one doubts whether much progress has been made.

Regarding the organization of learned societies, there is a national association called the Association of Science and Technology of the Chinese People's Republic. In this Association are many learned societies, such as the Chinese Mathematics Society, Chinese Physics Society, and a whole chain of Chinese societies of chemistry, geology, archaeology, oceanography and lake study, meteorology, botany, zoology, psychology, astronomy, geography, dynamics, automation, mechanical engineering, civil engineering, architecture, hydraulics, electrical engineering, surveying, textile engineering, chemistry of silicates, electronics, aviation, agriculture, agricultural mechanics, soil science, forestry, entomology, pharmacology, physiology, microbiology, and anatomy. These societies have their branches in the different centres of the country and hold regional as well as national conferences from time to time. It is reported that there were some fifty conferences of a highly specialized and technical nature on the national scale in the year 1965.[24]

Political thinking, that is, Mao Tse-tung's thinking, must be

[24] See *China Monthly*, Hong Kong, April 1966.

the foundation of all scientific research in China today. There is no way of getting round it even in pure mathematics and the pure sciences. Scientists have to read Mao's writings and be able to come forth and tell the great difference between scientific research with Mao's thinking and scientific research without Mao's thinking and how they have been benefited in their scientific research by studying Mao's great thoughts. Some old Chinese scholars in Chinese classical studies thought that they could keep their peace of mind by burying themselves in the old classics and living in a secluded world among the book stacks. They could do so for the first few years, but they have been unearthed and found that there is no refuge from the invasion and bombardment of Marxism–Leninism and Maoism.

Maoism has also gone into revolutionizing the classification of knowledge. All former systems of book classification in Chinese libraries were criticized as unfit for use. In many schools and universities books are now classified under a new system devised by the China People's University in Peking which is said to be based on the scientific classification of knowledge as revealed by Chairman Mao. This system classifies all books under seventeen headings in four main groups.

*First group: Integrated Knowledge.* 1. The works of Marxism–Leninism and Mao Tse-tung. 2. Philosophy, dialectical materialism and historical materialism.

*Second group: Social Sciences.* 3. Social science and political science. 4. Economics, political economy, and economic policy. 5. National defence and military affairs. 6. The State, the law, and legal science. 7. Culture and education. 8. Art. 9. Language and philology. 10. Literature. 11. History and the history of revolution. 12. Geography and economic geography.

*Third group: Natural Sciences.* 13. Natural science. 14. Medicine and health. 15. Engineering and technology. 16. Horticulture, animal husbandry, marine products.

*Fourth group: General Reference.* 17. General reference.

What is of most interest is that under every heading the first few sub-headings are always assigned to Marxism–Leninism. For example : under Heading 3, "Social science and political science", sub-heading 3(1) is "Social science and socialism", sub-heading 3(2) is "Marxist–Leninist political science"; under heading 9, "Language and philology", sub-heading 9(1) is "Marxism and linguistics"; and under heading 12, "Geography and economic geography", sub-heading 12(1) is "The theory of geographic science and Marxism–Leninism", sub-heading 12(2) is "Communistic construction, socialistic construction and the reform of natural geography". In other words, even the classification of knowledge has to be reshuffled to conform to a Communist pattern of thought according to Mao's thinking in terms of materialism, proletarian outlook, and his own way of thinking.

Research work in China includes, of course, other branches of learning than natural science and technology. In anthropology and archaeology, for instance, accomplishments are also very outstanding. However, evidently research work in China today is not well balanced, and achievements are not evenly attained. It may be of interest to quote here the observation of a Swedish scientist, Professor Arne Tiselius, Nobel Prize winner for chemistry in 1948, and President of the Nobel Foundation from 1946 to 1965, who visited China in March and April 1966. He said in Hong Kong after his visit :

> What I saw has led me to believe that in many places the Chinese are doing excellent work in bio-chemistry and fundamental medical research. They are making impressive efforts to build up and intensify scientific research in general and they are also paying great attention to the practical application of their research to agriculture, industry and public health.[25]

It was also reported that he said he had seen many remarkable achievements the Chinese had made in the research field,

[25] *South China Morning Post*, Hong Kong, 12 April 1966.

though he thought Chinese research was very uneven, and in certain fields it had shortcomings though in others it was well advanced. He said that though the younger Chinese research scientists lacked training, this was amply compensated by their enthusiasm.

# CHAPTER 7

# Social, Technological, and International Change

THE modern world is characterized by change. The social, economic, political, and cultural life in the modern world has not only changed, but is still in the process of change, and the change seems to be proceeding at a greater and greater momentum. The academic world today places special emphasis on the phenomenon of change. So a chapter on social, technological, and international change in China is well in place.

If by adaptation to modern change is meant catching up with the advance of the progressive world, and if by that is implied that the advancement of the backward countries in Asia and Africa is to be measured according to the degree they reach to the pattern of the United States which is supposed to be at the frontiers of human experience, one may say that China, under the Communists, has not made and does not aim to make such an adaptation. In fact, the Communists in China challenge the proposition that the Western world is leading mankind forward. The Communist contention is that the Communists are the only people who are capable of leading mankind, and it is only by negating the West that mankind can attain peace and prosperity. Adaptation to social, technological, and international change according to the Western pattern is considered to be unrevolutionary and anti-revolutionary. So that we shall not get ourselves involved in this controversy as to which way of life is to be the mode, we shall disengage ourselves from the question of adaptation altogether and be content with the phenomenon of change alone.

As we have intimated before, agrarian civilization is conservative and static in nature. In as much as Chinese civilization has been essentially agrarian up to modern times, one may say that Chinese life and Chinese society have been stationary and almost changeless for thousands of years. This view of changelessness was expressed by a Western writer at the opening of this century when she said :

> Such a crisis, a mere break-up or change of dynasty, is nothing new to Confucius's people, and China will continue to break up at intervals for thousands of more years to come; the Chinese remaining the one same, homogeneous, unchanging, incomprehensible people— the Chinese, only the Chinese, forever the Chinese, no matter under what alien flag they toil, by what outer people they are conquered, or benevolently protected in inalienable spheres of influence. . . . Defying age and time and progress and the harsh impact of Western civilization, China continues, and will continue, to be China.[1]

What seemed to hold true at the opening of the twentieth century does not hold true in the second half of the century. China is China, but it has certainly changed, and changed to a most astonishing degree—and in certain aspects almost beyond recognition.

One may argue that China has not changed and the Chinese have not changed even now, just as Africa is still Africa and the Negroes are still Negroes. One may also argue that the characteristics of the Chinese have not changed in spite of the apparently sweeping changes under the Communist régime, and that the characteristics of the Chinese will again prevail when the revolutionary storms are over. Whether or not this contention is justified and to what extent it is, only time will tell. Even then, it will depend on one's criteria of change and the aspect of life which one has in mind. We are contented, however, in this chapter with confining our discussion to the presentation of the social, technological, and international changes that have taken place in Chinese society in the last two decades, once more evading another dispute.

[1] *China: The Long-lived Empire*, by Eliza Ruhamah Scidmore, Century Co., New York, 1902. p. 2.

Before we proceed further, a word may be said of the concept of change in the mind of the Chinese. Whether or not the Chinese mind is dynamic and whether or not dialectics is native to Chinese philosophy, is a question we shall not take up here. But we must say that the concept of perpetual change is definitely not alien to Chinese thinking. One may recall that among the six classics[2] of China, there is *Yi Ching* (the *Book of Change*), which though very difficult to interpret, is, without doubt, on the principles of Change. It has often been quoted from *Yi Ching, chiung tse pien, pien tse tung,* which means "when one change has run its course, alteration follows; and by resorting to change, the way is open again". Being freer from religious dogmas and from the concept of the absolute than the way of thinking in other cultures, the Chinese mind might be more susceptible to change. It is perhaps with this unrestrained mood of mind that the Chinese people have been able to survive their trials and adversities. This view is supported by the fact that the Chinese are found in almost every corner of the world. It is probably their ability to adapt themselves to new situations that accounts for their successful migration. They adapt themselves to alien situations instead of demanding that the native peoples change their situation to suit them, as Western colonialists have been doing.

While it may be true that the Chinese are not a static people, one must submit that there had been considerable conservatism towards any change that was being introduced. This conservatism was seen in the attitude of the Chinese leaders during their adoption of modern education in the Ching Dynasty. Though they realized the need to accept Western learning, they were unwilling to forsake their own native culture. So we see that Chang Chi-tung, the chief exponent of the modern schools at that time, advocated in his famous treatise *An Exhortation to Learning,* published in 1903, the dualistic policy *chung hsueh*

---

[2] The six ancient classics are: *Shi Ching* (Book of Odes), *Shu Ching* (Book of History), *Yi Ching* (Book of Change), *Li Chi* (Book of Rites), *Yo Ching* (Book of Music), and *Chin Chiu* (The Annals of Spring and Autumn).

*wei ti, hsi hsueh wei yung* which may be translated as "Chinese learning as principle and Western learning as practice". In spite of criticisms from time to time, Chang's motto has never been completely repudiated. There have been times when Western culture was exalted and Chinese culture was attacked, such as the call for "wholesale Westernization" in the 1930's and the call for scrapping all remnants of the old culture by the Red Guards in 1966. Yet, in the main, the desire to retain the native culture has always been strong. In the final analysis, one must admit that conservatism is characteristic of the Chinese.

With these introductory remarks, let us proceed to the discussion of social, technological, and international change in China in the last 19 years since the establishment of the People's Republic.

## SOCIAL CHANGE

In the foregoing pages we have separately touched on two factors in China which have been deterrents to change : one is the conservative nature of its basically agrarian civilization, and the other is the Confucian outlook of returning to the ways of the ancients. In spite of such deterrents, there have been changes from time to time. The contact with the West in the last 100 years has accelerated change in many directions. We shall be speaking here in this section of the major features of social change in China since the Communist assumption of power; but we must not forget that there had been social changes in China all along prior to the Communist régime. For example, Western books on China 50 years ago used to contain illustrations of the Chinese men with queues and Chinese women with bound feet as outstanding Chinese features. But such features had passed into oblivion long before the appearance of Communists in China.

Social change in China in the last 19 years, however, has taken a new line. It has been brought about in accordance with Communist ideology. We have discussed this in part, in connection with social and economic complex and with formative institutions. In order not to over-repeat, we shall take up here the aspects of social change in connection with the series of social movements which have been sweeping through China.

Naturally it is the goal of all revolution to destroy the old order and to set up the new in its place. It would not be revolution if it did not do so. For the Chinese Communists the goal is to destroy the old social order of feudalism, capitalism, landlordism, imperialism, compradorism, and to set up in its stead a new social order of the working class, of the proletariat. In upsetting the table, the order of social values is turned upside down, and, in a real sense, as the Bible says, "The first shall be last, and the last first".

For the non-revolutionaries, there was a period of a year or so of relative peace of mind after the establishment of the People's Republic in October 1949. Except for the prominent Kuomintang officials and their army officers who had been outstanding in anti-Communist activities (particularly those who had blood-debts to be paid) the population was in relative peace. One may recall that in 1949 and 1950, people were free to move about, not only within the country, but also to leave China for Hong Kong and from there abroad without any restriction. Many Chinese went in and out of China as before. Indeed, many businessmen, bourgeois, and intellectuals who had fled from Shanghai to Hong Kong because of fear of Communist restriction returned to Shanghai to live. It was only after January 1951 that permits were required to leave the country, and permits were not too difficult to get in the early years. We mention the relatively free movement of persons in the first 2 years just to show the atmosphere of social ease in China in that period when the bourgeois classes and the intellectuals were enjoying a rightful place in the new régime.

But to the revolutionaries, of course, that was not how things should be. To the Chinese Communists that state of affairs was just marking time. It was their tactic to keep the bourgeoisie and intellectuals from being scared away so that they would have a larger "catch" for later use and transformation. For them the *status quo* must not be maintained. The population must be converted into a revolutionary mass which must not only be changed but must be in perpetual change. It has to be kept stirred, as it were, so that it cannot be at rest, just as a basin of muddy water is kept stirred so that no particle has a chance to precipitate. We shall not speak of the rectification campaigns which take place from time to time within the party to streamline the members' thinking, nor of the ceaseless campaign to liquidate what they call anti-revolutionary elements. We shall review the outstanding campaigns or social movements which affect the masses. We shall take them up in their sequential order as far as feasible. The movements which we have already discussed or which we shall discuss in other connections will only be mentioned briefly just for the sake of completing the picture. We shall give a fuller acount of the latest movement, the Great Proletarian Cultural Revolution.

### The Land Reform (1950)

We have spoken of the land reform before. What we want to stress here is its nature as a social movement. It is wrong to conceive of it as something that involved only the landlords and rich peasants and only those who lived in the countryside. As a social movement, everyone was thrown into it whether he was a landlord or not a landlord, whether he was a rural dweller or a city dweller. No one could stand aside to watch as a spectator. If he was not an object of struggle, he must be an active participant on the side of the revolution. Now, though landlordism has been abolished and the Chinese farm has been completely transformed, the social labels of the former landlords and the rich and middle peasants still give them a political handicap whenever a social movement is on. Besides, their sons and daughters and their kinsmen still have to suffer from their damaging social status.

## *The Anti-American Aid-Korea Movement (1950–3)*

We have also mentioned the Anti-American Aid-Korea Movement. We must add that, internally, it was used to intensify the image of America as the leading imperialist and the "paper tiger". It tried to mar all the pretty images that had existed in the minds of the Chinese people regarding America, American people, and things American. In spite of the fact that America has never had any colony or concession in China as had Great Britain, France, Germany, Italy, Russia, and Japan, the Chinese Communists have succeeded, at least apparently, in portraying America as China's No. 1 enemy and the greatest imperialistic country in the world. This is in agreement with the Stalin line of tactics for world revolution, in which the United States is portrayed as the major symbol of imperialism.

## *The Three-anti and Five-anti Movement (1951–2)*

The Three-anti Movement was for the purification of the cadres in the government while the Five-anti Movement was for the re-education of the bourgeoisie in private industry and private business in the early stage of the People's Republic. In December 1951 when the Three-anti Movement was launched by the People's Government among its cadres, the people (particularly the city folk and bourgeoisie) were happy to watch the cadres whom they had disliked being purged. But no sooner were they spectators than they were thrown into the Five-anti Movement in January 1952 which was created for them by the Government. As a result of the Five-anti Movement many suicides were committed in the cities in China by businessmen and proprietors. The Chinese Communists never permit the people to be idle and interested spectators of their party purges or government purges.

By "three-anti" is meant anti-graft and corruption, anti-wastefulness, and anti-bureaucracy. And by "five-anti" is meant anti-bribery, anti-evasion from taxation, anti-theft from State property and money, anti-cheating by means of substandard work and substandard material, and anti-theft of the State's economic information. By means of discussions, lectures, criticism, self-criticism, group struggles against individuals, public denunciation and trials, the Chinese people who had been slack in public discipline, whose government had been known for corruption, whose officials had been used to graft, and whose civilians had been used to bribery, took a stimulating lesson for a more regulated way of social living and economic living. As we have said, people are now brought to such a high degree of consciousness in the new socialistic ethics that the offering of a cigarette or a cup of tea to a visitor is considered to be associated with bribery on the part of the giver and graft on the part of the receiver, and associated with social corruption in general. These two movements, like other social movements, did bring in a lot of good to Chinese society; but again, as in other social movements, the price the people had to pay, many of them innocent, was too high.

## *The Patriotic Sanitation Movement (1952)*

One may wonder why a movement for health and sanitation should have to be connected with patriotism. The reply is that the Chinese Communists like to use powerful and captivating terms for whatever they want to do. Besides, the movement was launched at the time of the Anti-America Aid-Korea Campaign and there were good causes to associate sanitation with the anti-imperialistic war, when the Chinese were accusing the Americans of employing bacterial warfare in Korea.

Since 1952 the sanitation movement has persisted, at certain times more vigorously and at other times less vigorously. For instance, as a measure to prepare for the celebration on 1 October every year the Patriotic Sanitation Campaign is revived to welcome the National Day. The Liberation Army people have been very useful in the example they set and in their insistence on cleanliness. Of course the Liberation Army is not the only body that took an active lead. Organizations of all kinds, occupations of all kinds, and people of all kinds, not the least the medical personnel and the people who handle food, also played an important role. This movement has brought about a change in people's conceptions of social and personal living as well as in their social and personal habits. One may note that among all the social movements in China in the last 19 years, it is perhaps only this sanitation movement which has saved rather than caused many lives. However, birds such as sparrows and domestic animals such as dogs were killed in huge numbers in the name of patriotism and sanitation. The success in killing off flies won the high praise of foreign visitors to China who came out to tell the world of this clean land which had been notorious for over a century for its unsanitary conditions.

*Thought Reform (1952– )*

It can be said that the thought reform began to take its form as a social movement as early as 1952. We must hasten to say that thought reform should not be regarded as a movement which took place once upon a time and is now over, nor as a movement independent of itself or unaffected by other movements. Whenever the question of ideology is involved, there is thought reform. What the Communists are doing in China is instilling the new ideology in the minds of the people as a basis of the Communistic social order. Since their method is so thorough and yet so crude, it has been called "brain washing". The term depicts most accurately the mental and spiritual torture which the American prisoners of war in Korea once went through and which the Chinese intellectuals have been undergoing all these years.

In the earlier days thought reform was for the general correction of people's habits of thought and manners of life. One of the common practices in those days was for an individual to relate to the group to which he belonged his life history from the age of 10 and to criticize his past "sins" of commission and omission from the standpoint of the new society's ideals as far as he understood them. If he had been rude to his servant, if he had feared communism, if he had been indulged in luxurious living, if he had tried to make a name for himself, he would make his repentance, not only by self-flogging but also by pointing out the ideological basis of his unbecoming behaviour. If his story was incomplete, that is, if he had only mentioned the minor things in his past life, leaving out the major ones, or if he had failed to trace the causes of his past errors to their deeper roots, or if he was not earnest in his self-criticism, he would have to give another account in another group meeting, until his case was accepted by the group.

In every case the confession was under the supervision of a Communist cadre who had been trained to conduct the thought reform campaign. Younger persons who had little history, or those who had no social enemies, or those who had never been prominent in any way, had their cases dismissed in the first round. Older people who had lived in the Kuomintang régime or who were socially prominent or who had offended people of proletarian status, would be accused of being liars and hypocrites, of concealing their history and being evasive. They had to write pages and pages of their history as many times as necessary to satisfy the group and the cadre in charge. Since the jury was composed of the mob, those who had cases to answer were tremendously worried.

It may not have been the intention of the Communist Party to waste so many lives in the campaign. But since the people had never experienced such mob rule before, which went far beyond the realm of reason and decency, many conscientious people simply could not stand it. Many suicides were committed because of the strain and the torture. Now, with more experience, some Chinese have become wiser and learned to adapt themselves to such reformative processes.

Another form which the thought reform took at that stage was the denunciation of certain outstanding intellectual figures who had nationwide influence, such as the great Chinese scholar

Hu Shih, and an outstanding philosopher, Liang Shu-ming, for their idealistic philosophy and capitalistic, bourgeois, and individualistic thinking.

Thought reform in Communist China deserves a study of its own. As a matter of fact, it may require many intensive studies to give the subject an adequate treatment. Interesting as it is to see how Hu Shih, particularly, was attacked in 1955 as a case study of the thought reform, we find no space to go into that subject here.

Without going back to the pre-1949 days of the thought reform of intellectuals in the Communist capital of Yenan, we may cite the first act of thought reform in China which started in 1951 in connection with the case of Wu Hsun. Wu Hsun was an illiterate in Shantung Province in the Ching Dynasty who had used all the money he obtained from begging to establish free schools for children. He had been praised all along as a saint of the poor and a champion of popular education. After the Communists came into power, the story of Wu Hsun was made into a motion picture as a new venture of art to praise the efforts of the poor. Comments on the film were very favourable. Editorials in the newspapers were giving the man as well as the film high praise. Kuo Mo-jo was among those who gave loud eulogy. Soon the matter caught the attention of the theorists of the Chinese Communist Party who pointed out that Wu Hsun could not be the symbol of proletarian heroism. He was, indeed, an enemy of the proletariat. He was a hound of the landlords and officialdom. At once articles and editorials appeared in newspapers all over the country attacking Wu Hsun and the ideology harboured by those who had expressed the former views. The film was suspended. Kuo Mo-jo came forth to admit his error and to denounce himself. So did the others. We shall not go into the subject further, except to point out that the case of Wu Hsun was studied in the whole country as a first lesson of proletarian ideology from which to learn discrimination between what is a worthy man and what is not a worthy man, between what is good social behaviour and what is poor social behaviour.

Thought reform came in a big sweeping way in the Anti-rightist Movement of 1957, the Socialist Education Movement of 1958–9, and in the Great Proletarian Cultural Revolution of 1966. In every case, the intellectuals, particularly the high intellectuals and the old intellectuals, were the hardest hit.

### The "Hundred Flowers Bloom and Hundred Schools Contend" Movement (1956–7)

This was not exactly a social movement; but its "come-back", the Anti-rightist Movement, was. Since we cannot understand the Anti-rightist Movement without reference to this event, we must treat it as a movement for the sake of convenience.

To the old Chinese intellectuals this brief period of the blossoming of art and the contention of thought was a period of vitality and optimism. They compared its short appearance to the transitory opening of the night-blooming cereus which fades as soon as it blooms.

The phrase, *Pei Hua Chi Fang* (Hundred Flowers Bloom) and particularly the phrase *Pei Chia Tseng Ming* (Hundred Schools Contend) were originally phrases of praise of the *Chan Kuo* (Warring States) period known also as the Period of the Philosophers, prior to the unification of China by Chin Shih Huang, when there was the free play of ideas which has made Chinese philosophy so rich and won for that period the name of "the golden age" in spite of its political turmoil.

As we have said, the phrase "The Hundred Flowers Bloom", or "Let the Hundred Flowers Bloom", referred to operatic and dramatic art. As a slogan to encourage theatrical art it was used by Mao Tse-tung very early when the Communist capital was still in Yenan. In a banner which he presented to the artistes at that time, on the occasion of the establishment of the Peiping (Peking) Opera House there, he inscribed these words : *Pei hua ch'i fang, t'ui ch'en ch'u hsin*, which mean "[Let] the hundred flowers bloom; pushing out the old comes the new". In the First National Operatic Exhibition in Peking in 1952, Mao again wrote those words to indicate his pleasure over the performances and over the way operatic art was being promoted. Many other national theatrical exhibitions then took place in Peking in the following years.

In 1956, when Mao was still pursuing a liberal policy, that is before he adopted the hard line of the Socialistic Main Line, he was thinking of giving the intellectuals the same freedom as he allowed the artistes. He announced a parallel motto to be applied to learning. The phrases "Let the Hundred Schools Contend" and "Let the Hundred Flowers Bloom" pair very well, and their connotations are very familiar to the Chinese traditional world. If we trace the date when those two phrases were used in People's China, we would find their first appearance in Mao Tse-tung's address at the Supreme State Council Meeting on 2 May 1956 in which he summoned the people to put into practice the policy "[Let] the Hundred Flowers Bloom; [let] the Hundred Schools Contend" for the furtherance of creative works of literature and art and of learning and research. Mao, supported by those who were close to him at that time, was probably very confident of the prospects of communism—that communism was not afraid of being challenged. As he had said, since Marxist ideas had triumphed over bourgeois ideas even under the bourgeois régime in the past, they would undoubtedly triumph under the Communistic régime today. He was not aware of the seriousness such a motto might lead to. That was before the uprising in Hungary and the emergence of the leftists within the ranks of the Chinese Communist Party.

However, the Hundred Schools Contend Movement freely ran its own course under the leadership of the old intellectuals (many of whom belonged to the minor democratic political parties); and as it soon seemed to be getting out of bounds, the propaganda chief of the Chinese Communist Party, Lu Ting-yi, came out to give his warning. He said that the Hundred Flowers Bloom Movement was to be confined to the realm of art and the Hundred Schools Contend Movement was to be confined to the realm of natural science. By that he meant that the contention was not to be for the realm of politics, economics, and philosophy. He said that just as atheism was not allowed in a temple, so idealism could not be allowed in a Communistic Society. In spite of his warning in a speech on 26 May 1956, some old intellectuals and minor political partisans continued their free expression through a misunderstanding of some of the statements Mao Tse-tung had made. This brought them endless trouble when the Anti-Rightist Movement came.

## The Anti-Rightist Movement (1957–8)

The official order for the launching of the Anti-Rightist Movement came on 22 June 1957 in the editorial of *Renmin Ribao* (*People's Daily*) entitled "An Unusual Spring". The editorial came at the time when the convention of the First National People's Congress's Fourth Session was held in Peking. The word "spring" in the title of the editorial was for the purpose of rebutting some earlier articles by leading writers who were later branded as rightists and whose articles had the word "spring" in their titles, which had been used to glorify the free air of that year's early spring. The convention was immediately turned into a barrage of speeches directed against the rightists under the general theme : "To crack down and shatter the Rightists' Attack". The movement's main targets were the leaders in the academic, educational, cultural, literary, and political circles who had been outspoken in their criticism of the Government and the party, the great majority of whom were not Communist Party members. One of the immediate results was removal from their posts as delegates to the National People's Congress. Among the most outstanding figures were Lo Lung-chi, Tseng Chao-lun, Lung Yun, and the Communist woman writer Ting Ling.

The movement went on for a full year in the vigour of a revolutionary struggle. Many public and intellectual leaders of the past were labelled as "rightists" and were sent to labour camps for hard labour. They were practically never heard of again. The lesser "offenders" were excommunicated until they were rehabilitated after a number of years, at which time the "rightist cap" was removed from them and they were permitted to live a normal social life again. Sympathy for the rightists was so severely punished that the rightists' mental and social sufferings of excommunication were very real. A visitor from Hong Kong saw a Chinese pastor whom he had known sitting in a far corner of the church in Canton. As he wanted to approach him, he was stopped by his companion, who told him that the pastor had been named a "rightist", and any contact with him would only bring trouble to himself and greater persecution to the pastor.

Now that to be a rightist in China is criminal while a leftist is not, one may say that the Chinese Communist Party has now committed itself to leftism. It has gone to the extent that even what should be properly called "leftist infantile sickness" or "leftist infantilism" is encouraged, though Lenin had criticized it and Mao Tse-tung had once agreed.

## The Three Red Flags (1958– )

The Great Leap Forward, the People's Commune, and the Socialistic Main Line formed what the Chinese Communists have called "the Three Red Flags". The Socialistic Main Line was really the main flag. In spite of the fact that it is many years now since the three flags were hoisted, they are still being waved. Indeed, the Socialistic Main Line red flag is waving higher. It was under that banner that the Great Proletarian Cultural Revolution arose in the spring of 1966. The three red flags policy evidently did not have the unanimous support of the leaders of the Chinese Communist Party. It is because of their scepticism of this party line at this stage of China's development that they have been purged in the Proletarian Cultural Revolution. Among them are Peng Te-huai, Chou Yang, Peng Chen, and Teng To. They are accused of criticizing the Great Leap Forward, the People's Commune, and the Socialistic Main Line, calling the three red flags the three black flags.

The three red flags are not three separate goals of achievement. The People's Commune was a definite agricultural institution, which has already been set up. It was to replace individual farming, co-operative farming, and semi-socialistic farming. It is a flag that has already been planted on the Chinese farm since 1959. Although, evidently, individualistic inclinations or what the Chinese Communists call capitalistic thinking have to be weeded out from time to time on account of socialistic neglect, the People's Commune is, by and large, a settled affair. The flag of the Socialistic Main Line, as the name indicates, is a line of thought and a line of action which could apply to the farm (as in the case of the People's Commune), or to the school (as in the case of preferential admission for children of the proletariat). It was not only the main flag but also the ever-waving flag.

The flag of Great Leap Forward is a matter of the bounding spirit required in a revolution; that is to say, it is the spirit "to do and to dare", to do and to dare what the conservative would consider to be too early, too quick, too much, too fast, too far, too extreme. It is rather a sub-flag of the Socialistic Main Line, to indicate the spirit in which the movement should be launched. To leap forward means not to go at a slow pace and speed or to wait and see. It is more a matter of accepting the impulse of a subjective urge than of acting according to objective and careful consideration. It indicates a certain amount of anxiety, impatience, and aggressiveness on the part of those who are in command. To leap is not to walk on two feet; it is to jump and to skip.

One has little right to question the hoisting of the Socialistic Main Line red flag in Red China. Since the whole world, including the capitalistic countries, has been moving toward the direction of socialism, there is no reason to question China for moving to this direction, particularly since its adoption of the 1954 Constitution. People may question, however, the wisdom of the speed and manner in which it should move. One may say that it is principally in this matter of speed and manner that the Chinese Communist leaders disagree. It is perhaps also in this matter of the speed and manner in which the world revolution should be brought about that the Chinese Communist leaders and the Soviet Communist leaders disagree. It is because of this disagreement that some Communist leaders in China are purged by the Red Guards, and perhaps also because of this disagreement that the rift has widened between the Chinese and the Soviet Union. Since the Great Leap Forward and the Socialistic Main Line, like the People's Commune, arose from Mao Tse-Tung's initiative, we find the clue to the intensive study of Mao Tse-tung's thoughts in recent years, and to the Great Proletarian Cultural Revolution which has shocked the world since the year 1966.

## *Movement for the Study of Mao Tse-tung's Thoughts (1960– )*

Mao Tse-tung's writings had been documents of study by the Communist Party members at various times as they were published and as occasion arose. Mao's line of thought has become the party line since he gained leadership in the party, particularly after he had defeated the Li Li-shan Line or Li Lishanism. This line Mao had criticized in 1930 as too radical and extreme.[3] The great prominence given to Mao's works came only after the Communist Party succeeded in completely taking over the Chinese mainland. The success won for him the unprecedented prestige within as well as outside the party. The truism is: "Nothing succeeds like success." A personal cult developed gradually in the image of Russia's Stalin. Following the example of Stalin, whose works were compiled in the Soviet Union, Mao's *Selected Works* began to be compiled as early as 1950, the first volume of the standard four-volume edition

---

[3] Mao Tse-tung's own words, as he was recounting the history of the Chinese Soviet government in 1929 and 1930, said: "In expanding Soviet areas [in China] in general the programme of the Red Army favoured wave-like or tidal development, rather than an uneven advance gained by 'leaps' or 'jumps', and without deep consolidation in the territories gained. The policy was pragmatical, just as were the tactics

appeared as early as 1951.[4] In order to boost their significance, they have been translated into many languages,[5] implying that they contain a universal truth for international communism.

The enthusiasm for a personal cult lapsed for some time when such a cult was under attack in the Soviet Union in connection with the movement of de-Stalinization. However, as the Sino–Soviet split came into the open, the personal cult was resumed in China. It was to fulfil both the ambitions of a dictator and the longings of hero-worshippers. Now it has become official as an open challenge to the line taken by the Soviet Party since the death of Stalin. What had taken place in the Soviet Union during the Stalin era in the glorification of Stalin, as revealed in the book *I want to be like Stalin*,[6] is now repeating itself in China today.

The study of Mao Tse-tung's thoughts became intensified after

---

*Footnote 3 (continued)*

already described, and grew out of many years of collective military and political experience. These tactics were severely criticized by Li Li-san, who advocated the concentration of all weapons in the hands of the Red Army, and the absorption of all partisan groups. He wanted attacks rather than consolidation; advances without securing the rear; sensational assaults on big cities, accompanied by uprisings and extremism. . . . But Li Li-san overestimated both the military strength of the Red Army at that time and the revolutionary factors in the national political scene. He believed that the revolution was nearing success and would shortly have power over the entire country. . . . With the events in Hunan, the Red Army's return to Kiangsi, and especially after the capture of Kian, 'Lilisanism' was overcome in the army; and Li himself, proved to have been in error, soon lost his influence in the Party." (Edgar Snow, *Red Star Over China*, Chapter 6, "Growth of the Red Army", pp. 159–163, Random House, New York, 1938.)

[4] Vol. 1, containing Mao's writings from 1926 to 1937, arranged in historical order, as all the four volumes are, was published in October 1951. But Volume 4, containing his writings from 1945 to 1949, was not published until September 1960.

[5] Mao's articles were translated into many foreign languages. The *Selected Works* of Mao Tse-tung in the standard four volumes have been officially translated and published in English, French, Spanish, and Russian. For internal use they have been translated into many languages of the national minorities. Imitating the Christian Bible, they are now also published in Braille.

[6] *I want to be like Stalin*, by B. P. Yesipov and N. K. Goncharov, translated and prefaced by George S. Counts, John Day, New York, 1947.

1960. This study is done in two ways. One is to study Mao's works directly; the other is to study indirectly through the exemplary heroes whose claims to "Communistic sainthood" lay in their devoted study of Mao's writings and their faithful observance of his words.

Mao's works appear in several forms. There are Mao's *Selected Works* in four volumes, Mao's essays in pamphlets, and the quotations of Mao Tse-tung. The quotations are in the most concise form, now often read in unison by groups and mass meetings, as one would repeat the classics in the Chinese schoolrooms in the past or recite catechisms in the Catholic Church. We should note that all along there had been political lessons in the schools and universities. But Marxism–Leninism was taught, and not Mao Tse-tung's works. In order to give the study of Mao's thoughts its new emphasis, it has been decided to specify it in the curriculum. Schools and universities are naturally criticized for having neglected the study of Mao's works in the past. So are the government publication houses criticized for failing to supply enough copies to meet the demands of the public.

Even Mao's picture is now associated with Maoist study. This is designed to associate the study of Mao's works with hero worship or even divine reverence. It is surprising that such a reactionary mentality could be entertained, being so different from the spirit of the Chinese Renaissance and so diametrically opposed to the essence of the anti-feudalistic revolution which is supposed to be going on in China today. Now it becomes a fashion or even a "must" to have Mao's works displayed prominently on one's desk, to hang Mao's picture in a respectful place in one's room, and to post Mao's sayings on the walls of one's home and office. These are the outward signs of study. To go deeper one has to learn his thoughts thoroughly and to apply them in a lively way.

By upholding the examples of heroic figures whose attainments were attributed to having learned Mao's teachings well, the significance of Mao's thoughts for everyday behaviour is demonstrated. The first case came into use in the campaign "Learn from Lei Feng" in February 1963. It was followed by "Learn from Ouyang Hai" in February 1964, "Learn from Wang Chieh" in November 1965, "Learn from Mai Hsien-te" in February 1966, and "Learn from Liu Ying-chun" in March 1966.[7] We cite five among a dozen of such examples of national heroes. With the exception of Mai Hsien-te, who is still living, all of them have died and were unknown before their heroic deeds. These heroes were picked from the Liberation Army, partly to co-ordinate the campaign "To Study Mao Tse-tung's Thoughts" with the campaign "To Learn from the Liberation Army", and partly to pacify the Liberation Army by stepping up their social and political status.

The fact that all these heroes were in their early twenties is significant. It indicates the desire to select from among the budding generation dauntless youths as successors to the Communist Revolution. In many cases the source of their virtues and their strength is traced to their daily devotion to the study of Mao Tse-tung's thoughts, reading Mao's writings, pledging to obey Mao's words, helping others to love and to follow Mao's teachings, and carrying with them wherever they went the pictures of Chairman Mao as symbols of loyalty. Diaries are

[7] Lei Feng, a native of Hunan Province, died on 15 August 1963 at the age of 22. He was an army truck driver attached to an engineering unit, who was killed while directing a driver to back a truck.

Ouyang Hai, a native of Hunan Province and a corporal in the People's Liberation Army, died on 18 November 1963 at the age of 23. In preventing the collision of a passenger train and an artillery carriage drawn by a frightened horse, he lost his legs and died.

Wang Chieh, a native of Shantung Province and a corporal in the Liberation Army's engineering corps, died on 14 July 1965 at the age of 23. He threw himself over an exploding bomb which killed him but saved his comrades from injury.

Mai Hsien-te, a native of Kwangtung Province, and a mechanic in a gunboat, while in action in a sea battle with the Nationalists, received a brain injury. With superhuman endurance, he bore the pains of his wounds to perform his duties for 3 hours until the battle was over.

Liu Ying-chun, a native of Heilungkiang Province and a soldier in an artillery unit of the Liberation Army, died on 15 March 1965 at the age of 21. In his efforts to restrain a horse, which was drawing an artillery cart, from running into six children he was fatally injured.

published which are alleged to have been written by the young heroes during their lifetime, indicating how their lives had been indebted to Mao's guidance and enlightenment. The glorification of the dead heroes whose lives are already sealed is safe, but it seems a bit risky to glorify a young man who is still living and whose age in 1966 is only 21, as the case of Mai Hsien-te.

It is not inconceivable that out of millions of Chinese youth there could not be found some activists who subscribed so completely to Mao's thoughts that they found themselves transformed through the inspiration of Mao's life and teaching, particularly as such youth came from families which had had no chance of an education and as Mao's works were the only intellectual material available to them. The fact that such heroes are so few as to require national exaltation is a reflection of the great efforts sustained in picking out good examples.

The older people whose thinking is more seasoned cannot subscribe to Mao's thoughts in the same naïve way. To them the validity of Mao's ideas is questionable. There are, after all, many self-contradictions. Li Ta, one of the four living founders of the Chinese Communist Party and chancellor of the University of Wuhan[8] (Hupei), and chairman of the China Philosophical Society until he was recently purged, was asked in 1962 to express his views regarding Mao's articles "On Practice" and "On Contradiction". He made the following remark: "Chairman Mao's articles 'On Practice' and 'On Contradiction' were written 20 and more years ago. As they were written when he was extremely busy, the ideas expressed there are not necessarily very accurate." He continued by quoting a famous phrase from the great scholar of the Tang Dynasty, Han Yu, *wei chen yen chih wu chu* (which means "the old writings should be cast aside"), implying that Mao's works were "old stuff" and should be discarded.

---

[8] Wuhan is an abbreviation for the three cities Wuchang, Hankow, and Hanyang in Hupei Province at the Yangtze River. Though the romanization is the same as that of the name of the deposed vice-mayor of Peking, the Chinese characters are entirely different.

Again, when a young activist went to the University of Wuhan to talk on Mao Tse-tung's philosophy, Li Ta said: "This is a satire on the University of Wuhan and a big joke. If a 14-year-old kid talks about philosophy when he is not clear as to what matter is and what ideology is, how can it be philosophy worthy of the name?" It is because of his maturity that Li Ta finds such works and such study campaigns questionable; and it is exactly because of this attitude of his that he was attacked as anti-Mao and anti-party in the Cultural Revolution of 1966. Li Ta is not alone. He is only one among a great many old Chinese intellectuals sharing these views. Again, it is because of the large number of old intellectuals who hold such views, particularly those in the high places of the party, that a purge was necessary, the criterion of which was submission to Mao's thoughts.

## *The Great Proletarian Cultural Revolution (1966– )*

We speak of the Great Proletarian Cultural Revolution[9] here as a sequel to the series of social movements that have gone before. We have touched on this subject before, and we shall try to avoid unnecessary repetitions.

Since the policy of the Socialistic Main Line was announced in 1958, there had been pressure all along to forge this hard line of action. More recent instances were the attack on the *Hsi Chu P'ao* (*Dramatics Magazine*) which was published under the directorship of Tien Han, one of China's greatest modern dramatists, in October 1964; the general attack on Chinese classical operas by Tao Chu in July 1965; the attack

---

[9] The Great Proletarian Cultural Revolution is sometimes translated as Great Socialist Cultural Revolution, as has been done by the Foreign Language Press, the Communist Party organ for foreign propaganda in Peking. The term *wu chan tseh chi*, as it appears in the Chinese, should be translated only as "proletariat". Certainly "socialist" is not identical with "proletariat". It is probably that for Western consumption the Chinese Communists want to tone down the pitch of their movement.

on Wu Han which appeared first in the *Wen Hui Pao* in Shanghai in November 1965 by Yao Wen-yuan; and the attack on Tien Han's opera, *Hsieh Yao Huan*, by the *Renmin Ribao* (*People's Daily*) in Peking in February 1966.

The sharp turn of events came in February 1966 when the *Renmin Ribao* (*People's Daily*), which had been commenting favourably on Wu Han's play, suddenly changed its attitude and attacked it as a "poisonous weed", a term now used in China, following Mao's usage, to brand all literature which they consider to be anti-socialistic in nature. This sudden change brought about not only the change in political policy of the party organ but also the change of top authorities who had been in control of the party mouthpiece. Following the denunciation of Wu Han's play, came the denunciation of Wu Han himself; then came the denunciation of Wu Han's thoughts; then came the denunciation of those who tolerated Wu Han's "anti-party" line of thought as well as those who had been writing along the same line. This line of thought the leaders of the Great Proletarian Cultural Revolution call bourgeois, unrevolutionary, anti-socialistic, anti-revolutionary, and thus pro-revisionist, contrary to Mao Tse-tung's thinking, anti-Mao, and anti-Party.

*A case study of Wu Han and his play.* As an aid to our understanding of the events which unravelled in the Great Proletarian Cultural Revolution, let us direct our attention to the case study of Wu Han and his play. We may be able to see there the thread that runs through the whole campaign.

Firstly, Wu Han's play, *Hai Jui Dismissed from Office*, was a historical play, giving high praise to a great official of the Ming Dynasty by the name of Hai Jui (1514–87) who, because of the outspoken and straightforward manner in which he appealed on behalf of his suffering people, was dismissed from high office. The play was written in late 1960, one year after Peng Te-huai, the famed commander-in-chief of the Chinese Volunteer Army in the Korean War, was dismissed from the office of Defence Minister on account of his outspoken criticism of Mao Tse-tung's policy of the three red flags in the Conference of the Eighth Session of the Eighth Congress of the Chinese Communist Party at Lu Shan (Kiangsi Province) in August 1959.

For 3 years after Wu's play was written and performed, it was very well received. The critics were happy about it; so also, of course, was the playwright himself. But literature and dramatics in general began to be attacked after 1962, following the Conference of the Tenth Plenary Session of the Eighth Central Committee of the Party, for not serving the proletarian cause. The writers, most of whom were Communists, were accused of glorifying some dynastic figures, sketching portraits of neutral figures and serving the bourgeois cause. Among the critics were Peng Chen, the recently deposed Mayor of Peking, who might have been forced by circumstances to be critical too, in spite of the fact that Peking had been the centre of such literature, operatic art, and publications, for many years. In late 1965, *Hai Jui Dismissed from Office*, written by Wu Han, underwent sharp political scrutiny. He was accused of using events of the past to criticize the affairs of the present, using the dismissal of Hai Jui to reflect on the dismissal of Peng Te-huai,[10] and using double talk to attack the Government. This was serious. This meant criticism of Mao and the party. It is interesting to note that the chief spokesman of the Great Proletarian Cultural Revolution was none other than Lin Piao, the very man who replaced Peng Te-huai as the Minister of Defence after Peng's dismissal.

Secondly, the official position of Wu Han as a vice-mayor of Peking was of immense significance—not because of his own importance as a vice-mayor, but because of the importance of his superior, Peng Chen, who was the mayor. Again, Peking is

[10] The accusations were based on the allegation that the events were of a "double talk" nature or contained ambiguity directed against the party. Persecutions of the intellectuals were common in Chinese history. Chinese history has a special term for persecution of this kind. It is called *wen tze yu*, which means "imprisonment on account of literature". The most notorious cases are found in the history of the Han Dynasty, the Ming Dynasty, and the Ching Dynasty.

the capital and Peng Chen was mayor of Peking ever since the establishment of the People's Republic in 1949 until his removal in the summer of 1966. Peng Chen was the chief executive of the Communist Party Municipal Committee in Peking, which is by far the strongest and most influential regional party committee in the whole country. Many top Communist leaders are registered in Peking, and their membership to the National People's Congress originate from the Peking electorate. These delegates include Mao Tse-tung, Liu Shao-chi, Chou En-lai, Teng Hsiao-ping, and Peng Chen. Of course, since the Central Government is there, and all the ministries, and since all big national events take place there, Peng Chen's position was obviously very strategic. He could easily take over the reins of National Government should Mao Tse-tung pass away. If another person aspired to be Mao's successor, and particularly if he were not one of Peng Chen's group, he would have to break down the Party Municipal Committee in Peking before Mao dies. This is what Lin Piao seemed to be doing in the name of the Great Proletarian Cultural Revolution.

Thirdly, the fact that Wu Han was a high intellectual and a well-known writer made his position more delicate. In attacking his historical play, other historical plays are attacked: this involved a play on a historical event of the Han Dynasty, *Hsieh Yao Huen*. In the attack on Wu Han, other writers of similar views were attacked. This embroiled Teng To,[11] who was the writer of a series of short articles in the *Peking Evening News* entitled "Evening Chats at Yenshan",[12] and a contributor to the series of short sketches on Chinese cultural topics in the *Chien Hsen (Frontline)*, a fortnightly magazine, entitled "Notes of the Three Family Village". This then envolved Liao Mo-sha in turn; he is a prose writer and author of a series of free-lance, free-ranging articles on miscellaneous subjects which he calls *Luan*

[11] Teng To was chief editor of *Hsin Hua Yih Pao*, a Communist Party newspaper in Chungking during the Sino–Japanese War and chief editor of the *Renmin Ribao (People's Daily)* 1954–9, the official organ of the Chinese Communist Party.

[12] "Yenshan" is another name for Peking.

*Tan Tsa Chi.* Teng To, Wu Han, and Liao Mo-sha are now called "the trio" by their opponents. They are given the nickname "the Three Family Village", which is taken from the title of the series of short sketches by them under the joint pen name, Wu Nan-hsing, in the *Frontline* magazine under the title "Notes of the Three Family Village".

In the attack on writings and writers, the newspapers which published them were involved. As a result, the *Peking Daily* was suspended, the *Peking Evening News* was changed from a daily to a semi-weekly, and the magazine *Frontline* was suspended. In the attack on these newspapers their overseers were involved— that is, the Propaganda Department of the Peking Municipal Party Committee and the Peking Municipal Party Committee itself. This put Chou Yang, Minister of Culture, and Lu Ting-yi, Head of the Department of Propaganda of the Chinese Communist Party, into jeopardy. So it continued in an endless chain. The attack naturally was not confined to Peking, nor even to writers, but the curtain of the first scene of the first act was raised in Peking. This is definite, and is significant.

*The significance of army leadership.* In order to assess the meaning of the Great Proletarian Cultural Revolution properly, the underlying forces and motives of this revolutionary movement must be made clear. In order to do so, let us recall some dates and some documents connected with this movement. As everybody knows, the *Renmin Ribao (People's Daily)* has been the official organ of the Chinese Communist Party as *Pravda* is the official organ of the Soviet Party; its editorials have therefore always been looked upon as party policy and studied as directives and guide lines. It was always the *Renmin Ribao* that took the lead in announcing any national movement. It was the job of the other newspapers to echo *Renmin Ribao* or to reprint its editorial and not vice versa. Again, it is the Communist Party or the Central Committee of the Chinese Communist Party which is the decision-making body, and it is the *Renmin Ribao* which must propagate whatever is decided through its editorial machine.

However, what happened in the case of the Great Proletarian Cultural Revolution was most unusual.

Let us take a look at the dates and events. The earliest announcement of the Great Proletarian Cultural Revolution is traced to 18 April 1966 when the *Jiefanjun Bao (Liberation Army Daily)* in Peking carried this editorial : "Hold High the Great Red Banner of Mao Tse-tung's Thought and Actively Participate in the Great Socialist Cultural Revolution." It was a long article of over 6000 words, outlining the goals and programme of the revolution.[13] Then the next day, 19 April, we found the *Renmin Ribao* reprinting it on its front page. This shows that in this revolution, it was the army that led the party and not the party the army. This was odd. It showed, also, that the army was now strong enough to subordinate the party and particularly the non-army elements of the party. What was odder still was that *Jiefangjun Bao* through its editorial sparked off the Great Proletarian Cultural Revolution, as early as 18 April 1966, whereas the "Decision of the Central Committee of the Chinese Communist Party Concerning the Great Proletarian Cultural Revolution" was adopted on 8 August 1966, 3 months later.[14] It seemed strange for the party to have taken so long to catch up with the ideas of the army, if one could put it that way. Though calling it a cultural revolution, it is clear that it was instigated by political consideration. This is, it was based on internal politics more than on cultural and social considerations. It was evidently a contest for power within the hierarchy of the Chinese

---

[13] The sectional headings were : Sharp Class Struggle on the Cultural Front; a New Situation in the Great Cultural Revolution; Create New and Original Socialist and Proletarian Works and Foster Good Models; Emancipate the Mind and Overcome Superstition; Practise Democratic Centralism and Follow the Mass Line; Encourage Revolutionary, Militant, Mass Criticism of Literature and Art; Use Mao Tse-tung's Thought to Re-educate Cadres in Charge of Literature and Art; and Reorganize the Ranks of Writers and Artists.

[14] We must say, however, that in September 1962 at the Tenth Plenary Session of the Eighth Central Committee of the party, it was decided to launch a "Socialistic Educational Movement". But the idea of a "great revolution" was not suggested.

Communist Party, the victims of which were principally men who were armed with pens and were without guns. This, however, does not preclude implications for international communism. We shall take up this point in the section on international change.

*Mao's thought and the Cultural Revolution.*  We may say that the movement to study Mao Tse-tung's thoughts and the movement of the Great Proletarian Cultural Revolution are closely related. By this, we do not mean that following Mao and his ideas necessitates the denunciation of Chinese traditional culture, as the Red Guards now claim. What we do mean is that the campaign to proclaim the personality of Mao and to study Mao's writing is related to the campaign of destroying the images of the party leaders whose high cultural accomplishment has won the esteem of the masses. What the manipulators of the campaigns aim for is not a study of all Mao's writings as such, nor the development of a new proletarian culture as such. In that sense, Mao is a tool and the cultural revolution is a pretext. The real factor is greed for party power among a group who have no cultural backing but have army backing. Now only certain selected quotations from Mao are studied, omitting other parts (such as his insistence on the use of persuasion instead of coercion in matters of ideology, and the use of mild methods "like breeze and light rain" when it comes to matters of contradiction within the people). One can therefore suspect the authenticity of the respect for Mao and his thoughts, particularly as his lips are kept sealed when people want to hear what he has to say here and now.

We have given much space to the development of the Great Proletarian Cultural Revolution and it may be out of proportion to usual subsections. The only excuse for doing so is that we may need this background to assess the significance of the Cultural Revolution and to interpret recent events in China. Now, having done so, we can be briefer in the presentation of what has been happening in the cultural revolution, what its effects are and what will probably be its consequences.

*The Red Guards.* Reports of events in China since the Great Proletarian Cultural Revolution started in April 1966 have astonished the world. What creates this astonishment is not so much the attack on the old traditions as its occurrence at this stage of Communist rule. Attacking foreigners, ridiculing people in foreign dress, destroying idols, renaming streets, the sort of thing the Red Guards are now doing, have happened in China time and again since China's contacts with the West. One may recall that in 1900 the Boxers killed the foreigners and missionaries in China and at the birth of the First Chinese Republic in 1911, all men who had been wearing queues were forced to have them cut. In the Chinese villages the children used to jeer at those who wore Western clothes as "foreign ghosts". In 1925, after the so-called massacre in Canton by British troops in Sha Kei Road (which meant Sand Embankment Road) on 23 June, the road was renamed "June 23 Road" or "6–23 Road". As for the demolition of idols, Sun Yat-sen did it in his childhood in his own village—90 years ago.

What is astonishing is that the Chinese Communists should do all these things when they had been in power for 17 years, when party government was outwardly at least well established and secure, and when there was apparently nothing in the country to challenge the Communist Party's power. It is amazing that to do these things they had to rely on the teenagers.

Rightly or wrongly, the Great Proletarian Cultural Revolution in China is associated with the *Hung Wei Ping* or the Red Guards. These guards are principally boys and girls from 12–13 to 17–18, ages popularly known in the West as adolescence and teenage. This period is known to Western psychologists as the time of storm and stress, as a period of bubbling energy, and of discontent and unrest. It is a period of transition from childhood to adulthood and of revolt against the older generation. The sudden rise of these youngsters into prominence as vanguards of the cultural movement in China shatters the picture of submissive Chinese youth which many people have painted in contrast to the rebellious juveniles in Western societies. These Chinese youths are no longer as passive as their ancestors were when they were young. The case of the new youth in China may be used in support of John B. Watson's boastful statement : "Give me a dozen healthy infants, and my own specified world to bring them up in, and I'll guarantee to take any one at random and train him to become any type of specialist I might select—doctor, lawyer, artist, merchant-chief, and yes, even beggar and thief, regardless of his talents, penchants, tendencies, abilities, vocations and race of his ancestor."[15]

The Red Guards first appeared on the scene at the first of a series of mass rallies in Peking on 18 August 1966. The *Peking Review* called them the revolutionary mass organization set up in the Great Proletarian Cultural Revolution by the capital's college and middle-school students. The most noticeable sign of the Red Guards is the red armband with the words *Hung Wei Ping* (Red Guards) printed in black. They always carry Mao's book, *Quotations from Chairman Mao*,[16] in their hands, and they wave it in the parades. The Red Guards are selected from youngsters who are activists by disposition and proletarian in family status; that is, children of the workers, peasants, and soldiers. Those who are qualified in all other ways but in parental status have become targets of the struggle among the ranks of youth. The fact that the pattern is so uniform shows that it was not a spontaneous mass movement of youth, but one engineered, organized, and directed by a group which has the power to let young people go ahead without interference. The total number of the Red Guards who journeyed to Peking before the end of

[15] John B. Watson, *Behaviorism*, Norton Book Co., New York, 1925, p. 82.
[16] *Quotations from Chairman Mao* is a pocket-size book, with a red cover. It contains 420 quotations under 33 subject headings with approximately 88,000 words in 270 pages. It is edited and published by the Political Department of the Chinese People's Liberation Army. After the portrait of Mao Tse-tung is an inscription by Lin Piao, which is followed by a foreword signed by the Army's Political Department, dated 1 August 1965. The publication was originally intended for the Liberation Army.

November 1966 has been reported to be 11 million. They went from all parts of China and were reviewed by their leader, Mao Tse-tung, in a total of about eleven rallies. They were given free transportation to the capital to pay homage to their great leader, whose life and whose thoughts they are supposed to guard. After their pilgrimage they returned to their own districts to further the cause of the revolution.

Theoretically, the leadership of the Red Guards should come from the Communist Youth League and the Young Pioneers Brigade, in accordance with the administrative structure of the Communist Party; but it is definitely not so. If the regular party organizations had been trusted, there would have been no new institution of the Red Guards. However, the Red Guards' pilgrimage to Peking gave the promoters a lot of headaches. They interrupted transportation, which was a great setback to industry and production. Feeding and housing them in Peking presented a problem and many became ill or had to leave before it became too cold. These are only some physical aspects of the problems which confronted them.

*The sixteen points and the Red Guards' activities.*   What the Great Proletarian Cultural Revolution tried to do may be seen in the "Decision of the Central Committee of the Chinese Communist Party Concerning the Great Proletarian Cultural Revolution", which is commonly referred to as the sixteen points, adopted on 8 August 1966. We shall summarize the contents under five points :

1.  The Great Proletarian Cultural Revolution is recognized to be a new stage of the socialist revolution now unfolding. Although the bourgeoisie has been overthrown, it is still trying to use old ideas, culture, customs and habits to corrupt the masses, and to stage a come-back. The object of the struggle at present is to crush the persons in authority who are taking the capitalist road, to repudiate the reactionary bourgeois academic authorities and their

ideology, and to transform education, literature, and art. Some of those in authority wormed their way into the party and are actually hidden representatives of the bourgeoisie. The main targets are those within the party who are in authority and are taking the capitalist road.

2. The main force of this revolution is from the masses of the workers, peasants, soldiers, revolutionary intellectuals, and revolutionary cadres. The young people are courageous and daring pathfinders. It is unavoidable that they should show shortcomings of one kind or another, but the main current is correct and they will profit from experience. Revolution, as Chairman Mao has said, cannot be very refined, or so gentle, temperate, kind, courteous, restrained, and magnanimous.

3. The cultural revolutionary activities should be concentrated on cultural and educational units, leading organs of the party, and government in large and medium cities. For the other units and regions such as the productive units and the countryside, the original socialist education movement should go on as before and should not be upset, unless the movement there has not been going well. However, the great proletarian cultural revolution may add to its momentum.

4. The mass line must be thoroughly applied. The tactics are to rely firmly on the revolutionary left, isolate the handful of anti-reactionary bourgeois rightists and counter-revolutionary revisionists, strike at them and expose their crimes. A distinction should be made between the reactionary bourgeois scholar despots and authorities and the ordinary bourgeois academic class. No measure should be taken against students at universities, colleges, middle schools, and primary schools during the movement. Scientists and scientific and technical personnel who have made contributions should be helped to transform their world outlook gradually. To them the policy of "unity, criticism, unity" is still to apply.

5. Regarding educational reform; the most important task is to transform the old educational system and the old principles and methods of teaching. The phenomenon of domination of the schools by bourgeois intellectuals must be completely changed. Education must serve proletarian politics, and education must be combined with productive labour so as to enable those receiving an education to develop morally, intellectually, and physically, and to become labourers with socialist consciousness and culture. Schooling must be shortened and courses become fewer and better. Criticism must be directed against reactionary views in philosophy, history, political economy, and education, in works and theories of literature and art, and in theories of natural science. Materialist dialectics must be fostered in opposition to metaphysics and scholasticism.

The sixteen points are not new or surprising in the sense of transgressing the Communist programme's general frame of reference as we have understood it all along. They do formulate a composite treatise of what socialistic or communistic or proletarian culture means in all its amplifications. It is a bitter dose for the Chinese people, and particularly for the Chinese intellectuals, who have to take it in all at once.

After all, let us mention some of the things the Red Guards have been doing. They paraded the streets with banners, beat drums, cymbals, and gongs, shouted slogans, with Mao Tse-tung's book in their hands as they went. They stuck up posters and handwritten "big character" wall newspapers; from the standpoint of the Proletarian Revolution they criticized party leaders, public leaders, or individuals having followers of some kind. They used every chance they had to deface the picture of the Soviet Union in the eyes of the people by calling Soviet leaders revisionists and collaborators of American imperialism.

Red Guards shouted "Long live Chairman Mao", "Long live the Cultural Revolution", and "Long live the Communist Party". They broke down what they considered to be the "four olds".[17] They molested people in public for unbecoming modes of dress and attire. They changed the names of historic places, streets, buildings, and shops which they said were of feudalistic, superstitious, or imperialistic origin and association. They broke into people's homes to destroy their old pattern of bourgeois living by removing their objects of art, comfortable furniture, fine clothing, and sometimes even silver and gold. They burnt their idols, tablets of ancestral worship, and their sacred books. They took away other books including novels which were accused of carrying bourgeois ideology. They entered the churches and temples to break anything they found disagreeable. They organized meetings in the form of public trials to denounce in person people who were on the black list and humiliated them, spat on them, hit them, hung disgraceful signs on their necks or on their doors. They invaded and sacked local party headquarters whose cadres were not enthusiastic supporters of Red Guards' activities.

So wherever the Red Guards went, people tried to hang Mao's portrait on the walls in their homes, stuck up posters of Mao's sayings, displayed Mao's works on their desks, or showed at least in outward form that they did not resist the movement. The amount of fear and unrest that exists in the cities among the non-proletarians today is tremendous, leaving only those in relative ease of mind who have never had anything—anything in terms of wealth, possession, education, culture, and reputation.

From those who are unsympathetic to the Proletarian Cultural Revolution, the employment of youngsters as a spearhead of the revolution invites more criticism. They criticize it as a crude method of revolution by which greater suffering has been inflicted on the people than absolutely necessary. They also criticize it as an unwise method of revolution because the Chinese people have always had a great regard for age, and have looked down upon the youngsters as persons "whose mother's-milk smell has not yet faded away".

But the logic of those who led the proletarian cultural revolu-

[17] See Chapter 5, "The Chinese Cultural Heritage" (pp. 144–145).

tion is different. They are out-and-out revolutionaries whose very object is to defile traditions. What they want above everything else are people with abounding enthusiasm, reckless courage, simple-minded loyalty, utopian idealism, and bubbling energy. These teenagers, particularly the selected teenagers who excel in all these qualities as the Red Guards do, offer the most useful material. To the leaders of the revolution, their lack of experience, lack of education, and lack of culture, seem not liabilities but assets. Such youths have no drawbacks or social and cultural burdens. What experience they lack will be supplied by close supervision, and experience will be gained anyway as they grow older. By the time they are older and wiser they will have lost fervour, enthusiasm, courage, idealism, and energy. As conservative and reactionary thinking creeps in, they will be weeded out and new innocent teenagers will fill their places. The revolutionaries do not worry about weeding out the old. If they can purge their comrades-in-arms like Peng Te-huei, Peng Chen, Chou Yang, and hundreds of others like them before, need they worry about when these Red Guards become older and wiser? The Chinese Communists in power today are out for their programme. They are not trying to be nice to the youngsters, who are only useful instruments. The Chinese Communists learned during their guerrilla days that youngsters in the *Hsiao Kuei Tui* (Little Devil Teams) were instrumental in their army. The Red Guards today are a new type of youth who were either born in the Communist régime or were in very early childhood when the Communists came to power and have never had a glimpse of China's better days.

What the Red Guards have done by way of positive construction of the new proletarian culture has not been seen yet. Indeed, Soviet leaders have condemned what the Red Guards have done as a hindrance to the building of a new proletarian culture and to the proper understanding of the proletarian cause in the eyes of the world. The movement of the Red Guards again illustrates the saying that it is easy to destroy but difficult to construct. As the Chinese saying goes: "What thousands of people find it difficult to construct in hundreds of years, a man can easily destroy in a single day." It is fortunate that the momentum of the Red Guards in their destruction of the old things was not sustained after one or two months of reckless drive; otherwise much more serious damage would have been done. As to the social and psychological effect the movement has on the Chinese people, one's estimate must depend a good deal on one's own attitude toward revolution in general and toward the Cultural Revolution in particular.

Social movements of mass dimensions will continue to arise, as they have done so in the last 19 years. In the opinion of the revolutionaries, the masses of the people must not be given time to pause and ponder. If no movement comes naturally when revolutionary changes are needed, one has to be created; which is always easy to do. A Chinese has to go through an endless chain of social movements in his lifetime. He will only be emancipated from this ordeal when he gets out of the life-cycle altogether or, if he is lucky enough to do so when he quits the Communist society.

## TECHNOLOGICAL CHANGE

When one compares the technological changes that have taken place in agriculture, industry, and business in China today against the previous background, the changes have been remarkable; but when one compares them with what one finds in the advanced countries of the world such as the United Kingdom, Germany, the United States, Canada, etc., they are but commonplace phenomena, and not so incredible. Again, the improvement in the national life of China is great, but the improvement in the individual life of the Chinese is trivial. The nation has been enriched at the expense of the people.

Modernization in the sense of adaptation to technological change has made great progress in China in the last 19 years. Whereas in the past almost every innovation in the countryside was opposed because of superstition, conservatism, and conflict with local vested interests, today the bases of such opposition have been swept away by the land reform. Modernization in the second half of the twentieth century is no longer an unwelcome process anywhere in low-income countries, as it used to be in the nineteenth and early twentieth century. So there is no special merit in China's having adapted itself to modern technological change.

The earlier ambition of Communist China was immense. In 1953, when the first five-year plans was announced, it promised to catch up with England's steel production and other major industries in 15 years. Now Chinese leaders are more realistic, and aim to catch up and to surpass "the advanced *levels* of science and technology" of the world in 20–30 years.

In our previous discussion of the schools and universities, of teaching and research, of scientists and technicians, of "redness" and "experts", we touched on certain aspects of the subject of technological change which we shall not repeat here. We shall take up some other features which seem to deserve special mention.

## *The Five-year Plans*

The five-year plans in China are programmes for the development of the national economy. So far China has launched three five-year plans : the first one was for the period from 1953 to 1957, the second for the period from 1958 to 1962, and the third for the period from 1966 to 1970. We notice that the third plan did not follow the second immediately, and there was a lapse of 3 years. While it is claimed that the first five-year plan exceeded its target, and the second five-year plan was basically completed in 1960 (2 years ahead of schedule), it was admitted that delay in the launching of the third five-year plan was due to natural calamities in three successive years from 1959 to 1961. Leaders also acknowledged and admitted their errors and shortcomings, and pointed to the withdrawal of Soviet specialists, with curtailment of important supplies and cancellation by the Khrushchev revisionist clique of over a hundred projects contracted with Russia.[18]

It is a Chinese Communist propaganda technique to boast of accomplishments and to conceal defects, while leaders expose the shortcomings of the capitalistic countries and keep silent about their accomplishments. We seldom hear such an open admission of errors and shortcomings on their part as appeared in that *Renmin Ribao* new year editorial of 1966, but even this did not specify what the errors and shortcomings were. As to their accomplishments, the government's words speak louder than their deeds. They tell of increased production in terms of percentages, in comparison with other periods, concealing the actual figures, so it is difficult to tell what the exact conditions are. Whether these are in figures or in percentages, there is no way to check the validity of the statistics, so we shall not bother ourselves with their data.

### The Nuclear Explosions

If mastery of the nuclear device is a sign of technological advance, then China is entitled to that claim. It must be pointed out that the most outstanding Chinese scientists in nuclear research were all trained in the West and returned to China only in recent years, and that it was through Russian assistance that the work first started. It is to China's credit, however, that the Chinese have succeeded with nuclear explosions, four of which took place within a period of 2 years in spite of Russian withdrawal since 1960. The first three explosions took place on 16 October 1964, 14 May 1965, and 9 May 1966 respectively; the fourth, with a missile-guided warhead, succeeded on 27 October 1966; and a fifth on 28 December 1966. When one bomb is successful, many more can be made; when small ones are successful, bigger ones can be made; when the missiles can

[18] According to the editorial of *Renmin Ribao* (*People's Daily*) of 1 January 1966 on the initial date of the third five-year plan.

deliver over a short distance, others can be made that will deliver over longer distances. The question is of time and the heavy cost the Chinese have to pay, with the sacrifices they have to make for such production in a country which has other appalling needs. It does not change our earlier proposition that the nuclear weapon may be as much a blessing to China as it is a curse.

## Industrial Development

China likes to show off her industrial accomplishments to the outside world as well as to the people within the country. We see photographs of factories, machinery, and industrial scenes on display everywhere, whenever an opportunity for propaganda is available to the Communists, with the exception of things connected with national defence which are considered military secrets. The people, particularly the rural people, hear so much about what machines can do and yet see so little of them, that when tractors and generators are brought to their locality either for use or for demonstration, they welcome them with cheers and tears. This reflects the positive attitude of the people toward machines, mechanization, and industrialization, as against the negative attitude attributed to the rural folk in China in the past. This attitude has taken such an extreme form that a kind of machine-worship, of looking at the machine as an emancipator seems to develop—a phenomenon one does not find in the West, where (in the United States, for example) heaps and heaps of discarded automobiles and refrigerators lie on wasteland.

Those who are familiar with Communist China propaganda abroad must have seen pictures of China's new industrial developments such as the long Yangtze River Bridge at Hankow; the iron and steel works at Anshan and Taiyuan; the textile mills at Shanghai and Wusih; the skyline of towering derricks and refineries in the oil fields at Ta Ching and Yu Men; the big dams and hydroelectric plants at Hsinanchiang and Chechi; the heavy machinery plants at Taiyuan and Shenyang; the tractor plant at Lingshan; the coal-mines at Kailan; the fertilizer works at Wuching, and so on. It does not seem worth while to describe them here or to give statistical figures of the size and growth of China's industrial development.

Instead, we shall mention a feature of China's industrial and technological output which might reflect, in a specific way, China's accomplishment within the last two decades. We refer to the Chinese Exhibition of Export Machinery and Instruments in Hong Kong in August 1966. It demonstrates that China is now able to make not only objects of art but also good quality products in machinery and scientific instruments. For a country where machinery had always been an imported item and never an export item, this progress is highly applauded. In our footnote we shall quote what a Western reporter has said of the exhibition.[19]

It is obvious that such exhibitions and such exports have their economic value as well as their political value in drawing the developing peoples and uncommitted peoples to the Chinese orbit.

### Agricultural Development

The greatest change in the agricultural life of the Chinese people has certainly been in the ownership of land which we have discussed in the previous chapters in connection with land reform and the People's Commune. Abolition of private ownership of farmland has at least this advantage : it increases

---

[19] *South China Morning Post*, Hong Kong, 10 and 11 August 1966.

More than 1,000 pieces of machinery and technical instruments for the Exhibition of Export Machinery and Instruments of the People's Republic of China to be opened here today were shown to the Press yesterday in a preview sponsored by 14 local dealers here. . . .

Among goods on display will be machine tools of various categories, marine diesel engines, generators, generating sets, heavy duty air-conditioning equipment, high and low tension porcelain, insulators, switchgear, printing machines, wire stitchers for book binding, high speed paper cutting machines, and electronic equipment. . . .

Some of the products on display are being distributed in Australia, Belgium, the United Kingdom, Iran, Iraq, Norway,

the farming area automatically by reclaiming all the boundary paths between small farm lots of different ownership into productive use in larger farming units. There is a great change in the picture, in that we do not see small lots which used to characterize the Chinese farm, but the transformed land in large areas as we would in Canada and in the United States. What was inaccessible to tractors is now accessible. Following the change in ownership is the change in organization and management of farming. What poor individual peasants would not attempt to do nor landlords risk investment in, such as the installation of large scale irrigation systems, the state farms and communes can do today.

Without going into details, let us outline some of the things which science and technology are doing in China to boost agricultural production. Large dams and reservoirs, canals and ditches, are built almost everywhere to improve irrigation, to direct water-flow, and to regulate water levels, in order to decrease damage by flooding and to remedy shortage during drought. With the utilization of hydraulic power, much of the formerly unproductive land has become arable, particularly the terraced land on hillsides. It is true that such installations and

---

Pakistan, Singapore, Sudan, Ethiopia, Finland, Holland, Jordan, Japan, Kenya, Lebanon, New Zealand, Syria, Tanzania, United Arab Republic, and other countries. . . .

[It was further reported the next day] Europeans were prominent among the hundreds of Hong Kong businessmen who went to the opening of the Chinese Exhibition of Export Machinery and Instruments . . . yesterday.

The Britons who were among the visitors said they were impressed with the quality of the exhibits. . . .

One European visitor remarked the heavy machinery showed influences of German design. He said: "Some of the smaller lathes are extremely good. . . . China is making good sales here, I believe. . . ."

Other sections include equipment for hospitals, the sciences and higher education; marine gear; photography equipment; car accessories; and radio and electricals. . . .

An attendant said export orders would be taken for any of the displayed items throughout the period of the exhibition. . . .

improvements require much manual labour; but, happily, China has an almost unlimited supply of manpower which has been fully utilized. As we have noted, people from the cities have been mobilized every year to work on farms.

To improve methods of farming, besides the introduction of machinery such as tractors, the method of "fewer rows and closer planting" has been tried out in rice fields. Deep ploughing and crop rotation are done on a large scale. Chemical fertilizer is used in addition to the utilization of manure accumulated from local sources. Seed selection is in use in horticulture and breed selection in animal husbandry and pest control is extensive. Though anti-pest spraying is employed, pest control is largely done by labour which, nevertheless, has its special effectiveness. It is reported that the campaign to kill sparrows resulted in an increase of insects on the farms which sparrows had helped to control. Reafforestation begins to show results in the conservation of soil and many productive advantages, besides its own timber supply. With all these scientific and technological advantages plus the optimal use of human resources, agricultural output has been on the increase in spite of other shortcomings and the serious floods and droughts which have been China's misfortune for some years.

China is still short of grain to feed its increasing population and although improvements have been made in agriculture, China has to import grain from other countries, the largest suppliers being Canada, Argentina, and Australia. According to the announcement of the Chairman of the Australian Wheat Board, China was to buy another $1\frac{1}{2}$ million tons of wheat from Australia, exceeding £36 million in value, to be delivered in the period from December 1966 to June 1967.[20]

There is one factor which China has overlooked : that of incentive. The Chinese Communists in power insist that political motive is the strongest incentive and should be the only legitimate incentive. They attack material inducement as capitalistic ideology which must be ruled out if they do not want to fall into

[20] See *South China Morning Post*, Hong Kong, 3 November 1966.

revisionism. We admit that there are people who do not work for personal gain, but work for a nobler cause at great personal sacrifice. History is full of records of such sages and saints, heroes, and martyrs, but such people are very few. We cannot expect such high moral attainments from everyone in the common masses or everyone in the Church. Few would work hard when it does not make much difference whether they work hard or not. Even if the common run of people can do it for a time, they cannot keep it up indefinitely, and this is the sort of thing which troubles the Chinese farm today. Whether there will be a change in the future, or when, will depend upon the chances of the so-called revisionism.

## Experience in Socialization

The traditional Chinese society had been known for its extreme individualism; organization and discipline were the weakest spots in the life of the people. Take census-taking as an example : in the Ching Dynasty as well as in the early years of the Chinese Republic it was practically unknown. Births and deaths were not recorded and it was in the Sino–Japanese War that registration of males was first required because of military service. Movement within the vast territory was entirely free. Chinese movement abroad and re-entry was entirely free. No restriction was imposed and no permit required. The Chinese had a general dislike for organization and regimentation. People did not know how to organize themselves or to conduct public meetings and parliamentary law was practically unknown. Even when there were organizations, they were loosely organized, thus many Westerners called the Chinese "a basin of loose sand" which implied a huge number of Chinese people and an absence of the quality of cohesiveness. Chinese patriots have admitted this fundamental weakness of their national character and have looked upon it as a national disgrace that must be removed.

It is most surprising that the same people have, within two decades, transformed themselves into such a high degree of unification and socialization in their social and economic life as well as in their personal and political life. It is most surprising that this people, with no experience of industrialization or of collectivization, has come up as a highly organized mass, posing as a single giant. This people, used to a free economy and *laissez-faire*, is now geared to the machinery of national economy and to the rationing of food and clothing. This change is all the more startling in view of the fact that the population has been mostly illiterate, and systems of transportation and communication have been so inadequate for this massive land.

If the Chinese people have failed in their first and second five-year plans they have amply made it up by the invaluable experience they have gained in public planning and in its execution. China has been able to put its house in order. With the cumulative experience of nationalization and socialization, what it will be able to do cannot be minimized.

We must not forget one thing in our assessment of the accomplishments of the Chinese People's Republic over these years. What slavery can accomplish by way of productivity, of uniformity, and of maintenance of discipline and order, socialism in Communist China can and should be able to achieve. What glory is there in order and in discipline themselves which prisons and concentration camps can also boast? Slavery in the pre-emancipation days of America also accomplished productivity and industry, discipline and order, in the cotton, corn and tobacco plantations in the south. In fact, there was also a great deal of mirth and gaiety, music and dancing, among the Negro slaves. The Chinese peasants are now driven to work much harder in return for less reward than the peasants of the landlord days, when they could be lazy or quit for a better chance of life in the town. Now they cannot do even that. What was lacking then among the American Negroes was freedom as it is lacking now among the Chinese. It is a price which many people value higher than productivity and even dearer than life itself. It is doubtful that a supposedly free people can bear this virtual slavery for ever.

## INTERNATIONAL CHANGE

There is nothing more illustrative of the extent to which international change affects the social, economic, and cultural life of a nation internally in the time of peace than the difference in China in the last 19 years, between the days of friendship with the Soviet Union and the days of quarrelling. On the establishment of the Chinese People's Republic, the Union of Soviet Socialist Republics was the first to recognize China. It became the mainstay of China, of the latter's international, military, technological, and economic position in the early years of the People's Republic, when the nations were on the closest fraternal terms. Everything Russian was good and excellent. Russian leaders and government, Russian science and scientists, Russian education and educators, Russian literature and writers, Russian art and artists were just and superb. To criticize Russia and things Russian was considered almost blasphemy.

Such a situation lasted for almost a decade. Even as late as 1957 when Lun Yuen, the former Nationalist governor of Yunnan Province and a member of the Kuomintang Revolution Committee who participated in the People's régime, criticized the Soviet Union in the Hundred Schools Campaign, accusing Russia of taking away the machinery from Manchuria during their occupation, of charging high interest on its loan to China, and of giving low prices for China's products, of requiring a refund of its loan to China for the Korean War. He was "capped" as a rightist for obstructing the friendship with Russia and was removed from the membership of the National People's Congress.

But now that China and Russia are not on friendly terms, everything which is Russian and good is kept silent. No one dares to speak a good word of Russia for fear of being suspected as a revisionist. Such a change is startling. With this international change in international alignment, social, economic, political, and cultural change followed. As a challenge to Soviet policy of moderation in agriculture, the Chinese announced the policy of the Socialistic Main Line and drastically communized their farms; as a demonstration of its resoluteness in face of the threat of Soviet withdrawal of technological assistance, the Chinese staged the Great Leap Forward Movement and employed the "backyard furnace" method; as an indication of distrust of Soviet methods of military organization, the insignia in uniforms distinguishing military ranks which had been adopted from the Soviet system was abolished; as a repudiation of the Soviet denunciation of the personal cult, the person of Mao was brought to even higher exaltation; as an attack on the Russian view of literature and art China purged the classical opera and classical literature; as a warning of the extent to which reversal could go, the Russian language was replaced by English in the schools. It looks as if the Chinese Communists have adopted an extreme position : "Don't do what the Russians do, and do what the Russians don't."

We shall speak of international change in China in the last 19 years under these topics : (1) China's relations with the Soviet Union, (2) China's relations with the United States, and (3) China's relations with other countries. We shall take special notice of those features which have bearing on education.

### China's Relations with the Soviet Union

When people speak of the Soviet Union or the Union of Soviet Socialist Republics (USSR), it is often taken for granted that it is synonymous with the Soviet Government, the Soviet Union Communist Party, the Soviet people, and the Russians, just as when they speak of China, or the People's Republic of China, it is often taken for granted that it is synonymous with the Chinese Government, the Chinese Communist Party, the Chinese people, and the Chinese. But we should be aware that they are sometimes synonymous and sometimes not. Even within the Communist world, when the Soviet people and the Chinese are in accord, the Soviet Communist Party, the Soviet Government, the Soviet Union and the Soviet people are looked upon as having the same identity just as the Chinese Communist Party, Chinese People's Government, the Chinese People's Republic, and the Chinese people are looked upon as having a single identity. But when they are in discord, the Russian Communist Party, according to the Chinese Communist Party, does not represent the Russian people; and the Chinese Communist Party, according to the Soviet Communist Party, does not represent the Chinese people, and so on. It is probable that both are correct, though neither side is willing to admit the fact in its own case. We shall, however, use the terms interchangeably and indiscriminately.

*The "fall on one side" policy.* To "fall on one side" means to fall on the side of the Soviet Union. This became China's major foreign policy and China's national policy at the establishment of the Chinese People's Republic. "To fall on one side" was first advocated by Mao Tse-tung in his treatise *On the People's Democratic Dictatorship* written for the occasion of the 28th anniversary of the Chinese Communist Party on 1 July 1949, 3 months before the establishment of the People's Republic. It was composed during the process of preparation for the convening of the Chinese People's Political Consultation Conference (CPPCC), the formulation of the Common Programme, and the establishment of the People's Republic. Mao put forth his idea of the nature of the new government as a People's Democratic Dictatorship which served as the basis of thought for the participants of the Conference.

Mao's proposition of falling on one side was part of his platform or the Chinese Communist Party platform. It was a sharp reply to commentaries, criticisms, and misgivings about the Chinese Communist Party's foreign policy by other factions which took part in the foundation work of the conference.[21]

[21] The treatise *On the People's Democratic Dictatorship* contains a series of replies to the commentaries, criticisms, and doubts regarding certain Communist policies as expressed by the non-Communists who were in preliminary consultation. There are seven paragraphs in succession, each of which starts with a quotation of such commentaries and criticisms and doubts. The quotation "You are falling on one side" is the first of the series.

Some democratic leaders who participated in the CPPCC, notably Li Chi-sen, Chairman of the Kuomintang Revolutionary Committee, had hoped that China would maintain an uncommitted international policy so that it could play the role of arbitrator or mediator between the USSR and the United States. But after the publication of Mao's treatise, the debate on foreign policy was closed. Let us quote Mao's paragraph in that article in full :

> "You are falling on one side". Exactly. The forty years' experience of Sun Yat-sen and the twenty-eight years' experience of the Communist Party have taught us to fall on one side, and we are firmly convinced that in order to win victory and consolidate it we must fall on one side. In the light of the experiences accumulated in these forty years and these twenty-eight years, all Chinese without exception must fall either on the side of imperialism or on the side of socialism. Sitting on the fence will not do, nor is there a third road. We oppose the Chiang Kai-shek reactionaries who fall on the side of imperialism, and we also oppose the illusions about a third road.

It is an extreme measure to fall on one side. For those who were more cautious it was too risky a step to take and it was going too far. But Mao was so sure and determined although he was a bit naïve, as we see it now. He overlooked an important factor. He did not realize that Joseph Stalin would die; and, more specifically, he was not aware that the Russian Communist Party could depart so far from the ideas of its great dictator after his death.

*To accept Russians as teachers.* According to Mao Tse-tung's way of thinking, the Chinese had been searching for the way to national salvation since the Opium War. They sought it from the West, but they failed to find the solution. Then the October Revolution of Russia broke out. There the truth of Marxism was revealed. The Russian path was the Chinese path. China must learn from the Russians.

The slogan "To accept the Russians as Teachers" in fact was first advocated by Sun Yat-sen in 1924. Mao was only reiterating what Sun had said. Let us quote a few statements from Mao's *On the People's Democratic Dictatorship* to illustrate his ideas on the subject. In doing so we do not want only to show Mao's logic on learning from Russia but also to show on the reverse side of the coin the almost unsurmountable difficulties he had set before himself when he decided to denounce the Soviet Union and the Russian Communist Party. To quote from Mao :

> From the time of China's defeat in the Opium War of 1840, Chinese progressives went through untold hardships in their quest for truth from the Western countries. . . . Imperialist aggression shattered the fond dream of the Chinese about learning from the West. Doubts arose, increased and deepened. World War I shook the whole globe. The Russians made the October Revolution and created the world's first socialist state. . . . It was through the Russians that the Chinese found Marxism. Before the October Revolution, the Chinese were not only ignorant of Lenin and Stalin; they did not even know Marx and Engels. The salvos of the October Revolution brought us Marxism–Leninism. Follow the path of the Russian—that was their conclusion. . . .
>
> Only once in his whole life did Sun Yat-sen receive foreign help, and that was Soviet help. Let readers refer to Dr. Sun Yat-sen's testament; his earnest advice was not to look for help from the imperialist countries but to "unite with those nations of the world which treat us as equals". . . . We should remember his words. . . . Internationally, we belong to the side of the anti-imperialist front headed by the Soviet Union, and so we can turn only to this side for genuine and friendly help, not to the side of the imperialist front. . . .
>
> But the Communist Party of the Soviet Union emerged victorious and . . . it learned not only how to make the revolution but also how to carry on construction. It has built a great and splendid socialist state. The Communist Party of the Soviet Union is our best teacher and we must learn from it. . . .

Those were his words in 1949. Let us further quote his words in 1953. In his tribute to Stalin in the article "The Most Precious Friendship", published in the *Renmin Ribao (People's Daily)* on 8 March, we find these words :

> The Soviet Union Communist Party is the Party nurtured by Lenin's and Stalin's own hands; it is the Party which is the most advanced in the world, and most experienced, and the most cultivated in theory. This Party has been our model in the past as it is at present, and will also be in the future.

*The glamorous days of Sino–Soviet friendship.* There was a chain of happy events which followed the Soviet Union's recognition. Russia was the first foreign country to recognize China, the day after the establishment of the People's Republic. The Culture, Art, and Science Delegation from the Soviet Union arrived in Peking on the National Birthday itself. They took part in the opening of the China Association for the Protection of World Peace. On 5 October 1949 the Sino–Soviet Friendship Association was inaugurated. Then Mao Tse-tung went to Russia and arrived in Moscow on 16 December 1949 to attend Stalin's 70th birthday celebration, which took place on 21 December 1949. The Mutual Assistance Treaty between the Chinese People's Republic and the Soviet Union was signed at Moscow on 4 February 1950 by Chou En-lai and Vyshinsky in the presence of Mao Tse-tung and Joseph Stalin. The effective period of the treaty is 30 years.

Another agreement signed on the same day was the Soviet Loan of US $300 million to the Chinese People's Republic for industrial development at an interest rate of 1 per cent per annum.[22] With the provisions of this loan, Soviet equipment came; Soviet installations came; Soviet advisers, specialists, and technicians came. This was a great boost to China's economic recovery after 8 years of anti-Japanese war and 4 years of civil war. The mere presence of Soviet personnel and arrival of Soviet supplies were enough to stir up nationwide enthusiasm. The fact that China spoke of her relationship with the Soviet Union as an unbreakable fraternal bond and named Russia as her unfailing ally kept the world guessing whether Russia was not committed to go to war if China should go to war. With the benefit of that doubt, China escaped the bombing of its north-eastern region across the Yalu River by the United States in the Korean War. In the years 1950 to 1954 when China was on the receiving end and without yet having to be on the paying end, the tone of its economy was jubilant.

In the field of education, as we have noted, Russian was

[22] The loan was to be made in five instalments from 1 January 1950 to 31 December 1954 with refunds to be made in ten instalments from 31 December 1954 to 31 December 1963.

taught in the schools in place of English. The fervour for learning Russian was running high. Russian textbooks were translated into Chinese for school use. Russian stories became popular in the Children's readers. Long Russian names became familiar to the students' ears and lips. Russian scholars came to lecture in the universities and institutes of higher education through interpreters while Russian science was deemed to supersede all Western science. Russian theories were accepted as better theories. Russian biologists such as Michurin and Lysenko replaced the Western authorities in the biological sciences and Pavlov replaced the Western psychologists. The Russian method of "tissue transplantation therapy" was used for every cure. The Russians had the last word in all branches of knowledge. All inventions such as telegraphy, electricity, X-ray, photography, were claimed to be of Russian origin so that some old Chinese intellectuals commented secretly with sarcasm that some day Chinese history would be traced to Russian origin. Students and scientists were sent to Russia to study and those who were chosen considered it the greatest privilege and honour. It made many returned students from the United States, the United Kingdom, and other countries of Europe regret not having studied in Russia. Such was the picture of Russia-worship in China in the early years of the Chinese People's Republic.

*The Sino–Soviet split.* Such a booming state of affairs for the Russians does not exist now. Then it was like honeymooning. Now that the Sino–Soviet quarrel has developed into an almost irreparable rift, the bitterness between one another is similar to that between a couple on the verge of divorce. Like a disappointed couple, both China and Russia perhaps wish that no one would speak of their early days. We speak of them here, not because we want to be hostile to either or to both sides, but because we want to be accurate.

The Sino–Soviet rift developed its gravest and most serious proportions as the year 1966 was drawing to a close. The most spectacular scenes were at the celebration of the 17th anniversary of the Chinese People's Republic in Peking on 1 October 1966 when the Soviet Diplomatic Corps walked out as the Chinese speaker, Marshal Lin Piao, the Chinese Defence Minister, attacked the Soviet Union's policy over Vietnam; and, reciprocally, in the celebration of the 49th anniversary of the Russian Revolution in Moscow on 7 November 1966 during which the Chinese Diplomatic Corps walked out as the Russian speaker Marshal Rodion Malinovsky, the Defence Minister, attacked the Chinese People's Republic's policy over Vietnam. Other incitements were the renaming by the Red Guards of the road in Peking where the Russian Embassy is situated, calling it the Anti-Revisionist Road, and the expulsion of Chinese students from Russia in retaliation. Both sides attacked the other for strengthening the American imperialist's hands in the Vietnam war. Tension grew as each accused the other of agitation, of hostility and territorial aggression at their border. This is a totally different picture from the one we saw in the early years of the Chinese People's Republic in both Peking and Moscow.

This rift did not come suddenly. It had been in the process of development. At first it was an undercurrent, but later it came to the surface; at first it was reserved—now it is unrestrained.

But how did this split come about? What was the real cause of the rift?

Of course the death of Stalin accounts for much of the reshuffling of policies in the Soviet Union which had a tremendou impact on China's national policy. But why could not China follow the Kremlin instead of Stalin after the death of Stalin China could have followed Soviet policy, and by so doing it coul have maintained the fraternal bond with its great socialist neigh bour. This would have benefited Communist China as well as the International Communist movement. But this China did not do It was probably the greatest blunder Mao Tse-tung has made. W might say that he miscalculated the power of Khrushchev and the power behind the new Russian leader. Mao's ignorance of Sovie politics was perhaps the reason behind his blunder. He was no aware of the undercurrents in the Soviet Union Communist Part when Stalin died. Mao, however, is not too much to blame, because he was relying on Stalin who apparently did not know himself what was going on in the hearts of his subordinates.

We may recall that as Stalin was approaching 73 he was thinking of naming a successor. At the 19th Congress of the All-Union Communist Party in October 1952, which Stalin also attended, he delegated the delivery of the party report to Malenkov. It appeared in everyone's eyes that Malenkov was his logical and favoured successor. Mao also took this for granted.

If one would bring to memory the picture of Stalin's funeral and recall the fate and destiny of Stalin's coffin's pall-bearers, one realizes the strain which was going on in the minds of the close associates of Stalin in their struggle for power. From this angle, we may be able to see the special significance of Mao Tse-tung's tribute to Stalin in connection with the Sino–Soviet split which came about later.

Stalin died on 3 March 1953. Mao Tse-tung in tribute to Stalin wrote the article "The Most Precious Friendship" which we have quoted. There was this statement in its closing paragraph :

> We completely believe that the Soviet Communist Party and the Soviet Government under the leadership of Comrade Malenkov is certainly capable of upholding the will of Comrade Stalin and of pushing forward the great work of Communism and amplifying it to greater glory.

This statement might have pleased Malenkov, but it certainly did not please Khrushchev. Mao thought he was taking the opportunity to assure the Soviet Party, the Soviet Government, and the Soviet People of his continued allegiance and at the same time to indicate that although Stalin had died and the personal leadership in the Communist world was left vacant, he was willing to endorse the leadership of Malenkov of the Soviet Union. In Khrushchev's mind, Mao's statement was probably uncalled for, because the leadership of the Soviet Union was Soviet internal business. It was out of place for Mao as a Chinese to pledge his support to any person, especially as Khrushchev was planning to depose Malenkov. Khrushchev might have made a certain reservation regarding Mao's real intentions until he had a chance to talk to Mao in person. In tracing the split to personal factors, we may be justified on the ground that personal factors do weigh quite heavily in the affairs of totalitarian states.

While Malenkov took up the premiership (chairmanship of the Council of Ministers) after Stalin's death, his post of First Secretary of the Soviet Communist Party was won by Khrushchev in September 1953. As Russian Party First Secretary, Khrushchev headed a party delegation to visit Peking in October 1954 to attend the 5th anniversary of the Chinese People's Republic. Although he was the first party chief from the Soviet Union ever to visit China, he was not so colourfully received as a man of his position should have been. Probably Mao was still thinking of Stalin, the Stalin line, Stalinists, and was anticipating an early return to power of Malenkov and the Stalinist group. Evidently Mao was unaware that Khrushchev was not alone and was backed up by the Kremlin hierarchy. In their 1954 meeting, either Khrushchev was trying to sound out Mao's inner thoughts in the matter of world communism (in which he was disappointed) or he was trying to persuade Mao to subscribe to the new line of communism (in which he failed). Whatever it was the meeting sowed the seed of disharmony. From the events which followed it is reasonable to speculate that Mao paid little heed to Khrushchev and entertained the idea that such a jovial character as Khrushchev, who seemed to have nothing in common with Mao's image of a Communist leader, could not remain in power long, and he might as well mark time and wait for his downfall.

Then events unravelled. On the Soviet side we saw the resignation of Malenkov from the premiership in 1955, the denunciation of Stalin and of the personal cult in 1956, the demotion of Molotov, a staunch Stalinist, to be ambassador to Mongolia in 1958, the increase of power of Khrushchev in his assumption of premiership in 1958, and the removal of Stalin's coffin from the

Lenin Mausoleum in 1961. On the Chinese side we saw the purge of the rightists in 1957, the launching of the People's Commune, the Great Leap Forward, and the Socialistic Main Line in 1958, and so forth.

In Sino-Soviet relations, much of the conflict was kept under cover for a long time. One could sense that the climate was changing. The lack of the former enthusiasm for Russia and things Russian was apparent. When Stalin was being denounced in the Soviet Union, his portrait was still on prominent display in the parades in Peking. Anyone could tell that there was something wrong between China and Russia. Then reports in the newspapers on Russian events and on speeches of Russian leaders appeared without the usual editorial enthusiastic support and comment. Later mutual attacks came into the open. It was no longer possible to pretend or to conceal. Finally, Russia withdrew all its technical personnel from China in 1960 and cancelled the contracts for industrial installations. The desire to discontinue co-operation was evident. Then the correspondence between the Chinese and Soviet Communist parties on their controversies were published in the *Renmin Ribao (People's Daily)* in 1963. As the last visit of Teng Hsiao-ping to Moscow in 1963 failed, hostility mounted both in the use of words and in the techniques employed. The events in autumn 1966 which we have mentioned show that the situation is getting worse and worse.

There is nothing strange about a country changing its policy. All countries change their policies from time to time. What makes it strange in the present case of China is that such a radical change is brought about in time of peace by the same party, by the same leaders, and, indeed, by the same man within a relatively short period of time.

## China's Relationship with the United States

The Chinese Communists cite the United States as their greatest enemy. This attitude and this policy have not changed since the founding of the People's Republic in spite of many other international changes. Indeed, hostility seems to be intensi-fying and the possibility of reconciliation is becoming more and more remote.

Some commentators on Sino–American affairs have offered the notion that the United States' defence of Taiwan and the Korean War were factors which contributed to the Chinese anti-American attitude. This is not correct, as we shall show. Commentators on that line of thought seem to suggest that more contacts between the Chinese people and the American people, and particularly between the Chinese Communist leaders and the American leaders, would help to remove the misunderstand-ing. This contention is only wishful thinking. The major issue, we must be clear, is the Communist outlook on the world and the Communist strategy of world revolution, adhered to by both Stalin and Mao. According to them, capitalism must be destroyed.

The United States is the chief exponent of capitalism and the only capitalistic country which really matters. If the United States is crushed, then all the other capitalistic countries would collapse automatically. The strategy is to split the capitalistic camp, isolate the United States from the other powers as much as possible, and feature it as the target of attack. Since the capitalis-tic countries are rivals among themselves, many would enjoy seeing the United States beaten while they would be enjoying a period of relative peace and prosperity. Human nature being what it is, particularly in a capitalistic and individualistic society, there is a good deal of ground for their optimism. This strategy of dividing enemies and singling the major one for attack has worked wonders in internal revolution; it seemed it would also work in world revolution. But one must work fast, according to the Chinese Communists, lest the capitalistic countries become wiser and this strategy loses its magical power. This strategy is not worth a penny if every person and every nation is awake to its devilishness.

In support of the view that China's policy toward the United States was formulated before the United States came to th defence of Taiwan and before the Korean War in October 1950, we have a concrete evidence.

> In October 1949 when the Province of Kwangtung was being taken over by the Chinese People's Liberation Army, Communist propaganda slogans were posted in all liberated areas. In the city of Hsiao-Ching, about 60 miles west of Canton, among the slogans found on the walls was this one: "Down with British-American Imperialism." The Chinese people in general had been used to that slogan since the early days of the Sun Yat-sen's anti-imperialistic campaign. And, in fact, for more reasons than one, Great Britain had been thought of as more of an imperialistic aggressor to the Chinese than the United States. Apparently there was no harm in grouping Britain and America together in their attack of imperialism. Considering the political consciousness of the Chinese people at that time, the slogan was flawless.
>
> But this slogan caught the eyes of the Communist propaganda cadres. They tore down the slogan and traced the man who put it up. The official slogan of the Communist Party was "Down with American Imperialism" with "British" deliberately left out. Finally this man was arrested. He was asked to account for his motive in putting up a slogan in variance with the official slogan. He was suspected of being a Trotskyist, trying to use a twisted slogan to mislead the people. However, after investigation, they found that the man was innocent. He had been living in an isolated rural area in the past few years and had not kept up with Communist thought.

The Stalin–Mao tactics of isolating the United States have been bearing fruit. While the United States is imposing an embargo on Chinese goods, the United Kingdom, together with Canada, Australia, France, etc., are doing good business with China. Such countries would act very differently, in which case China would have greater difficulties, if China had opposed all capitalistic countries *en bloc*.

Unless there is a radical change in Chinese Communist leadership, an improvement in Sino-American relationships is a forlorn hope. It is not a matter of understanding or misunderstanding between peoples, so much as a matter of interpreting or misinterpreting world affairs on the part of the Communists. If the Chinese Communists care to understand America as it should be understood, there are many returned students in China who can tell everything about America that the leaders care to know. But if they do not care to understand America then not even many times that number of Americans coming to visit China would be of any avail.

It is the matter of ideology which is the crux of the problem. Chien Hsueh-sen (Tsien Hsue-shen), probably China's nuclear test master-mind, who got his Ph.D. in physics in 1939 from the California Institute of Technology and returned to China in 1955, should be able to help the Chinese Communists understand America after having lived there for 20 years. In fact the "man who knew too much" of America has not been of much use in the promotion of Sino-American goodwill when something else, which goes deeper than knowledge plays havoc.

We like to note here that ideology is one thing and reality is quite another. It is one thing to speak of world revolution, it is another to speak of diplomacy. For China to continue to pursue Stalin's foreign policy toward America does not seem to common sense to be wise diplomacy. That policy was of Russian origin; but even the Russians have given it up, while China discontinues the policy of falling in on the Russian side.

## China's Relationship with Other Countries

In its relationship with other countries, China has been travelling a very rough international sea. There was a time when China's international prestige was at high tide, winning many friends to its side and being looked upon as the leader of the peoples of the formerly oppressed world. The Afro-Asian Conference in Bandung in April 1955 marked a very glorious page of Chinese diplomatic history. China had been able to hold out against the Americans with its "volunteers" at Panmentie (Panmunjom) and obtained an honourable truce at the 37 parallel. Many developing countries which had broken away from the yoke of colonialism and imperialism since World War II were heartened by what Communist China was able to do. But ever since its friction with the Soviet Union, followed by the anti-rightist movement, communization, the "back-yard furnace at home, persecution of the lamas in Tibet, tension at the border with India, and infiltration in Indonesia across the seas, its international position has been on a rapid decline. The recent Great Proletarian Cultural Movement as associated with the activities of the Red Guards has brought China's prestige to its lowest ebb. It is no wonder that the Soviet bloc accuses China of weakening the International Communist Movement by giving a wrong impression of the nature of the Communist cause in the eyes of the world.

There is a bright side and a dark side of the international picture of China. On the bright side, in 1965 there were forty-nine countries[23] which had diplomatic relations with the Chinese People's Republic. With the exception of the United Kingdom and the Netherlands which are represented by chargés d'affaires, Yugoslavia which has no representatives at present, and certain exceptional cases arising in 1966, ambassadors are exchanged with all the other countries. Friendship associations, such as the Sino-Soviet Friendship Association, Sino-Korean Friendship Associations, Sino-Polish Friendship Association, and so on, are established as semi-official organizations with many countries to promote such relationship. Protocols and agreements, bilateral and multilateral, have been signed between China and the other countries. Foreign delegations have come to visit China. Large delegations came to attend the National Day Celebration of the Chinese People's Republic and Chinese delegations have been abroad frequently in recent years, some of which were led by China's top leaders such as Liu Shao-chi, Chairman of the State, Chou En-lai (the Premier), and Chen Yi (the Foreign Minister). On the bright side of the picture one may say that China has made many friends and has won the support and respect of many nations and peoples.

On the other side of the picture, one must not forget what has happened to the contrary in China's diplomatic relations in these areas.

[23] According to the *People's Handbook*, 1965, published by the Ta Kung Po, Peking.

*With socialistic countries.* Among the socialistic group in eastern Europe, China's relations with Bulgaria, Hungary, Czechoslovakia, Poland, and East Germany, which flourished in the first decade, has been deteriorating. The relationship with Yugoslavia has always been very bad : though there is mutual recognition, there is no exchange of diplomats. There is mutual recognition with Rumania, while Albania, with a population estimated in 1964 to be only 1,814,000, less than half of that of Hong Kong, is the only socialist country in Europe which remains on China's side. In the attempt to win over Cuba, China lost finally to the Soviet Union.

*With capitalistic countries.* Among the capitalistic countries, the United Kingdom was the first to recognize China in January 1950. In spite of Britain's enthusiasm, China has given it only a lukewarm reception. Exchange of diplomatic personnel has been confined to the chargé d'affaires category. Later, the United Kingdom's protest to Peking's expulsion of Catholic nuns in August 1966 led to the absence of the British chargé d'affaires in Peking from the Peking National Celebration. The expulsion of the Chinese chargé d'affaires from The Hague in July 1966 for violation of diplomatic practice in connection with the death of a Chinese engineer, has strained the relations of the two countries.

In China's relationship with the capitalistic countries, the greatest gain was the establishment of diplomatic relations with France in January 1964 and the inauguration of an airline link between Paris and Shanghai in September 1966. De Gaulle won the appreciation of Mao, not because France has any reputable record in the history of colonialism and imperialism, but because he had set out to impair the United States' domination over the affairs of Europe, in line with Mao's policy of splitting the West and isolating America.

*With the Afro-Asian countries.* There was a time when China posed as the champion of anti-colonialism and anti-imperialism amongst the formerly oppressed peoples of Asia and Africa. The

Bandung Conference was helpful in boosting China's position. The missions of Liu Shao-chi, Chou En-lai, and Chen Yi to the Asian and African countries were designed to rally the countries there to China's side.[24] They were designed also, in the race with Russia, to foster their position as better spokesmen of the Asian and African peoples. It was as much a counter-measure to weaken Russia as a sign of over-aggressiveness in the Chinese Communists. In the event, however, efforts proved to be unrewarding. The Chinese have not succeeded in convincing these emancipated peoples that the Chinese have anything better to offer for their freedom and well-being than the converted ex-colonists and ex-imperialists are capable of, with the exception of revolution and more revolution. It was reported in November 1966 that Ghana and China had decided to withdraw their embassies from each other's capital after some months of tension between the two countries since the current Ghanaian régime overthrew President Kwame Nkrumah while he was on his way to Peking early in 1966.

China's relation with Laos, Cambodia, and North Vietnam, the new independent states from former French Indo-China, close to China and embittered with colonialism and imperialism as they are, have much to be desired. Even in North Vietnam, China has failed to win over Ho Chi-min to opposing the Soviet Union in the Sino-Soviet dispute. China's relations with Pakistan, Ceylon, and countries in the Near East are at best not unfriendly. Unless there is a miraculous change, the image of Communist China as the rising sun in the east, is growing dim.

There are two countries whose relationships with China have changed so much that may deserve individual mention. One is India and the other Indonesia.

[24] The missions were mainly led by Chou En-lai, Premier of the People's Republic. The countries he covered from 1954 to 1966, some of which he visited more than once, were : in Asia : India, Burma, North Vietnam, Mongolia, Indonesia, Cambodia, Pakistan, Afghanistan, Nepal, Ceylon, North Korea, Syria, and Palestine. In Africa : United Arab Republic, Algeria, Morocco, Tunisia, Ghana, Mali, Guinea, Somalia, Sudan, Tanzania, and Ethiopia.

India's position in Asian affairs became prominent when it was accepted by both sides of the Korean War, by the Americans as well as the Chinese, as the Chairman of the Commission to enforce the terms of truce in the cease-fire of 1953. In the attempt to promote Afro-Asian solidarity, any gesture of Sino-Indian solidarity should go a long way. So when Nehru, the Indian Premier, went to Peking at the invitation of China on 19 October 1954, he was given a big welcome. Two hundred thousand people lined the street to cheer him as he entered the capital from the airport. Then the historical friendship between China and India was played up. It was said that for over 2000 years there had been no incident of war between the two countries in spite of a long common frontier of 3000 miles. Both peoples were said to be peace-loving and at the same time to have the largest population in the world. This was the situation in 1954. Such a friendship did not persist long; it was interrupted even while Nehru was alive. The two countries went into armed conflict at the border in October 1962. Probably India felt that China was bringing pressure on her all the time; and with the nuclear weapon in China's hand, it was logical for India to accuse China of using nuclear blackmail. The cause of anti-colonialism and anti-imperialism would have been much advanced if China had been able to retain close ties with India, a great symbol of rebirth from colonialism.

The case of Indonesia, though somewhat different from that of India, has the same demoralizing effect on the prestige of China. Here is another Asian people which won its independence from the Dutch after World War II. Although it has a population smaller than that of India, still it is 82 million strong. The Afro-Asian Conference held on its territory in April 1955 was attended by twenty-four countries, and is known as the Bandung Conference. Sukarno, president for life and national hero of Indonesia, whose life-term presidency has now been terminated and whose hero image has waned, is probably Communist in aspiration but not in confession. The prospects of Communist expansion in Asia would be so much better if Indonesia, with its strategic base in the southern Pacific, were at China's side. One may recall the importance attached to Sukarno's visit to China in 1955 when he was given the welcome not only of a head of state but also of a comrade. But, unfortunately, things in Asia do not seem to turn out in the way the Chinese Communist leaders have wanted. The failure of the Indonesian Communist Party in the *coup d'état* in October 1965, which is said to have had the fore-knowledge of Sukarno's most trusted men and the support of the Chinese Communist Party, has given China another setback. Hatred of the Chinese in Indonesia seems to have mounted, which we do not find in countries without Chinese Communist infiltration. That is enough to reflect the change of attitude of the Asians towards the Chinese Communist Party—from admiration to hatred. The Chinese Communist Party is now "eating its own fruits".

*China and Japan.* Finally, let us look at the Sino-Japanese situation. There is no diplomatic relation between China and Japan. There is a Japan–China Friendship Association in Japan, but no China–Japan Friendship Association in China. Although there is no such association by name, its functions are taken care of by the China Association of Cultural Relations with Other Countries. The Chinese People's Republic has not yet taken up any major issue with Japan. Contacts have been confined to the minor ones such as the return of Japanese prisoners of war, returning the ashes of cremated bodies of Japanese soldiers who died in China in the Sino-Japanese war, the exchange of athletic teams, exchange of news reporters, delegations to conferences of a non-diplomatic nature, the signing of certain industrial and commercial contracts, and the like. The two countries have refrained from antagonizing each other. Both seem to be marking time.

A militaristic or anti-Communistic Japan would possibly be the greatest threat to Communist China. One may recall that when the Japanese attack on China was imminent in 1936, a year before the Sino-Japanese war broke out, Mao Tse-tung, realizing that Japanese militarism was more detrimental to the Communists' existence than the Nationalists, was willing to collaborate with Chiang Kai-shek in the united front against Japan in spite of the fact that Chiang had killed so many of the Chinese Communists and was still planning to encircle them. That is to say, Mao considered Japan as their most deadly enemy.

One might speculate that if the present policy of the leaders of the Chinese Communist Party remains largely as it is, and if the world situation worsens, it is conceivable that the greatest enemy to Chinese communism will still be Japan, which has a population of over 100 million. The Japanese are a highly efficient, patriotic, solidified, organized, and unique people, who are too clever for the Chinese Communists to infiltrate. They have no racial barrier in China and, in a way, very little language barrier. They have always had great ambition in China. Besides, they have a masterly knowledge of Chinese culture, Chinese history, Chinese society, and, on top of that, 8 years' experience of occupation in China. Japan had to give up China not because of Chinese superiority in war, but because of American intervention. When the time really comes, particularly if the United States is plunged into war with China, it will not be the Americans who will have to fight on the Chinese soil but it will be the Japanese whom they once restrained. The Japanese would come to China then, not as imperialists but as crusaders to free the Chinese from communism. Japan, with its high level of industrialization and with its talented people, would not be contented with being a silent member in the affairs of Asia forever. This silent neighbour of Communist China remains the real threat to the latter. One must remember that Japanese lost pre-eminence not by China's dictate but by the dictate of China's former friend and present enemy, the so-called "paper tiger", the United States.

Speculation about the shape of things to come will be of no significance if Japan also becomes Communist. Though that is not an impossibility, it looks rather remote. Even if Japan becomes Communist, judging from the recent expulsion of the pro-Mao elements from the Japanese Communist Party, it would be more likely to become pro-Russia than pro-Mao. The role of the Chinese Communist Party as well as the role of Japan in Asia's future is precarious.

But which is worse for the Western world, or for the cause of freedom if you will—a Communist China or a non-Communist China with a united China–Japan Oriental Entente? Would the latter not invite the danger of "yellow peril"? Such worries are perhaps only the worries of those who take a traditional view of human history.

# CHAPTER 8

# Problems and Crises

IN OUR review of the development of society and education in People's China many problems have presented themselves. Some of them are more or less of a social and cultural nature, while others are more or less of a political and economic nature. But whatever they are, in their amalgamation, they constitute a situation of grave magnitude which, unless duly remedied, will create serious crises.

We are aware that what we consider to be problems may not be problems in the eyes of the Chinese Communists, at least in the eyes of those who steer the Chinese Communist Party. For our every expression of concern, they may have their rebuttal. For example, when we say that the Chinese people are not having enough to eat, they would say that the Chinese are eating plentifully; when we say that the People's Government is losing the support of the people, they would say that it is gaining greater and greater support; when we say that the international situation is becoming more and more unfavourable to China, they would say that it is growing more and more favourable. They would also rebuke our concern as malicious slander, or, at best, regard it as bourgeois worries which do not trouble those who look at things from the proletarian standpoint. Even if they concede the existence of certain problems, they would say that such phenomena are of a minor nature and that these exist in all countries and are in no sense critical for China.

In the democratic countries where there is freedom of speech, there are many channels for public opinion, but in Communist China, where the only opinion is official, and dissenting views are suppressed even on the highest levels of the party, there is no public opinion in which to reflect its problems. It is fortunate that there were two occasions where some public opinion was expressed in the Chinese newspapers and publications, though they were of a milder nature and expressed in a guarded manner. One was in the "Hundred Flowers Bloom and Hundred Schools Contend" Campaign of 1956–7 when certain criticisms were recorded; and the other was in the earliest stage of the Great Proletarian Cultural Revolution of 1966 during the attack on certain Communist writers, whose writings reflected indirectly the general dissatisfaction over certain policies of the Government. From these and other sources, we shall try to present some of the problems in China today.

We shall list the problems under several headings, but although they are placed under separate headings, in reality they are all interrelated.

## FAITHLESSNESS OF THE GOVERNMENT

Keeping faith has been upheld in China as the minimum condition of responsible government throughout the ages, just as keeping one's word has been the minimum condition of integrity of personality. This was taught by the sages and exemplified in history.[1] It may be that good faith is not in the Chinese Communist code of ethics, for they do not seem to talk about it in Communist China. The promises of the Chinese Communists on the establishment of the People's Republic have been broken heedlessly one by one, as if their promises were meant to be

---

[1] Chinese students are familiar with this story in their history. In the fourth century B.C., Duke Hsiao of the Kingdom of Chin (great-great-grandfather of Chin Shih Huang) was afraid that the people would not trust him. Therefore he placed a 30-foot post at the southern gate of his capital and said that whoever would move it to the northern gate would be awarded ten pieces of gold. Nobody ventured to move it. He then said: whoever moved it would be awarded fifty pieces of gold. A man moved it. He was immediately awarded fifty pieces of gold. This was to show he practised no deceit. Henceforth his decrees were observed. (See *Shih Chi (The Historical Record)*, Vol. 68.)

deceit. We have referred to the five-star flag as the greatest mockery in modern political history. The Communist Government says one thing and does another. To paraphrase a Communist slander : "They wave the five-star flag to attack the five-star flag."

At the time of the Hundred Schools Contend Movement, the old intellectuals were hestitant to voice their opinions for fear that it might be a trap, and even if it was not meant to be a trap, there might be reprisals later somehow, somewhere. Mao Tse-tung then gave his assurance with all earnestness that there would be no repercussions of their criticisms. He made three statements, taken from popular Chinese usage, each consisting of two sentences of four Chinese words which may be translated as follows :

> When one knows a thing, he will not be quiet about it,
> When he speaks, he will tell the whole tale.
> He who speaks is not guilty,
> He who listens is thus warned.
> He who has faults should correct them,
> He who has no faults should endeavour to do better.

With Mao's assurance, many democratic leaders came forward to express their views. Lo Lung-chi, Fei Hsiao-tung, and Chang Nai-chi were among a long roll of high intellectuals who were more vocal in their criticism. But in June 1957, when the Hundred Schools Contend Movement was replaced by the Anti-Rightist Movement, they were severely persecuted. Since then we have heard nothing from them except their repenting self-criticism. One wonders whether the Communists have lost their sense of responsibility or, to be cynical, whether they have lost their memory.

The Chinese Communist leaders are now conscious of the people's grudges over their breach of promise. They have become so sensitive to criticisms of this kind that they consider any talk on untrustworthiness as double-talk directed against them. For this reason, Teng To has been the target of attack for this alleged double-talk. In an article written by Yao Wen-yuan, a leader of the recent Proletarian Cultural Revolution, entitled "Teng To's *Evening Chats at Yenshan* is Anti-Party and Anti-Socialist Double Talk", Teng is accused of "Slandering our Party as 'Going Back on Its Own Word' and Being 'Untrustworthy'". Since we have mentioned Teng To more than once, and since he is an interesting writer, whose sketch on "Special Treatment for 'Amnesia'" makes a fascinating story, a longer quotation from this piece of writing[2] may not be improper :

> There are many people afflicted with diseases . . . one of which is called "amnesia". This is a very troublesome ailment, and whoever suffers from it cannot be cured easily.
> Such a patient . . . often shows such symptoms as going back on his own word and failing to keep faith, and people are even inclined to suspect that he is feigning idiocy and is therefore untrustworthy.
> In *More Stories Told by Ai Tzu* by Lu Cho of the Ming Dynasty, there is a tale which presents a typical case of amnesia :
>
> > There was a man in *Chi* State who was so forgetful that he forgot to stop once he started walking and forgot to rise once he lay down. His wife was much worried. She said to him, "I have heard that Ai Tzu is a witty and clever man and can treat the most baffling diseases. Why don't you go and consult him?" The husband replied, "Very good." He rode away on horseback, bringing his bow and arrow with him. Having gone a short distance, he felt a call of nature and dismounted. He thrust his arrow into the earth and fastened his horse to a tree. Having eased himself, he looked to the left and then exclaimed on seeing his arrow, "My God! What a narrow escape! Where is this arrow from? It nearly hit me!" He looked to the right and at the sight of his horse, cried in joy, "Although I am badly scared, I have got a horse." When he was about to start off again, rein in hand, he suddenly trampled on his own leavings. Stamping his feet, he complained, "I've trodden on some dog's dung and ruined my shoes! What a pity!" He whipped the horse and rode home. Soon he reached his house and hesitated before the gate, wonder-in to himself, "Who lives here? Is this Master Ai's House?" His wife saw his bewilderment and knew that he had lost his memory again and gave him a scolding. The man was puzzled, asking: "We are not acquainted, madam. What do you swear at me for?"
>
> Apparently this man was a bad case of amnesia.

---

[2] This sketch appeared in the *Frontline*, Peking, 14 November 1964. The English translation is adapted from *The Great Socialist Cultural Revolution in China*, Vol. 2, Foreign Language Press, Peking, 1966.

> According to ancient Chinese medical books . . . one of the causes of amnesia is the abnormal functioning of the so-called breath of life. In consequence, the patient not only suffers from loss of memory but gradually becomes capricious, has great difficulty with his speech, is irritable and finally goes mad and runs amuck. . . . Unless treated in time, he will become an idiot. Thus if anyone finds either of these symptoms present in himself, he must promptly take a complete rest and say nothing and do nothing, and if he insists on speaking and acting, he will come to grief.
>
> Are there then really no positive methods for treating this disease? Certainly there are. . . . According to modern Western medicine, one way is to hit the patient on the head with a specially made club to induce a state of "Shock" and then restore him to consciousness.

Whether Teng To was talking medicine or talking politics, the fact that a government should be so intolerant toward his writing is enough to show that trustworthiness could not be its indisputable virtue.

A government cannot survive long by deceit. The Chinese Communists like to pose as truthful and often quote from Abraham Lincoln without naming him : "You can deceive some people some of the time, but you cannot deceive all the people all the time." It is the Chinese Communists themselves that should take this to heart.

## HARDSHIPS OF LIFE

There is a great deal of hardship for the people in China today. They are driven to work hard while they have little time to relax and few provisions to meet the necessities of life.

One can well understand that for a country in its endeavour to make progress in a shortened time, without much foundation, the people have to work harder and to live in austerity.

If the demand for more work and less comfort for the people is within reason, the Government should be praised instead of blamed; many governments have had to make similar demands in times of emergency such as in times of war and calamity. But if there is no restraint, and the people have to work harder and harder with no end in sight, and at the same time receive less and less, year in and year out, then such a system of society should be challenged.

In China, since the adoption of the five-year plans, targets for production have been set. In order to drive the people to exceed the targets, the slogan *sheng hao to kuai* (which means saving more material, doing better, producing more, and finishing faster) was advanced. The result is that the people are constantly being spurred by the driver. After one target there is another target; and after one set of goals, there is another set of goals.

The Communists are fond of looking upon production as a form of warfare. They call the labour force "labour army", the productive units in the communes "production brigades", and the productive enterprises "the productive front". They praise workers who continue to work in spite of having sustained injuries as heroes who do not withdraw from the "firing line". The military climate in production adds much more strain to the life of the people.

Besides heavy work in the day-time, people are required to attend political meetings and study groups in the evenings. They are kept so busy that by the time they go home they are dead tired. There is no leisure and no enjoyment in life. Fun, to the Communist cadres, is only bourgeois luxury. In the labour camps the situation is even more deplorable.

The Chinese Communists boast of the unlimited manpower at their disposal, but they feel no need to treasure it. The article which Teng To wrote in 1961 in sympathy of the people entitled "The Theory of Treasuring Labour Power"[3] reflects in a moderate

---

[3] This article was another of the series *Evening Chats at Yenshan* which was published in the *Peking Evening News* on 30 April 1961. We shall quote it in part as follows:

"As far back as the periods of the Spring and Autumn Annals and the Warring States and thereabout, there were many great statesmen who understood the importance of treasuring labour power. . . . Through the experience of their rule, they discovered the 'limits' on the 'expenditure of the people's labour power'; in fact, they discovered certain objective laws governing the increase and decrease of labour power.

"It is written in the 'Chapter on the Royal System' of the Book of Rites: 'The people's labour power should be used for no more than three days each year.' On this statement Chen Hao, a scholar of the Yuan Dynasty, glossed: 'The people's labour power was used to build city-walls, roads, lanes, ditches, palaces and temples.' This actually refers

manner the misuse of manpower in Communist China. For this writing he is now paying his penalty for "Slandering Our Party as Not Treasuring Labour Power During the Great Leap Forward".

One of the most obvious sights to visitors in China is the poor way the people are clad. Each person is rationed to only 3 yards of cloth a year which is not enough for a suit of clothes. As a recent observer has said, the cloth is only sufficient for a change of a pair of sleeves, the collar, and for patching. The variety of textile goods in the Communist stores in Hong Kong are for export and foreign exchange only. They are not obtainable or even seen in the stores in the mainland. The Chinese Foreign Minister, Chen Yi, has been reported as saying that China must build up its nuclear weapons even if the people have to go without pants.[4] If by pants is meant new pants, then truly the Chinese are already without pants!

It is true that people can live without pants, but they cannot

---

*Footnote 3 (continued)*

in our present-day language to the labour power to be used in all kinds of capital construction. According to the level of the social productive forces of their time, the ancients fixed an amount of labour power to be used in all kinds of capital construction—approximately only one percent of the total labour power available. . . .

"Drawing up plans for Prince Chung Erh of the state of Tsin, Hu Yen advised, 'After saving your strength for a dozen years, you can go far.' He was then escorting the prince past Wulu of the state of Wei, and even predicted that 'in twelve years you will conquer this land'. . . . From this story, it can be seen that a man like Hu Yen well understood how to accumulate strength in the historical circumstances of ancient times. If a man of the seventh century B.C. understood this truth, we who live in the sixties of the twentieth century should naturally understand it even better.

"We should draw new enlightenment from the experience of the ancients."

[4] In 1963 Khrushchev ridiculed the Chinese Government's policy of building up its war weapons at the expense of the people to the extent of five people to a pair of pants. In Chen Yi's interview with Japanese reporters, referring to the subject of pants, he said that without modern weapons, China would forever remain a second- or third-class nation. The Chinese must have modern weapons even if the people have to go without pants. (See *Sing Tao Newspaper*, Hong Kong, 29 October 1963.)

very well live without food. Food has been in short supply and people are constantly under the threat of not having enough to eat; half-filled stomachs have decreased people's vitality. Lack of meat and oil have brought about illnesses of many kinds affecting the eyes and the liver and causing swellings on the limbs. Fortunately, nature has been merciful in that the people's physique has the blessings of abundant sunshine and fresh air and the invigorating effects of manual labour.

The Chinese Communists never admit the shortage of food or that the people are not having enough to eat. At first when the city people complained that they were not having enough to eat, the Communists said that it was because the country people were eating much better than before. But later when the country people flocked to the cities in order to find more to eat, the Communists laid the blame on natural calamities. In 1957 a former public leader remarked that the people in the rural areas of Kwangtung Province were on the verge of starvation.[5] The great influx of refugees to Hong Kong in 1962 from the Chinese border which was known to the whole world was due chiefly to the shortage of food. Although the food situation has been improved since 1962, tight rationing is not yet relaxed.

It is true that human beings can bear greater hardships than is generally believed, and the Chinese people because of their cultural and historical background can probably bear even more. Still there is a limit to one's forbearance, just as there is a limit to what a donkey can bear and there is limit to the effectiveness of the whip. No one can work without rest, and few would work harder if it makes little difference to their well-being. None would prefer a social order of that kind if he had a choice. The Chinese Communists once painted a glorious picture of the beautiful Fatherland which was to be the people's and made

---

[5] This was a well known case. Lo Yih-chun, a member of the Kuomintang Revolutionary Committee, in his tour of the eastern part of Kwangtung Province in 1957, made the remark that the people were on the verge of starvation. He was immediately attacked by the local Communist Party and he had to disguise himself in order to escape. He was finally persecuted in Canton for this remark.

promises of a better living for all. After 19 years there is no indication of improvement, their promises have turned out to be
empty talk and the people have become disillusioned—the
enthusiasm of the early years in support of the government is
vanishing.

## UNREST OF INTELLECTUALS

All through Chinese history, the intellectuals have always
played a major role in public affairs. Without going too far back
into history, the modern events which we have spoken about in
an earlier chapter are good examples. Such were the 1898 reform
led by Kang Yu-wei, the 1911 revolution led by Sun Yat-sen, the
renaissance led by Chen Tu-hsiu, Hu Shih and others based on
Peking University, and the 1919 Student Movement sparked to
explosion by Liang Chi-chao in his telegram from Paris.

Whether the Communists like it or not, according to Mencius,
people are of two classes, those who do mental labour and those
who do manual labour. He said: "Hence, there is the saying,
'Some labour with their minds, and some with their strength'."
The mental labourers are the intellectuals. They form only a
small fraction of the population but their influence is all out of
proportion to their size. In modern terms they are the scholars,
university professors, writers, journalists, poets, novelists, dramatists, artists, scientists, specialists, doctors, engineers, and teachers.
In as much as those who use their pens are mental workers, the
intellectuals would also include, in a broad sense, the managers,
secretaries, and the whole group of clerks and office workers. The
Chinese Communists like to classify them as far as possible into
the workers' class or the peasant class according to the nature of
their employment and their place of work. Since such people
do not belong to the workers' and peasants' class, they could be
considered to be in the bourgeois class. The Communists do not
regard the intellectuals as a class, but they do look upon them
generally as of the bourgeoisie, partly because of their family
status and partly because of their ways of life and habits of

thought. As bourgeoisie, the intellectuals are looked upon with disfavour.

The fact that they are intellectuals implies that they are inclined to use their intellect, to explore new ideas, to indulge in intellectual engagements, in abstractions, and in the search for truth. They would not be intellectuals unless they did so. Their reluctance to conform to the dictates of Communist authorities is sufficient cause for their disfavour.

But the Chinese intellectuals, particularly the leading intellectuals, have always enjoyed high social esteem in Chinese society. They have their cultural contribution to make and they do not work for pecuniary motives; because of these characteristics they win special favour in society.

After the beginning of the Anti-Japanese War in 1937, the Chinese Communist Party pursued the policy of recruiting intellectuals. At first, it tried to draw the intellectuals, particularly the discontented and destitute intellectuals, such as teachers and students, who fled from the war zones. The intention was that, after they got into the Communist area, they should be gradually educated and transformed in accordance with the Communist design under the maxim "to unite and to educate". Before the intellectuals were under their control, the policy was "to unite"; after they were under control or after the iron curtain was lowered, the policy was "to educate". Before the Communists took over China, the Chinese intellectuals, the more progressive ones in particular, were hopeful of the new régime. But since the establishment of the People's Republic, especially since 1957, they feel that they have been discriminated against, distrusted, abused, humiliated, and persecuted. They feel out of place.

In the institutions of learning as well as in the government departments, service agencies, and productive enterprises, the high posts are not given to those who have knowledge but to those who have party or Liberation Army affiliation. Experts and specialists are being watched by party cadres, marking them as unreliable and even suspect elements. Professors are sent to farms to toil and run errands for the poor peasants. Scholars have to go through all kinds of ordeals and are denounced by their colleagues and students in addition to having to join in self-denunciation. Their reinstatement in society is attained only by favour of the party. Labour camps in far-flung areas are full of condemned Chinese intellectuals who are receiving their education there through hard labour, for having been critical or resistant. In the Great Proletarian Cultural Revolution of late, the intellectuals are again targets of attack. The suffering they have to go through could be more severe than in previous years. Even after this cultural revolution is over, other movements and purges of intellectuals will continue to come, with a new movement or purge growing from every previous one. There is no end to the intellectual's worry, thus unrest is rising. A university professor once said, as reported in a Peking newspaper : "When I see a party member, my heart trembles."

One has the right to ask how the energies and talents of the intellectuals could be released under such conditions; how any society could afford to look down upon its intellectuals and abuse them so heedlessly; and how any government could survive long with its intellectuals opposed to it.

## PEOPLE ARE CONFUSED

The people in China are confused. Since the people who are outside China, who are not under such emotional strain and who have other means of checking what is going on in China, are also confused by conditions in China, we can imagine how much more so are the Chinese people behind the iron curtain.

The Chinese people look at their national flag, the beautiful five-star red flag, but the stars need to be explained. Why are there five stars? What do the four small stars stand for? Where are the other two "twinkling little stars" now? Why should Mao choose that flag out of all flags?

In the 1954 Constitution there are these provisions :

> Citizens of the People's Republic of China enjoy freedom of speech, freedom of the press, freedom of assembly, freedom of association, freedom of procession and freedom of demonstration. . . . Citizens of the People's Republic of China enjoy freedom of religious belief. . . . The personal freedom of citizens of the People's Republic of China is inviolable. . . . Citizens of the People's Republic of China enjoy freedom of residence and freedom to change their residence.

But in actuality, as everyone who has been in China knows, such freedoms do not exist there. It would be closer to the truth if all those statements were changed into the negative : "Citizens of the People's Republic of China *do not* enjoy freedom of speech, freedom of press, etc." Then, why was freedom specified? Why was there the Constitution at all?

China speaks of practising democratic centralism. Article 2 of the Constitution states :

> All power of the People's Republic of China belongs to the people. The organs through which the people exercise power are the National People's Congress and the local people's congresses at various levels. The National People's Congress, the local people's congresses and the organs of the state practise democratic centralism.

Although matters concerning public control are the business of the State and are not the business of the people, yet the people can wonder why the State, which is at the behest of the party, does not practise democratic centralism. Why do the Communist Party Congress and the party-controlled National People's Congress not convene when such a big movement as the Great Proletarian Cultural Revolution has swept over the country and the cloud has been hanging over the land for over a year? Why should it be directed by Lin Piao and the Liberation Army? Why don't Liu Shao-chi and Teng Hsiao-ping speak? Why doesn't Mao Tse-tung speak? If personal dictatorship is to be the form of government, then why advocate "democratic centralism"? Why "democratic"?

The people are told to obey the party and look up to its members for guidance. With this the people have complied. They have trusted the party members in the belief that the latter represented the interests of the party. But now the people are told that many of the party members, including those in the top authorities, are actually anti-party elements who have wormed their way into the party. If the party had not been aware of it, how can the masses of the people know who are bona fide party members and who are not? People are bewildered about what is going on in the ruling house and what is going to happen next.

The people have been educated to respect the Communist Youth and Young Pioneers as the party's trusted assistants, but now with the new organization of the Red Guards, people ask what has become of the Communist youth and the red scarf pioneers? Are they no good? Are they unreliable? Has party education with these selected youths and children for all this time been a complete failure?

People were told that the road which the Soviet Union had travelled was what China was to follow, and that Russia was China's best teacher. They were told that the Soviet Union had no territorial ambition in China and that the postponement of the return of Port Arthur was at China's own request. They were told that Russian aid was selfless, and that the fraternal bond between the Soviet people and Chinese people was unbreakable. Now, having been educated in that way of thought, the people are told that Russia is the collaborator of American imperialism and Russia is the target of denunciation. Who is not confused?

Since the people have to accept certain ideas at one time and reject them at another, to respect certain leaders one day and scorn them the next, and what is true today becomes false tomorrow, it would be indeed strange if they were not perplexed. Who knows whether the present path will not be reversed again? As Mao Tse-tung is well over 70 and his vitality is evidently on a decline, who can be sure that what happened in Russia after the death of Stalin will not happen in China when Mao passes away?

There is no certainty and no security. People are held in suspense about what will or will not happen next. The people in China become more and more confused as the years go by.

## RULE BY FEAR

China is now controlled by force and the threat of force; behind that force are persecution, imprisonment, and hard labour; and behind the mob, the prisons, and the labour camps are the police and the Liberation Army. We do not need to mention the court, the so-called People's Court, because it exists only in name.

The labour camps are places of mental, spiritual, and physical torture, to which thousands and thousands have been sent and have perished without being heard of thereafter. Those who have lived in China can testify that the fear of persecution is real to most people. When they hear knocking at the door at night, fear swells in their heart, wondering whether it means police arrest and what the accusation is. Their heart is not at ease until they see that the man at the door is but a personal friend.

To control by force is to control by fear. To appeal to fear is to appeal to the lowest instinct of man and animal. Who is not afraid and who is not conditioned by fear? It is true that martyrs are not afraid, but martyrs are unknown in China today. Martyrs are known only in societies where righteousness still has a place and where righteous public opinion exists. In China today all mass media such as newspapers, publications, radio, printing facilities, and mimeographic apparatus are party-monopolized and party-controlled. Any dissenting opinion is prohibited and has no means of communication. The only opinion is official opinion. Martyrdom is reduced to the status of anti-revolution, anti-people, and anti-party, and, worse still, is branded as the anti-social activities of imperialism, capitalism, and landlordism. Since party control is so tight and the party has built up such a huge machine of control, if there are martyrs, so many martyrs would be so many worthless self-sacrifices. Bare arms are no match for fire-arms. The Chinese have learned through centuries of tyranny to bear it all, and they patiently wait for the coming of dawn in the belief that dawn will eventually come no matter how dark and how long the night.

According to the Chinese sages' theory of government, to control by force is the way of the warrior and to control by benevolence is the way of the prince. As Mencius said : "When one subdues men by force they do not submit to him in heart. They submit because their strength is not adequate to resist. When one subdues men by virtue, in their heart of hearts they are pleased, and sincerely submit."

If the Chinese traditional concept of human nature and of society still holds true, the basis of government of the Chinese Communist régime is contrary to what we know to be sound. The present régime can survive only in so far as it can maintain its force, but the antagonism of the people toward the party is inevitable. What people say with their lips is not what they feel in their heart. Indeed, when they shout "Long live the Communist Party", they may wish in their heart that it could soon perish. What appears to be, is far from being what it really is. The greatest danger to the Chinese Communist régime, as it is to all dictatorships, is that it has no way of telling the true supporters from the pretenders. The case of Stalin's dictatorship was the clearest Communist example, not to mention those of Mussolini and Hitler. Is a government safe which rests on the support of potential conspirators?

## QUALITY OF LEADERSHIP

Some like to call those who hold the reins of government in China, to which 700 million people are subjected, China's rulers, but it may conform more with common practice to call them leaders. Whatever we call them, the quality of leadership is involved.

When the Chinese Communists first came into power there was the general opinion that they were good at destruction but would not be good at construction, that they were successful in the arts of war but would not be successful in the arts of peace, that they were capable of managing the rural folk but would not be capable of managing the city folk. Although the Communists claimed that they were capable in both ways, affairs in China in the last 19 years seem to confirm the general opinion of the early days.

Leadership in China today is confined to members of the Communist Party and the Liberation Army who excel in political or military qualifications and in those qualifications only. As they say: "The political is the standard of the marshal." The social status of a *Chiai Fang Chun*[6] (Liberation Army member) is very high and if a person is both a Communist and a *Chiai Fang Chun*, his status will be the most enviable.

The Communist leaders today were revolutionaries to start with. For over a quarter of a century, from the time their party was formed to the time they took over the reins of government, the trials they went through were severe. They survived the Kuomintang's purges, arrests, imprisonments, encirclements, and persecutions of all kinds; they struggled, fought, escaped, and retreated. The most famous of the retreats was the famous 25,000 li (Chinese mile) long march of 1934–5. If they had not possessed the qualities of the warrior and been imbued with hatred, bitterness, resoluteness, ruthlessness, and violence, they would have acquired them in the years of adversity. As *Chiai Fang Chun* they were brought up to discipline, uniformity, rigidity, and collective habits of life, accepting orders without dispute and accustomed to resort to force.

With the Liberation Army basically recruited in the backward rural areas, the mentality of rural folk is predominant. This mentality is what the city people in China used to call *tu tou tu nao* (earth-head earth-brain), a state of mind which is easy to sense but difficult to define. These recruits lack the sense of culture, refinement, and education, and lag behind in their social, scientific, and international outlooks on life.

It is evident that the qualities of revolutionaries, soldiers, and peasants are not the same qualities one would look for in leader-

---

[6] The Chinese term *Chiai Fang Chun* (the Liberation Army) is used both as a collective noun and a common noun. For example it is correct to say "He is a *Chiai Fang Chun*".

ship for national reconstruction, in civil affairs, and in city growth, but the Chinese Communists claim that they are also capable in these aspects. They take control not only in the central government and in the key positions, but in everything : in units large or small, national or local, rural or urban, military or civil. As we have said, they dictate to the intellectuals; while they use the latter, they use them as tools; while they use them, they repeatedly disgrace them. The humiliation of the intellectuals, coupled with the arrogance of the Communists in China today, reminds one of when Greek scholars were subjugated as household slaves by their culturally inferior Roman conquerors.

Recently some Red Guards from the rural areas in North China, after paying homage to Mao Tse-tung in Peking, came to Canton for the "interlocking of revolutionary experience" with the local Red Guards. They found the bananas and pineapples hard to eat; because with their ignorance, they ate the bananas with the skins on and the pineapples without taking off the spikes. These are Mao Tse-tung's favoured youth who lead China's cultural revolution.

Those who do not know come forth to lead those who do. In this "Country of the Blind",[7] what is more tragic is not the blind leading the blind, but the blind leading those who have sight. The sentiment expressed at this point may represent the sentiments of thousands and thousands of Chinese intellectuals today.

The question of future leadership, of who will succeed Mao Tse-tung and how the new generation will take over from the present generation, is principally the concern of the Chinese Communists themselves. However if it is merely a change from one dictator to another, from one clique to another; or if the leadership is still confined to the qualifications of the political, the military, and to the peasants and manual workers; and if the national programme is circumscribed by political dogma, military discipline, and rural mentality, then any change is just a switch

[7] *Country of the Blind* is the title of a book on the Soviet Union by George S. Counts and Nucia Lodge, Boston, 1949.

from one tyranny to another tyranny. The Chinese situation would not be improved.

## COMMUNISM VERSUS CHINESE CULTURE

Are communism and Chinese culture compatible or incompatible? To what extent is Chinese national character favourable to communism and to what extent unfavourable? Answers to these questions will throw light on the prospects of communism in China.

Communism was forced upon the Chinese people by a small fraction of the Chinese population, by the Chinese Communist Party with the use of its Liberation Army. The fact that the people have had to be mobilized to learn Marxism–Leninism since the establishment of the Communist régime is evident of the people's ignorance of communism in the past. As we have said before, it was not communism and the Communist Party which the people particularly favoured, it was the Kuomintang Government under Chiang Kai-shek which the people wanted to be rid of. What the people wanted was a new government in the assumption that no government could be worse. It was exactly because of their ignorance of what communism was and what communism was not, that they were so easily misled by the deception of the Communists as well as by their own illusions.

Can a political philosophy be forced upon a people which has a cultural background of thousands of years with a philosophy of their own, with a long line of sages, thinkers, statesmen, and teachers, and with a rich endowment of classics, literature, ethics, and art? We should remember also that this new political philosophy is alien to them and is forced upon them by those who had not heard of it themselves before the 1917 Russian Revolution and who are in fact novices in the doctrine.[8]

[8] In the words of Mao Tse-tung: "Before the October Revolution, the Chinese not only did not know Lenin and Stalin, but did not know Marx and Engels either." (See Mao Tse-tung, *On the People's Democratic Dictatorship*.) The *Communist Manifesto*, the most important document of communism, was not translated into Chinese until as late as 1920 by Chen Wang-tao.

Chinese society is built on the principles of human relationship; between father and son, between husband and wife, between siblings, between friends, and between the sovereign and his subordinates. These relationships are as simple as they are natural where definition is not in dispute, but the communistic society is built on the idea of the class struggle between the proletariat and the capitalist. Who are the proletariat? Ignoring Karl Marx's definition of the proletariat, the Chinese Communists now define it as the peasants, the workers, and the Liberation Army soldiers. The peasants, workers, and soldiers have nothing in common in their ideology; the Chinese proletariat class is arbitrary and artificial. Yet, the revolutionary war in China is now waged according to the idea of the class struggle. The Chinese do have the concept of opposites as the *yin* (female principle) and the *yang* (male principle), or the negative and the positive; but, opposites, to the Chinese mind, are mutually admissive and complementary, as in the case of husband and wife and of night and day. It is harmony between opposites that the Chinese seek for and not antagonism.

There are many interpretations of communism. If Khrushchev, formerly First Secretary of the Soviet Union Communist Party, and Yang Hsien Chen, formerly President of the Highest Party School of the Chinese Communist Party, do not know how to interpret communism properly (as the Chinese Communist leaders allege), then what chance is there for the Chinese masses of semi-illiterates to understand communism properly? Before the Communists argue their case and come to an agreement as to what communism is and what communism is not, it is difficult to convince the Chinese that their old culture should be scrapped, particularly as the Chinese, as a people, are too practical to be bothered by theories and doctrines. While the Red Guards were scrapping Chinese culture and regard the old culture as fundamentally detrimental to communism, the old intellectuals in China, including certain prominent Communists, gave them warning that they must not blacken the faces of their ancestors and vilify their descent as offspring of wicked and unworthy ancestry.

In the contest between Chinese culture and communism, the world has yet to see whether Chinese culture will survive communism, or communism will survive Chinese culture.

## COMMUNISM VERSUS DEMOCRACY

Democracy, no matter how one defines it, is the trend of modern society, which has been accelerated by the advancement of science and technology. It answers the yearnings of mankind throughout the ages. It is a social current which sweeps over all phases of life as a result of which individuals as well as peoples have been emancipated. The demand for democracy is so strong that even dictatorships have to pay it lip service and it is for this reason that the Chinese Communists in their efforts to win the people to their side advocated the New Democracy which was later renamed the People's Democracy.

The cry for "liberty, equality and fraternity" of the French Revolution has become the motto of democracy. In China, it was the ideal of democracy which ushered the downfall of the Ching Dynasty and the establishment of the Chinese Republic. It was the ideal of democracy which gave birth to the Chinese Renaissance and incited the struggle against feudalism, colonialism, and imperialism. If after all these struggles, China can return to a state which denies liberty, equality, and fraternity, and succeeds, then the history of mankind of the last 200 years will have been meaningless.

Liberty or freedom, particularly individual liberty or freedom, is the real test of democracy. Without personal freedom there can be no democracy.

We have mentioned in an earlier section the provisions in the Chinese Constitution of 1954. Those who know anything about People's China will know that all these freedoms are denied : freedom of speech, of press, of assembly, of association, of procession, of demonstration, of religious belief, of person, of residence and change of residence, of the people's homes. No one would be so rash in Communist China as to ask for freedom of procession and demonstration. Indeed, not only is there no freedom of speech, there is not even freedom of silence. Recently the people's homes have been forced to house the Red Guards, and the ancestral tablets in the people's homes are taken out and burned. To say that People's China provides for personal freedom is a huge propaganda lie—a mockery.

The denial of freedom does not only intrude on the individual's human rights, it also blocks the channel through which public opinion and public sentiment would be reflected. As a result of this blockage, as years go by, no danger-signal will reach the administrator. From the standpoint of cultural, scientific, and technological progress, the greatest possible enemy is encroachment.

## INTERNATIONAL ENMITY

China has not only internal problems but also external problems.

There was a time when the People's China enjoyed growing prestige in the international world. It had the Soviet Union as its ally. It was able to withstand the Americans in the Korean War. It established diplomatic relations with more countries than China ever had in the past with its long list of ambassadors. Sticking to its firm foreign policy, it was able to enhance the diplomatic status of the countries of formerly oppressed peoples and play down the status of the formerly leading nations. India was boosted and Britain played down, to tilt the international balance. Delegations were sent to many countries, while foreign delegations enjoyed being invited particularly to participate in the National Day Celebration in early autumn to witness the magnificent parades in China's capital. They paid tribute to China's accomplishments among their own people as well as informing people in the rest of the world when they returned. The rising China kept the capitalistic countries perturbed, the socialist camp heartened, and the formerly oppressed peoples hopeful.

However, as general discontent in China developed, and

particularly as its rift with the Soviet Union widened, while its quarrel with India intensified and the Asian and African countries' resentment over China's aggressiveness increased, China's international position has declined; it now has more enemies than it has friends. If the enthusiasm of the foreign delegations to attend the October Celebration in Peking is an index of China's international prestige, we should notice that in the 17th anniversary of the People's Republic, several delegations walked out during the celebration. To go one year back, in the 16th anniversary in 1965, the only outstanding foreign guest to review the parade on Mao Tse-tung's side at the Tien An Men Gate rostrum was Prince Sihanouk of Cambodia, head of a small state which was only part of the former French colony of Indo-China, a state smaller than many Chinese provinces. Where are China's powerful allies?

In quarrels with the Soviet Union, the Chinese Communists have weakened their international position as well as the socialistic camp. It is not our business to be concerned for Chinese communism or international communism. Some may think that that is how things should be; but what we want to point out here is simply the fact that the position of the People's Republic is weakening and there is no indication of whether it is the Chinese people's curse or their blessing.

It may be correct to say that in as much as Mao Tse-tung stands out more and more clearly as a dictator of the Chinese Communist Party as revealed in recent events, the policy China has adopted for the last decade is largely his making. One does not doubt Mao's ambition and his staunchness as a revolutionary. As Russia's disciple he has the ambition even to be above his teacher. But one may doubt his wisdom. He does not seem to know what is really going on in the outside world. He still indulges in the old mentality of his guerrilla days and entertains the same outlook as when he was in the caves of Yenan. He is subject to the criticism in the old Chinese saying: "to make the cart behind closed doors". He seems to imagine that the people of the rest of the world are all like the simple rural folks in China who are so easily deceived and subjugated. To have a man so immersed by his own dogma and so limited in his mental horizon, steering the ship in the international sea is to invite peril. For us, what is lamentable is not the destiny of the "helmsman", nor his crew, the party, nor world communism, but the 700 million people who have to sail on this ship.

# CHAPTER 9

# Summary and Conclusion

IN BRINGING this study to a close, let us summarize certain points from the foregoing chapters and draw whatever conclusion may seem justified.

We shall present them under three headings : Society, Schools and Progress.

## SOCIETY

Let us review the characteristics of the Chinese society and its recent developments under the following points.

### A Massive Land and a Massive People

China is a country with a vast land and a huge population. This makes the Chinese case a colossal one as well as a unique one. With a land of almost all kinds of resources making it self-sufficient, the Chinese can be a contented people as they used to be. In an age of nationalism, mere size and numbers provide them with advantages over many other peoples of the world. If, however, nationalism leads to chauvinism and the Chinese become more and more aggressive, they might turn out to be a curse of mankind and an object of international contempt.

In terms of national construction, with this population many gigantic projects can be accomplished with relative ease. For instance, the contribution of a dollar from each person would make $700 million and the contribution of a day's work from each person would mean 2 million extra labourers for one year without cost to the State. But, on the other hand, any boastful figure of output of consumption goods would have to be divided by this astronomical denominator before it has any real meaning to the actual consumer. The increase in production of 700 million yards of cloth, enough to go around the world eighteen times, would entitle each person to only a yard; and the recent purchase of 1½ million tons of wheat from Australia would provide less than 5 lb for each person, or would be just enough to feed the population for 5 days.

## A Long History and a Rich Culture

China is known for its long history and a distinct culture of its own, rich in philosophy, literature, and art. Its culture has been firmly established and deeply rooted in the life of the people. It is obvious that to destroy the political structure of the Chinese people is relatively easy, but to destroy their old culture and replace it by an alien one by force is another story. It would be an easier task if the Chinese culture were primitive and there were not much in their history. Failing to take account of China's long history and its rich culture, dims one's hopes of handling the Chinese people and of understanding their society.

## The Opium War

The Chinese society is more immediately affected by its modern period. This modern period is marked by the Opium War; being the first imperialistic war in China, it is the symbol of imperialism which is identified with the "unequal treaties", imperialistic exploitation, foreign domination, and national humiliation. It may not be fair to lay all the blame for China's decadence, poverty, and backwardness in the past century on imperialism alone, as some people like to do. But it is certainly fair to say that without imperialism there would not have been this bitterness against the West in China and this discontent with its own society. Without imperialism, capitalism alone, which had been weak in China anyway, could not have opened the way to Communism in China.

## *The New Culture Movement* (the Chinese Renaissance)

The movement for Western democracy and Western science in the years 1915 to 1919 and onward which was associated with the publication of the *New Youth Magazine* by Chen Tu-hsiu and the literary revolution led by him and Hu Shih, is known to the Chinese people as *Hsin Wen Hua Yun Tung* (the New Culture Movement) and, to the Western world, as the Chinese Renaissance. It may be said that those years were the climax of the movement for individual liberalism in China since Western liberalism found its way there. If one wants to cite a single example to represent the appeal of the liberation of the individual to the Chinese mind at that period, the popularity of Ibsen's *A Doll's House* is as good as any.

The Student Movement of 1919, though a product of the intellectual awaking of the New Culture Movement, was diverted into the political channels of national and class emancipation. This gave birth to the Nationalist Movement of anti-imperialism and anti-warlordism and to the Communist movement of anti-capitalism and anti-landlordism. The founders of the Chinese Communist Party as we have noted were leaders of the New Culture Movement and the Student Movement who had been inspired by the Russian Revolution. It is most interesting that the New Culture Movement and the Student Movement seemed to have impressed Mao Tse-tung so much in his youth that, after half a century, he comes forth to repeat history by enlarging the cultural movement into what he calls the Great Proletarian Cultural Revolution and by using the revolutionary students as his Red Guards.

## The Two World Wars

The two world wars have had great consequences in Chinese affairs. World War I brought about the Chinese Communist Party. World War II brought about the Chinese People's Republic.

The Anti-Japanese War from 1937 to 1945 gave the Chinese Communist Party a good opportunity to build up its army, to consolidate its base, to win the goodwill of the Chinese people, and to infiltrate the Nationalist territory. After the war was over, with the corruption and inefficiency of the Nationalist Government, plus the social, economic, and political disorder which the Communists had succeeded in aggravating, the people were left with no other choice than to look for a new government. The Chinese Communists' victory over China was really too easy. They got the lion's share of the fruits of war.

## Coalition Government and the New Democracy

The Communists made many attractive promises. They advocated Coalition Government, the New Democracy, the collaboration of all patriotic elements and overseas Chinese and democratic parties, including the Revolutionary Committee of the Kuomintang. In 1949 the Chinese People's Political Consultative Conference (CPPCC) was convened, and the Common Programme was adopted. The People's Republic was inaugurated, admitting into the power structure of the State the petty bourgeoisie and national bourgeoisie in alliance with the peasants and workers, as symbolized by the five-star flag.

Five years later, in 1954, the First National People's Congress, an elected body, was convened to take over the legislative functions of the CPPCC which was a consultative body, as the name had signified. The new Constitution was adopted to replace the Common Programme. We should remember that the 1954 Constitution is not yet repealed. Legally, it is still the statute of the State; at least it was up to the end of 1966.

The People's National Congress and the Constitution put the affairs of the People's Republic on a stable and permanent basis. Things became regularized and looked promising. Prosperity was round the corner and the alliance with the Soviet Union increased the prestige of the People's Republic.

## The Three Red Flags

Since 1957, however, events in China have brought about many surprises, some of which turned out to be disappointments to its good wishers and supporters. The abrupt curtailment of the "Hundred Flowers and Hundred Schools" Movement in 1957 disappointed the intellectuals. In 1958 the People's Commune, the Great Leap Forward, and the Socialistic Main Line were forced upon the people, coming to be known as the three red flags. They were followed by agricultural and economic failures. As a result, differences within the Chinese Communist Party sharpened. On the international front, differences between China and Russia also developed. The rift was widened into open quarrel and mutual attack. The series of nuclear explosions since 1964 does not seem to have been able to win back for the People's Republic the former confidence of the people and the former prestige in the international world.

## Anti-Revisionism

What bothers the top authorities of the Chinese Communist Party most today is Russian revisionism, against which they are now putting up a life or death struggle.

"Revisionism" as the term indicates recommends the revision of the Communist Party line. It is still communism to be sure, but on the whole, it advocates a more moderate policy in economic, social, political, and cultural life in internal affairs, and a moderate policy of co-existence in international affairs. Since Mao Tse-tung insists on the Stalin "hard line" of communism and is not willing to lose in his contest with the Russians, he has stepped up the purge within his territory and among his own ranks. The Great Proletarian Cultural Revolution in 1966 was designed to eliminate all traces of Rightist inclination and the Red Guards were instituted to crack down upon the old guards. In his fight with Soviet revisionism, Mao is determined to go so far as to sacrifice international Communist unity and Chinese Communist Unity and to violate the Constitution of the Chinese People's Republic and the Constitution of the Chinese Communist Party.

In a desperate attempt to regain Mao's lost footing, Lin Piao came forth to support Mao as Aaron did Moses. The study of Mao's works and selected quotations is the last resort of the pro-Mao elements to reinstate Mao's prestige. But since Mao does not listen to his most able associates, he is more and more isolated. The Great Proletarian Cultural Revolution, with the unbecoming behaviour of the Red Guards, has ruined his prestige as well as that of China.

This was the picture of the Communist Chinese society as the curtain fell at the close of 1966, 17 years after the establishment of the Chinese People's Republic.

## SCHOOLS

### The School System

China abolished its traditional classical examination in 1905 as soon as it adopted the Western school system. Since then, the school system has been undergoing several changes. The American-type 6–3–3 system with a 6-year primary school, a 3-year junior middle school and a 3-year senior middle school, on top of which is the usual 4-year undergraduate college, was adopted in 1922. By now it has had almost 46 years of history. This is the system in operation in Taiwan and, in a large measure, as we have said, has been in operation in Communist China in the past 19 years.

### Demands for Change

There have been demands to bring about a drastic reform to the school system in conjunction with the Great Proletarian Cultural Revolution. The demands are : shortening the years of schooling, particularly in the arts and the social science course in the university; simplification of the curriculum; teaching fewer subjects but teaching them more thoroughly; the abolition of the college entrance examination; the admission of students to the schools with preference for the children of the proletariat; the removal of domination by bourgeois intellectuals in the schools; the reform of methods of teaching, and so on. After the demands were made, the college entrance examination was suspended. All the schools, colleges, and universities suspended classes after June 1966 to permit students and teachers to participate in the Cultural Revolution.

We have yet to see what kind of system will be devised, how drastically different it will be from the past and from other countries, and more important, how well the new system will work and how long it will last.

## *Education and Culture*

In a static social order, the school is usually the main educational institution and can be studied apart from other institutions. But in a society in revolution, such as that we find in China since the establishment of the Chinese People's Republic, the school is not the main educational institution, nor can it be studied independently.

Educational and cultural institutions work hand in hand. These include the press, radio, film, theatre, and literature, music, and art. They work under the same assumptions or guiding principles. We refer to the prevalent assumptions of education in Chapter 5, namely, education as the instrument of politics; education for the working class; the importance of the mass line in the revolutionary struggle; the importance of labour; education to be linked up with production; the importance of socialization and co-operate life; the integration of theory and practice; the use of criticism and self-criticism; the equality of the sexes; the necessity for discrimination in the treatment of Chinese culture; the place of patriotic appeal; the implications of internationalism and internationality; the use of repetition as a social method and the importance of persistent vigilance.

These assumptions tally well with three important documents which we have quoted or partially quoted : the cultural and educational policies of the Common Programme; the provisions in the Constitution of the Chinese People's Republic with regard to education and culture; and the so-called "sixteen points" or the "Decision of the Central Committee of the Chinese Communist Party Concerning the Great Cultural Revolution".

## *Nation is School*

Futhermore, education, de-education and re-education take place in other institutions besides those of education and culture. They take place in the social, economic, and political institutions as well, such as the family, religion, customs, the communes, factories, production agencies, the Liberation Army, workers' unions, governmental offices, neighbourhood organizations, and so forth. Since the new social order has to be established with this new ideology of the proletariat, no institution can be spared from use and no person can escape conformity. Every person is confronted with proletarian ideology at every turn. It is certain that if he is not bombarded at one turn, he will be bombarded at another, until he is rid of the old ideology. In a real sense, as the Red Guards advocated, the whole country is turned into a huge school with Mao Tse-tung as its great tutor. In this sense, education is life, real life, and the most embracing form of life.

## *The New "New Culture Movement"*

In the first decade of the First Chinese Republic there was a New Culture Movement which we called the Chinese Renaissance. Now in the second decade of the Second Chinese Republic, we have this New Culture Movement which is known as the Great Proletarian Cultural Revolution. In both cases, the old Chinese culture is attacked and the new culture introduced. The slogan now is "to destroy the 'four olds'—old thoughts, old culture, old customs, and old habits, and to estab lish the 'four news'—new thoughts, new culture, new customs, and new habits". In actual operation, it can be done on a wholesale scale and in a drastic manner or it can be piecemeal and mild. One must patiently wait to discover to what extent the "olds" will be destroyed and to what extent the "news" will be established. The crux of the problem, of course, is the question of how "left" they go.[1] If it is going to be mild and piecemeal, it would be like the Renaissance Movement stepping up; but if it is going to be drastic and wholesale, it might mean turning society upside-down; this, however, is not likely.

## PROGRESS

Has there been progress in China since the establishment of the People's Republic? The answer is probably "yes", but with reservations.

When we speak of China's progress we do not forget the many defects of the People's régime which we have intimated in the preceding chapter as its problems and crises. They are too fresh in our mind to require more than just naming : lack of faith in the Chinese Communist Government; the hardships of the people; the unrest of intellectuals; the confusion of the masses; control by fear; the inadequacy of Communist leadership; the irreconcilability of communism with Chinese culture and with modern democracy, and the aggravation of international enmity. These constitute the liabilities of the Chinese People's Republic and they fall on the debit side of the ledger.

It is not fair, however, either from the social and educational standpoint or from the academic standpoint to ignore China's merits, ignoring the credit side of the ledger. Let us now

---

[1] The question of "left" and "right" is a delicate one. When one goes o one extreme, it is extreme left; when one goes to the other extreme, t is extreme right. This is clear. But in between, left and right are only elative. What the Communists called rightists in the anti-rightist campaign in 1957 were, in fact, leftists in the days of the Nationalist régime. And what the Communists attack as anti-revolutionary writers today have been known in China all along as leftist writers.

outline some of the assets of the People's Republic. The reader will recall that these virtues which we shall mention have not been ignored in previous chapters. We shall try to repeat here as little as possible.

## National Prestige

China's prestige in the world is definitely higher than at any time since the Opium War. Many nations, including Canada, are insistent on seating the People's Republic of China in the United Nations. Many consider any world disarmament conference ineffective without China's participation. Remarks by China's Foreign Minister are watched carefully by the rest of the world and his words are analysed with care. If China is not respected, at least it is feared. A recent example is the riot in the Portuguese Colony of Macao in December 1966 in which the Portuguese Government there accepted unconditionally all the humiliating demands imposed by the left-wing constituents in Macao, which had the support of the Bureau of Foreign Affairs of Kwangtung Province. The Chinese Foreign Minister, Chen Yi, did not even have to bother to open his mouth. China since 1840 would never have dared to entertain the idea of having the grievances of its nationals in a colony redressed in such a triumphant way.

## Scientific and Technological Achievements

China has always been known for its scientific and technological backwardness and it has been considered so far backward that it could never catch up. If the Orientals deserved any word of praise in the field of science and technology, the award went to the Japanese. Now with the first nuclear explosion in 1964 followed by four others in 1965 and 1966, China became, a yet, the only country in Asia to master the device. To add to what has been said in the section on technological change, we should mention that in the field of Western medicine, China is able to perform heart surgery. In the field of Chinese traditional medicine, it has made great strides through the employment of new methods of scientific investigation and experimentation. Chinese medicine and Western medicine are now integrated into a new medical science and art.

## *Economic Stability*

In the last years of the Nationalist régime, the currency was changed from paper to a silver basis, and from a silver basis to gold; but in spite of the changes, the currency was literally depreciating every day. Since the assumption of power by the Communists, the currency has been stabilized. The price of commodities has been steady and the cost of living has remained at par. This is a phenomenon undreamed of in the Nationalist days and it is not found everywhere in the world.

Foreign trade is in balance. Exports even exceed imports, a condition which had never existed in China since the first import of opium. All machinery used to be imported, but now imports are chiefly limited to heavy machinery and machines and scientific instruments have become China's export items. China used to import a great deal of textile and consumer goods but now textiles are an export item, and consumer goods are reduced to almost nil. Cigarettes, luxuries, and cosmetics which were imported in large numbers are virtually prohibited as imports.

At the end of 1966 China had no standing foreign loan. In fact, it had loans to offer to other developing countries. There was little internal debt. No national bond has been floated for many years and people are encouraged to open savings accounts in the People's Bank which the State can draw for its capital use. It has a big gold reserve and enjoys good credit in international trade. China's status in the financial world is high.

## *Sanitation and Cleanliness*

China used to be described as a dirty place with a filthy people. It stood out as the most disgraceful thing in Chinese social and personal life. But now cleanliness seems to be one of China's spectacular virtues on which foreign visitors have constantly made favourable remarks, as we have mentioned in connection with the patriotic sanitation campaign.

The people's clothes, though patchy and drab, are frequently washed and kept clean. The houses are clean; streets are clean; restaurants, kitchens, parks, trains, and buses, and all public places are kept clean. People have acquired good habits of public and personal hygiene; they do not throw waste paper and rubbish into the street and spitting in public is far less common than among the Chinese in Hong Kong.

## Anti-Corruption and Anti-Vice

The Chinese Government of the past was known for its corruption. The officials squeezed and the people bribed. Such traits have been so prevalent in Chinese society that some Westerners in Hong Kong have called them second nature to the Chinese people. Before the Communists got into power, vice in Chinese cities (such as gambling, prostitution, heavy drinking, and drug addiction) was common. Racketeers, secret societies, and the underworld were so strong and well organized that even high government officials turned a blind eye. And, indeed, social vice was often associated with government corruption. Now in Communist China, the Government is clean and corruption and all forms of vice have been swept away. We find no betting on horses, greyhound racing, mahjang gambling, night clubs, bars, dancing halls, smoking dens, red-light districts, racketeering, hooliganism, anywhere in the land. Instead we find people with wholesome habits and simple living, who live on the legitimate returns of their honest labour and avoid anti-social tendencies. The moral tone of the Chinese society in this atmosphere of simplicity and self-restraint reminds one of the Christian community of the Puritans, which one seldom encounters nowadays in the Christian countries.

Communist Canton and the British Colony of Hong Kong

are only 90 miles apart, but in the matter of social vice and public corruption, they offer very sharp contrasts. It would be interesting to write "a tale of two cities".

China has undergone a thorough spring-cleaning and has set its house in order.

## Social Awakening and Political Consciousness

As we have said, the Chinese people used to be described as a basin of loose sand. But now after 19 years of Communist tutelage in socialistic mobilization, the Chinese people have been organized into a solid mass, apparently with a single mind and a single purpose.

They have been brought to a high degree of social and political consciousness. Though many of them are still illiterate, they are aware of what is going on in their own country and in the rest of the world. Subjects in the field of the social sciences in the Western universities, such as sociology, economics, political science, ethics, are becoming familiar to the man in the street in China. He understands, for instance, what feudalism, landlordism, socialism, imperialism, and capitalism is. He can tell the difference in political alignment between North and South Korea, North and South Vietnam, East and West Germany, India and Pakistan, the United States and France, and between Mao Tse-tung thinking and revisionism. He has also learned to tell the difference between bourgeois ideology and proletarian ideology, and between the roots of the old culture and the new culture. The Chinese have come to realize that the improvement of their living lies in the way they work together to harness nature instead of leaving it to the manipulation of fate. They are brought to see the goal of building a new nation and a new society, and the part they are to play. Thus their horizon is widened and their awareness increased. They are not merely members of their family, their clan, their local community, but also members of the great Society and the new world. What goes on in the world seems to have something to do with them, and what goes on in them seems to have something to do with the future of mankind. What is taking place in China, then, is a great social and political awakening. Such accomplishments in two decades must have astonished the leaders of mass education in China during the first half of the twentieth century, as they have amazed the world.

### Resumption of Self-respect

By resumption of self-respect we refer both to the individual and to the nation as a whole. The recovery of national self-respect and individual self-confidence in Communist China in the last two decades has been most remarkable.

The Chinese had been so frustrated by the chain of events of national humiliation since the Opium War that it has been difficult for them to envisage how they could ever come to be equal to the Western peoples. They had come to a state of such frustration as to consider anything Western superior to their own. What worried them was their own incompetence and unworthiness. The United States was looked upon as the champion of the world and as China's ideal.

However, the Chinese Communists have cured this national inferiority complex. They have come out to challenge this Western superiority and American image. In the Korean War, Mao Tse-tung ridiculed America as the "paper tiger"; and in order to cure this Americanophobia the Chinese people launched the campaign to "belittle America", "despise America", and "hate America". Whether or not this Chinese attitude is entirely justified, China, at any rate, is now one of the very few countries in the world today which exists and flourishes without American aid, and indeed exists and flourishes in spite of American economic sanctions. Ambition has taken a step forward, invoking "The East wind to suppress the West wind".

Through the elimination of human exploitation, of landlord over peasants, of capitalists over labourers, of one group over another group, of men over women, and of adults over th young, the dignity of man is being restored. Everyone is as good as anyone else provided he does not claim to be higher than another. A peasant does not have to apologize for being a peasant as he used to do. He will no longer have to say in timidity, "I am *only* a peasant" but says with full dignity, "I am a *peasant*". A worker does not have to apologize for being a worker as he used to. He will no longer have to say timidly, "I am *only* a worker" but says with full dignity, "I am a *worker*". A waiter in a restaurant or a porter at the station does not accept gratuities. He counts it his duty, his joy, and his pride to render good service. Gratuities, according to the Chinese Communists, are a practice of bourgeois society to humiliate the worker. In a real sense, here is an example of "the rediscovery of man".

## *Capital Construction and Proletarian Welfare*

In writing on technological change we have spoken about some major aspects of industrial and agricultural development in China. China has put a great deal of investment into its capital construction. Many industries, factories, plants, buildings, bridges, roads, railway lines, canals, reservoirs, dams, power stations, state farms, schools, universities, research centres, and towns have been built since 1949. Those which had existed before have been expanded and improved. With these constructions, China has taken on a new look. These are China's national assets which are the people's common wealth.

As to the people, those who had been at the bottom of the social stratum in the past have had much to gain. One does not find slums, a common sight in the cities before 1949. We now find them replaced by airy and sanitary workers' quarters with the former filthy gutters replaced by a well-kept drainage system. Places for public enjoyment such as the parks, recreational centres, theatres, scenic spots for excursions, museums, stadiums, and athletic grounds are sources of pride to the proletariat who know that they are the possessors of these facilities and that these facilities exist for them. Hospital, transport, and service agencies are exclusively at their service. The peasants, workers, and soldiers, who form the greatest bulk of the population, feel that they are masters of the land and have the priority in the use of the nation's facilities and services. What used to be the exclusive summer resorts of the rich are now open to the workers and to them only. Conditions of work in the factories and mines are greatly improved, providing the worker with much greater protection and safety. This is a land of the proletariat. While the old intellectuals and old bourgeoisie may grumble over the many deprivations compared with what they had, the masses of the people who had been underprivileged do not feel the same way. They are at least satisfied that no class of people rides over their heads to enjoy extravagant privileges. After sharing each other's poverty, the proletariat in China begin to share their common wealth, though very meagre it must be at the beginning. They cherish the hope of better days to come.

## CONCLUSIONS

Now after all is said, and particularly after an examination of the ledger, what have we to say?

### *The Pros and Cons*

To be engaged in an analysis of the schooling and society in China is like engaging in a great debate. There are the pros and cons. When it is good, it is very, very good; and when it is bad, it is very, very bad. The paradox is that both are true, depending on one's point of view and sense of values.

In the main, if one looks at Chinese affairs since the establishment of the Chinese People's Republic from a traditional point of view, from the standpoint of the intellectual class, the middle class, the propertied class, from the standpoint of the individual and his freedom, and from the standpoint of the established system of ethical, social, political, and spiritual values, one draws certain conclusions. But if one looks at them from a revolutionary point of view, from the standpoint of the Communists, the proletariat, the peasants, and workers, the masses, and from the standpoint of the Marxist–Leninist–Maoist concept of ethical, social, political, and materialistic values, one draws quite a different set of conclusions. One should not be surprised to find the conclusions of the Communists and Nationalists different, the new social leaders and the old social leaders different, those who had been downtrodden and underprivileged and those who had held the reins of government and society with their special status and different privileges. In fact the conclusions of those supporting the interests of the child and those supporting the interests of the adult would be different; so are those supporting the interests of women as against those of men. One may like to compare the state of affairs in China in the last 19 years with its past, and to compare them with the state of affairs in a wide range of countries during the synchronous period.

## At What Price?

Granted that there are many accomplishments worthy of praise in the People's régime, we must seriously ask : at what price?

Think of the millions and tens of millions of Chinese people, many of whom were innocent, who have been humiliated, persecuted, tortured, imprisoned, abandoned, and killed. Think of the amount of cruelty, injustice, inhumanity, and brutality the Communists have inflicted on the people. Think of the millions of people who, because of the unbearable persecution, have committed suicide. To them the cold-blooded Communists have never allowed a word of sympathy; conversely, they have called them criminals evading punishment with no courage to face their own crimes because of heavy feelings of guilt.

Think of the suspicion that has been stirred up between one and another : between members of the family; between father and son; husband and wife; between friends and between associates; between a man and his neighbour; and between him and a stranger. Think of the hatred that has been implanted in men

318 Society, Schools and Progress in China

between what they call classes, between nations and between peoples. Think of the ill-will they have created in the world toward the Chinese people. Although good-will in the world toward the peace-loving Chinese in the past had not spared China from imperialism, yet the world's ill-will would not help to improve matters.

The mass-line they follow is an appeal to the mob, and mob rule is always dreadful.

Individuals have been emancipated from former exploitation, but they are now enslaved by a much stronger and harsher exploiter, the State, in the name of "the people".

### Must it be so?

There are many ways of bringing about a strong and prosperous China. But must it be done in the way the Communists have followed? Granted that the Chinese Communists have done their best, but is that the best that men can do? We do recognize the first-rate quality of the Communists in political shrewdness and military ingenuity; but in other respects they represent second- and third-rate quality among Chinese talents. It is no wonder that, with these second- and third-rate talents, China's progress was brought about with such great distortion. We must point out that there is no credit in "some progress". Some progress does not deserve praise. Some progress at such a heavy cost and at such unnecessary suffering is even to be condemned. Taiwan also has made some progress. They have attained a reputable land reform but they did not have to kill people. Hong Kong has also made progress under colonialism. It has built up so much in the last 19 years that it has been almost unrecognizable even by its own inhabitants. The people there are well fed and well clothed. They make no fuss about their progress there.

### Will These Things Last?

Nineteen years is long and very long in one's life, but 19 years is short—and very short in Chinese history. Chin Shih Huang reigned for 37 years and the Manchus ruled over the Chinese for over 250 years. But, alas, for those who have to suffer, one day is long!

How long the Chinese Communist Party is going to stay in power it is hard to say. Without considering external factors, for the factor of age alone Mao Tse-tung's era cannot be very long. The fact that Mao Tse-tung had to count on his wife, Chiang Ching, a former film actress, to come to his support in the Cultural Revolution is a bad omen for him. As to what will be the state of affairs in China after Mao passes away or after he steps down, one's answer will depend on whether the power transfer takes place after he passes away or before, and when the transfer will take place.

Some people think that the Communist pattern of life in China is a transient phenomenon. They hold that when external conditions change, the pattern will give way. They allege that just as the refugees from Communist China change and return to their former ways of life as soon as they set foot in Hong Kong and put on a suit of Western clothes, so also will the society in Communist China discard its communistic ways of life as soon as another régime comes into being. Such an argument is not without support in the Communist theory that "existence determines ideology". However, it is unlikely that what has taken place in China during all these years will have no impact whatsoever on Chinese culture and Chinese society in the future.

## What Are the Prospects?

Whether we like it or not, it seems that the Chinese Communist régime is going to stay. The Chinese People's Government is still the strongest and best organized that China has seen for many centuries. There is no other political party in sight to challenge its power. The present hierarchy may change, as has happened in the Soviet Union, but it will be a Communist hierarchy and no other. It would be the abdication of the hierarchy, not of the party.

It seems that a more moderate form of communism is going to emerge in China *sooner or later*, giving the people an easier and better life and relieving the tension of people in the rest of the world. If it were to come *soon*, it would be when Mao dies or when he is deposed, if still living. If it comes *late*, it would perhaps have to be when another generation of moderates rise to succeed those washed out in this Great Proletarian Cultural Revolution. It does not seem likely that the Kuomintang will be able to take over China again or that the Chinese Communist Party will collapse.

## On the "Tiger"

The Chinese People's Government is definitely not a government of choice. It has now become a government which many have tried to avoid; this is reflected in the influx of refugees to Hong Kong and Macao, the only places out of Chinese jurisdiction along the whole coast of China and they are only accessible to those who live around the Canton delta. Hong Kong has a population of about 4 million, of which more than half are refugees who came since 1949. Some of them escaped, risking their lives and at the danger of being sent to labour camps in case of being caught.

One should remember that Hong Kong is a British Colony, and Macao, Portuguese. Colonies are certainly not the ideal home the Chinese would choose out of all places. If colonies are places of imperialistic exploitation, the reason why so many Chinese still come is clear. They want to avoid a government disliked even more.

Since the subject of the "tiger" has been brought to the fore through Mao Tse-tung's usage in calling America the "paper tiger", and all imperialists also "paper tigers", it may be of special interest at this point, and in conclusion, to cite a lesson on government as taught by Confucius, which is recorded in *Li Chi* (*The Book of Rites*):

> Confucius passed by the side of Tai Mountain. A woman was crying over a grave in extreme grief. The Master rose with respect

from the seat of his carriage to listen. He sent Tzu Lu to inquire, saying "The way you cry seems to indicate a multiple sorrow."

The woman replied, "Indeed, formerly my father-in-law was killed by a tiger; later, my husband was killed; and, now, my son has also been killed."

The Master asked, "Why don't you leave here?"

The woman replied, "There is no harsh government here."

The Master said, "Take this to heart, young men: a harsh government is more fierce than the tiger."

# Bibliography

*China Yearbook, 1937–1945*, compiled by the Chinese Ministry of Information, Republic of China, published by the Macmillan Co., New York, 1947.

*\*Chung Kuo Chin Tai Shih Shih Chi (A Chronicle of Chinese Modern History)*, published by the Shanghai People's Publishing Society, Shanghai, 1961.

*\*Chung Kuo Jen Min Cheng Chih Hsieh Shang Hui I Ti I Chiai Chuan Ti Hui I Chi Nien Kan (Commemoration Volume of First Plenary Session of the Chinese People's Political Consultative Conference)*, 1949, published by the Secretariat of the CPPCC, Peking, 1950.

*\*Da Gong Pao (L'Impartial Daily)*, Peking.

*The Great Socialist Cultural Revolution in China*, in 4 volumes, published by the Foreign Language Press, Peking, 1966.

*\*Hongqi (Red Flag)*, monthly, published under the auspices of the Chinese Communist Party Central Committee, Peking.

*\*Hsin Hua Yueh Pao (New China Monthly)*, Peking, 1949–55.

*\*Hsin Hua Pan Yueh Kan (New China Semi-Monthly)*, Peking, 1956–60.

*\*Hsueh Hsi (Study)*, monthly, Peking.

*\*Jen Min Chiao Yu (People's Education)*, monthly, Peking.

*\*Jen Min Shou Tse (People's Handbook)*, 1965, published by the *Da Gong Pao*, Peking, 1965.

*\*Kuang Ming Ribao (The Bright Daily)*, Peking.

*Peking Review*, weekly, published by the Foreign Language Press, Peking.

*\*Renmin Ribao (People's Daily)*, Peking.

*Selected Works of Mao Tse-tung*, in 4 volumes, published by Foreign Language Press, Peking.

*South China Morning Post*, daily, Hong Kong.

*\*Ta-Kung-Pao (L'Impartial Daily)*, Hong Kong.

*Ten Great Years*, Statistics of the Economic and Cultural Achievements of the People's Republic of China, published by the Foreign Language Press, Peking, 1960.

*\*Ti Erh Tzu Chung Kuo Chiao Yu Nien Chien (China Education Yearbook, second edition)*, published by the Ministry of Education, Republic of China, Nanking, 1948.

*\*Tsu Kuo (China Monthly)*, published by the Union Research Institute, Hong Kong.

*\*Wah Kiu Yat Po (Overseas Chinese Daily)*, Hong Kong.

*\*Zhongguo Qingnian (Chinese Youth)*, semi-monthly, Peking.

\* In Chinese.

Names of Chinese publications are romanized according to R. H. Mathew's system of romanization unless they have English names or their own way of romanizing.

# Index

Workers' universities  *see* Half-work, half-study schools
Working class  39, 46, 48–50, 67, 77, 129–131
World revolution  131
World War I  18–20, 23, 138, 176, 303
World War II  17, 23, 25–27, 40, 119, 303
*Wu Han* (person)  84, 119, 122, 235–238
*Wuhan* (place)  233, 234
*Wu Hsun*  223

*Yang Han-sang*  84
*Yang-tze* River  233
*Yao Wen-yuan*  235, 280
*Yenan*  94, 138, 223, 224, 299
*Yenching* University  110, 196
Young Pioneers Brigade  *see* Communist Young Pioneers
Youth Party  *see* Chinese Youth Party
*Yuan* Dynasty  8
*Yuan Shih-kai*  9
Yugoslavia  271, 272
*Yung Wing*  15